Revised Edition

WHEN ELECTIONS GO BAD

THE LAW OF DEMOCRACY AND THE PRESIDENTIAL ELECTION OF 2000

by

SAMUEL ISSACHAROFF
Harold R. Medina Professor in Procedural Jurisprudence
Columbia Law School

PAMELA S. KARLAN
Kenneth and Harle Montgomery Professor of Public Interest Law
Stanford Law School

RICHARD H. PILDES
Professor of Law
New York University School of Law

NEW YORK, NEW YORK
FOUNDATION PRESS
2001

COPYRIGHT © 2001

By

FOUNDATION PRESS

All rights reserved

ISBN 1–58778–233–2

TEXT IS PRINTED ON 10% POST
CONSUMER RECYCLED PAPER

FOREWORD

One of the best known truisms about the United States Supreme Court comes from satirist Finley Peter Dunne's turn-of-the-century fictional Chicago bartender, Mr. Dooley, whose adventures were chronicled in Mr. Dooley's Opinions (1901). In discussing the Court's decision in *Downes v. Bidwell*, 182 U.S. 244 (1901), one of the "Insular Cases" concerning how, if at all, the Constitution was to apply to the territories acquired during the Spanish-American War, Mr. Dooley remarked:

> "An' there ye have th' decision, Hinnissy, that's shaken th' intellicts iv th' nation to their very foundations, or will if they thry to read it. 'T s all r-right. Look it over some time. 'T is fine spoort if ye don't care f'r checkers. Some say it laves th' flag up in th' air an' some say that's where it laves th' constitution. Annyhow, something's in th' air. But there's wan thing I'm sure about."

> "What's that?" asked Mr. Hennessy.

> "That is," said Mr. Dooley, "no matther whether th' constitution follows th' flag or not, th' supreme coort follows th' iliction returns."

The events of the presidential election of 2000 turned Mr. Dooley's observation on its head, as the election returns followed a decision of the Supreme Court. For the first time in over a century, the presidential election was not decided in the beginning of November. Not until the Court issued its opinion in *Bush v. Gore*, 531 U.S. 98 (2000), the lawsuit, did we know the outcome of Bush against Gore, the campaign. And just as at the turn of the last century, we begin this century with a Supreme Court decision "that's shaken th' intellicts iv th' nation to their very foundations . . . ."

Election 2000 revealed two things. First, it exposed the frail underside of elections. Second, it exposed to the public at large, and to those parts of the legal profession and the academy that had focused on other issues, the pervasive way in which the judicial regulation of politics can shape electoral outcomes. As we frame the issue in The Law of Democracy: Legal Structure of the Political Process:

> Before the first vote is cast or the first ballot counted, the possibilities for democratic politics are already constrained and channeled. The election process is well under way before the formal stage of voting, for elections do not take place in a legal vacuum. Rather the election process emerges from previously fixed — and often carefully orchestrated — institutional arrangements that influence the range of possible outcomes that formal elections and subsequent policymaking can achieve. Thus a paradox rests at the core of democratic politics: this politics is in part a contest over the structure

of state institutions, and yet those very institutions define the terms in which the contest of democratic politics proceeds.

Samuel Issacharoff, Pamela S. Karlan, and Richard H. Pildes, The Law of Democracy: Legal Structure of the Political Process (2d ed. 2001). However, most of the scholarship and federal case law involving the political process prior to the 2000 election focused more on institutional arrangements than on the nuts-and-bolts of casting votes and having them counted. Much of the law of democracy turns on structures of the political process, conceptions of representation, the roles of candidates, political parties and money in elections, and the overriding constraints imposed by statutes and the Constitution. When all is said and done, however, the election process still comes down to masses of people casting their ballots with the expectation that they will be fairly and accurately counted. As with all participatory events involving millions of people, elections are fraught with the capacity for mistake, ineptitude, and outright fraud. Over time concerns about corruption of the electoral process have changed. For example, moneyed interests are much more likely to attempt to assert their influence at the wholesale level, through campaign contributions, rather than at the retail level, through buying individuals' votes. But the problem of the breakdown in the integrity, accuracy, and fairness of the actual processes of vote casting and tabulation remains an issue of significant dimensions.

The scramble for votes in Florida exposed what has long been the dark secret of the entire electoral process: significant inaccuracies and mistakes infect the actual process of recording and tabulating votes. In effect, elections have an unacknowledged "margin of error" – a concept that is readily identified with opinion polls and the Census calculation of the population. The existence of such error in elections rarely rises to the forefront. Most elections are not within the margin of error, and if they are so close to begin with, there appears not to be a compelling equitable consideration in allowing adjustments to the electoral process to be implemented retrospectively. After all, if the "wrong" candidate is declared the winner, the voters can cure the problem by voting her out of office the next time around. And absent fraud or willful manipulation, the error in any election might be thought random. Even if *ex post* analysis reveals systematic tendencies to make errors involving identifiable groups of voters, such as less experienced voters, as long as those systematic tendencies are not known in advance and not intentionally exploited by state actors who, for example, choose election technologies, there would be little reason to believe that the resulting error rate reflected a calculated political manipulation by those holding political power. In these circumstances, a judicial tendency to let the errors lie where they fall might be most understandable.

Moreover, most election processes are not subject to particularly penetrating public scrutiny. Voters may express concern and even outrage if, for example, tie-ups on election day cause the lines to swell and delays to mount. But rarely will mere inconvenience result in anything beyond the most fleeting attention. Nor is this an area where elected officials are likely to intercede. The one unassailable generalization that can be made about elected officials is that they were all elected. Once elections end and public attention fades, there is rarely any incentive for those who have succeeded in the electoral arena to alter the rules and procedures that put them in office.

But what happens when the consequences of electoral error have implications nationwide? What happens when error threatens to tip the scales of an election for president? What happens if public scrutiny brings to light pervasive inaccuracies in how the electoral process actually functions? What if the public demands accountability for electoral machines that function poorly, or ballots that are confusing, or counting processes that include rather fluid assessments of the now infamous "hanging chads," "pregnant chads," and the like?

Examining the legal foundations for these questions reveals a series of different concerns in the distinct remedial phase of the law of the political process. There are two overriding generalizations. First, when elections are challenged after the fact there are obvious difficulties with deferring to the political process to redress the defects. As the events in Florida showed, once the votes are cast, every potential procedural and substantive decision becomes outcome determinative. There are ample reasons to believe that every claim put forward and every decision made will be the product of an attentive eye to the bottom-line result — or at least will be publicly perceived as such. There is little reason to believe that partisan officials will cease to be that if they are given the chance to interpret or even alter the rules of the game after the election has occurred. Second, this is an area in which courts have been acting and must continue to act with tremendous circumspection. For just as the partisan effects of all potential courses of action are known to partisan political officials, so too are they known to judges who must adjudicate electoral challenges. The adjudication of claims that will alter the outcomes of high-profile elections threatens significant damage to the integrity of courts. At the same time, the failure to provide for a judicial forum threatens to undermine the legitimacy of the political process itself.

At the second, more abstract level, Election 2000 provides a signal opportunity to think critically about the complex interaction between democratic politics and the formal institutions of the state. The conventional understanding of democracy — which sees democratic politics as the *source* for public offices, officials, institutions, and policies — is misconceived and perhaps even unintelligible. The kind of democratic politics we have is always and inevitably itself a product of institutional forms and legal structures. There are many possible forms democracy can take, many different institutional embodiments of democratic politics.

And because politics is not independent of existing law and institutions, those who control existing arrangements can shape the outcome of the elections that purportedly legitimate their power. There is no way to take the law "out" of democracy. Rather, the law mediates the delicate dance between state and federal power, between courts and legislatures, and between government and individual citizens. What has been true at least since the Reapportionment Revolution of the 1960's remains especially true today: When courts become central players, this raises some of the most difficult questions about institutional role in all of constitutional theory.

This book – which consists of Chapters 4 and 12 of The Law of Democracy modified slightly so that they can stand alone – addresses the judicial and political remedial structures, state and federal, for resolving election disputes. The 2000 presidential election provides our catalyst and our focus, but we seek to integrate the issues that dispute raises into a more comprehensive framework for elections gone bad.

We begin, in Chapter 1, by examining the federal interests that might be thought implicated in election disputes of all sorts, from state to federal. Every dispute about state election processes necessarily involves voting, but that does not turn every election controversy into a "federal question." There are some situations – those in which a state's law unfairly excludes citizens from voting in violation of the due process or equal protection clauses of the Fourteenth Amendment or the antidiscrimination principle of the Fifteenth Amendment or in violation of the federal Voting Rights Act – where the federal interest is clear. But there are also more subtle problems – when, for example, states change their electoral rules in the middle of an election – that can raise federal constitutional problems. The first section uses the pivotal Eleventh Circuit decisions in *Roe v. State of Alabama* to illuminate these questions. We then turn to the additional federal interests implicated in elections for federal office. These materials consider the complexities introduced by the interaction of various federal constitutional provisions with state electoral processes. With respect to races for the United States Congress, we focus on *Roudebush v. Hartke*, in which the Supreme Court upheld the use of a state recount process to determine the winner of a House seat even in light of the Constitution's provision that each House be the judge of its own members. We contrast the judicial process with the more political processes that the houses of Congress use in challenges they determine themselves. We then explain the central constitutional and federal statutory provisions that govern Presidential elections, including the resolution of disputed Presidential elections.

Chapters 2 and 3 turn to the litigation over the 2000 election in Florida, in both its state and federal dimensions. Chapter 2 brings to center stage materials of Florida law that were central to the election dispute: the relevant Florida statutory texts and state Supreme Court decisions. Chapter 3 then presents the decisions of the United States Supreme Court. Together, these materials raise profound questions regarding the nature of the right to vote, the role of state legislatures in the Presidential selection process, and the relationship between federal courts and political institutions in resolving disputed Presidential or other elections.

Chapter 4 presents "Eight Views of the Cathedral" -- a collection of excerpts from recent academic commentary offering different perspectives on the dramatic decision in *Bush v. Gore.*

Chapter 5 considers the question of *when* federal courts should intervene to protect substantive federal interests. This Chapter is of particular interest for courses in federal court litigation. Given that the federal interest in most cases consists largely in a state's following the rules already laid down, the procedural issue of the timing of federal review raises important questions about federalism and the relationship between federal and state courts.

Finally, Chapter 6 considers the range of remedial possibilities open to federal and state courts when elections go bad. These range from setting aside elections after they occur, to stopping them beforehand, to changing the outcome of elections through excluding or including challenged ballots. In addition, we consider less targeted forms of relief, such as permanent injunctions banning or mandating specific election practices, damages actions, and criminal prosecutions.

Bush v. Gore has already produced a torrent of scholarship: several collections of scholarly essays including The Longest Night: Perspectives and Polemics on Election 2000 (Arthur Jacobson and Michel Rosenfeld eds. 2001); The Unfinished Election of 2000 (Jack N. Rakove ed. 2001); The Vote: Bush, Gore and the Supreme Court (Cass R. Sunstein and Richard A. Epstein eds. 2001); forthcoming symposia in many law reviews including the Florida State University Law Review, the Journal of Law and Politics, the Maryland Law Review, and the University of Chicago Law Review; and numerous articles. We have tried to cite and quote from a number of the already available articles in the notes and questions. Each of us has written about the case, and rather than including lengthy quotations from our own works, we cite them at the end of this foreword.

The first edition of When Elections Go Bad was put together under extraordinary time pressure. The luxury of a few months' time, plus the insights we got from teaching the materials during the spring semester – for which we thank our exceptionally talented students at N.Y.U. and Stanford law schools – enabled us to reorganize and rework the book. The material contained here is also incorporated into the second edition of our more extensive casebook, The Law of Democracy: Legal Structure of the Political Process (Foundation Press 2001), in Chapters 4 and 12. Readers who are interested in a more wide-ranging treatment of legal regulation of politics should consult that book.

In addition to the students who took our spring 2001 courses, we thank colleagues and friends, both at our home institutions and elsewhere, who helped us to think about the issues covered in this book: Richard Briffault, Viola Canales, Michael Dorf, Cynthia Estlund, Tom Goldstein, Penda Hair, Rick Hills, Larry Kramer, Cass Sunstein, Henry Weinstein, and John Yoo.

Paul Lomio and Erika Wayne in the Stanford Law Library were simply amazing, both in providing help with finding materials and in setting up a website that contains the pleadings in the Florida cases, other legal nmaterials, and links to social science sites: http://election2000.stanford.edu/.

Dina Hamerman, Jeff Hauser, Todd Lundell, Adam Morse, Tara Ragone, Paul Winke, and Saul Zipkin provided valuable research assistance.

Extra special thanks to Kristie Hart for heroic labors in the new, tortuous vineyards of camera-ready publication.

Our own scholarship on the election includes:

Michael C. Dorf and Samuel Issacharoff, *Can Process Theory Constrain the Courts?*, 72 U. Colo. L. Rev. ____ (2001)

Samuel Issacharoff, Bush v. Gore: *Political Judgments*, 68 U. Chi. L. Rev. 637 (2001)

Pamela S. Karlan, *Equal Protection: Bush v. Gore and The Making of a Precedent* in The Unfinished Election of 2000 (Jack N. Rakove ed. 2001)

Pamela S. Karlan, *The Newest Equal Protection: Regressive Doctrine on a Changeable Court* in The Vote: Bush, Gore and the Supreme Court (Cass R. Sunstein and Richard A. Epstein eds. 2001)

Pamela S. Karlan, *Nothing Personal: The Evolution of the Newest Equal Protection from* Shaw v. Reno *to* Bush v. Gore, 79 N.C.L. Rev. ___ (2001)

Pamela S. Karlan, *The Triumph of Expedience: How America Lost the Election to the Courts*, Harper's, May 2001, at 31 (transcribed discussion with Judge Richard Posner)

Richard H. Pildes, *Democracy and Disorder*, 68 U. Chi. L. Rev. 695 (2001)

Richard H. Pildes, *Disputing Elections*, in The Longest Night (Arthur Jacobson and Michele Rosenfeld eds. 2001).

Richard H. Pildes, *Judging "New Law" in Election Disputes*, 28 Fla. St. U. L. Rev. ____ (2001).

* * * *

The decision in Election 2000 is final, but we believe it opens rich opportunities for discussion and debate over issues of basic constitutional structures, electoral processes, the role of courts in overseeing democratic processes, and the future implications of this decision for other issues involving the vote. These materials are intended to prompt both a retrospective assessment of *Bush v. Gore* and a prospective engagement with the future implications of the decision and the issues it raises for the law of democracy.

TABLE OF CONTENTS

FOREWORD i

Chapter 1: The Federal Interest in Election Procedures 1

A.   State Elections 2
       1.   Lack of Sufficient Federal Interest 3
       2.   Sufficient Federal Interests 5
             Roe v. State of Alabama 6
             Notes on the Procedural Posture and Aftermath of
             the *Roe* Litigation 10
             Notes and Questions 11
B.   Distinct Federal Interests in National Elections: U.S. House
    and Senate Elections 19
C.   Distinct Federal Interests in National Elections: Presidential
    Elections 22
       1.   The Electoral College 23
       2.   Article II and the Role of State Legislatures 24
       3.   The Electoral Count Act of 1887 25

Chapter 2: The State Interest in Federal Elections 27

Palm Beach County Canvassing Board v. Harris 29
Notes and Questions 39

Chapter 3: The U.S. Supreme Court's Decisions 44

A.   The Federal Interest Potentially Asserted 44
    Bush v. Palm Beach County Canvassing Board 44
    Notes and Questions 48
       1.   Article II and the "Independent State Legislature
            Doctrine" 49
    McPherson v. Blacker 49
    Notes and Questions 54
       2.   Of "Safe Harbors" and the Electoral Count Act 58
B.   The Final Florida Court Decision and the United States
    Supreme Court Stay 60
    Bush v. Gore 61
C.   The Federal Interest Decisively Asserted 63
    Bush v. Gore 63
    Notes and Questions 85
       1.   The Constitutional Right to Vote and the Equal
            Protection Clause 85

2.   The Application of the Right to Vote and Equal
     Protection in *Bush v. Gore* 87
3.   Substantive Due Process and the Right to Vote 93
4.   The Federal Interest in State Judicial
     Interpretation of State Laws Regulating
     Presidential Elector Selection 96

Chapter 4: Eight Views of the Cathedral 98

Chapter 5: The Timing of Federal Court Intervention 107

Growe v. Emison 108
Notes and Questions 111
Siegel v. LePore 116
Notes and Questions 127

Chapter 6: Remedial Possibilities for Defective Elections 129

A.   Ordering a New Election 129
     Bell v. Southwell 129
     Notes and Questions 133
B.   Enjoining an Upcoming Election 137
     Chisom v. Roemer 137
     Notes and Questions 143
C.   Adjusting the Vote Totals 145
     In re the Matter of the Protest of Election Returns ... 149
     Notes and Questions 152
D.   Permanently Enjoining a Particular Election Practice 159
E.   Damages 164
     Wayne v. Venable 166
     Notes and Questions 168
     Hutchinson v. Miller 169
     Notes and Questions 177
F.   Criminal Prosecution 177

Documentary Appendix 180

Selected Provisions of the U.S. Constitution 180
The Electoral Count Act 188
Selected Sections of the Voting Rights Act of 1965 193
Selected Provisions of the Florida Election Code 195

CHAPTER 1

THE FEDERAL INTEREST
IN ELECTION PROCEDURES

Two key questions, one substantive, one procedural, arise regarding whether and when federal courts have a role to play in overseeing contested elections. The procedural question involves the *timing* of any federal oversight that is otherwise justified: at what stage in an election dispute is it proper for federal courts to play a role to enforce the relevant federal interests, if any, that the election dispute implicates. This question of the proper timing of federal intervention is addressed in Chapter 5. The substantive question is dealt with in this Chapter: what substantive *reasons* are sufficient to justify federal intervention in election disputes. What exactly are the federal constitutional interests (or, statutory interests, if applicable) in various aspects of the election process, including in potential disputes that arise post-election? To what extent does the federal interest vary, if at all, when what is at stake is national office, such as election to the House, the Senate, or even the Presidency? This became the critical issue for the Supreme Court decision that terminated the 2000 Presidential election dispute. This Chapter will provide the general legal framework within which courts have addressed these questions. This Chapter is designed to provide perspective on the eventual treatment of these issues in *Bush v. Gore*.

With respect to national offices, the answer might be thought simple: surely federal constitutional interests are implicated when national offices are at issue. But even here, the legal structure is counterintuitive and hardly simple. The unique legal architecture of American democracy — a product of the original Constitutional design and subsequent legal additions built upon that original structure — envisions a complex interlacing of federal and state interests in matters of voting, elections, and political participation. Many of the issues involving electoral structures are left to be resolved at the state level, even when national offices are at stake. Recall, for example, that the original Constitution only specifies voter eligibility requirements for one national office, the House of Representatives. This is then modified by the Seventeenth Amendment which mandates direct election for senators. And even here, the federal requirements are completely derivative of state-law suffrage requirements. For example, Art. I., Sec. 2 states that electors for the House of Representatives "shall have the Qualifications requisite for Electors of the most numerous branch of the State Legislature." Defining the boundary line, then, between issues left to be resolved as a matter of state law and issues that instead implicate distinct, federal constitutional interests, requires

working out the intricate relationship between federal and state law that has
long structured the American democratic system — even for national offices.

A. STATE ELECTIONS

We begin with the context of state elections. Before turning to the cases,
it is helpful to understand the general structure of the legal problem regarding
which aspects of state elections can trigger federal constitutional interests.
The central problem is this: every dispute about state election processes
implicates, by definition, questions involving voting and democratic processes.
In a colloquial sense, then, every dispute about state elections could be said to
implicate "the right to vote." But if every dispute implicated "the right to vote"
in *a constitutional sense* — under the Fourteenth Amendment, for example —
then every issue concerning state elections would be transformed into a federal
constitutional issue. Federal constitutional law would then be turned into a
detailed election code for state elections. This would hardly be unprecedented
in democratic countries. In France, for example, the Constitutional Court sits
as the election overseer for all elections and has broad administrative powers
over the conduct of local elections both before they are held and afterwards, in
cases of electoral challenges.

This has not, however, been the American experience. Just as the United
States Supreme Court has resisted constitutionalizing the vast body of state
tort law and has refused to permit the ordinary deprivation of state-law
property interests to be transformed into Fourteenth Amendment issues where
state procedures are adequate, *Parratt v. Taylor*, 451 U.S. 527 (1981), the
federal courts have also declined to transform most issues of the regulation of
state elections into federal constitutional matters. The question then becomes
where, precisely, the boundary line between state and federal interests ought
to be drawn.

On the one hand, the courts have recognized a number of discrete, quite
specific constitutional interests in the structure of elections. The courts
recognized most of these interests only beginning in the 1960s, after *Baker v.
Carr,* 369 U.S. 186 (1962). Thus, state election districts must comply with the
one-vote, one-person principle. The Constitution imposes some constraints on
partisan and racial design of all election districts. Since *Harper v. Virginia
Board of Elections*, 383 U.S. 663 (1966), the Court has also held that
definitions of who can participate in what elections, on what terms, are subject
to equal protection and due process review. Similarly, the Constitution
imposes some constraints on the conditions states can impose upon candidates
seeking access to being listed on the ballot. So, too, the Constitution's First
Amendment recognizes some degree of associational rights that protect the
integrity and autonomy of political parties from certain types of state
regulation. Of course, state election laws that discriminate on their face along
racial lines have been unconstitutional since The White Primary Cases (the
first of which is *Nixon v. Herndon*, 273 U.S. 536 (1927)), and election laws that
reflect an impermissible racial or ethnic purpose are unconstitutional under

either the Fourteenth or Fifteenth Amendments. Finally, the most important federal statute that overlays state elections is the Voting Rights Act, which prohibits electoral structures and practices whose purpose or effect is to dilute the voting power of certain statutorily-protected groups. These are most of the specific, targeted federal interests that the courts have recognized in election processes.

On the other hand, if there were a more generalized constitutional interest in ensuring "the integrity of the electoral process" or in ensuring "fundamental fairness" in elections, then every dispute over the running of state elections would, indeed, potentially be subject to federal oversight and control. Thus, federal courts have sought to map out the distinction between the discrete areas of federal legal interest in state elections and the rest of the issues that might be disputed about the structure of elections, with the latter being left to be resolved through the ordinary processes of state law. What follows are representative federal court cases that provide content to these general principles.

1. LACK OF SUFFICIENT FEDERAL INTEREST

A typical result, in an opinion written by the highly-respected, late Judge Rubin, is provided by the oft-cited *Gamza v. Aguirre*, 619 F.2d 449 (5th Cir. 1980). In a run-off election for a local school board, candidate Gamza discovered that there was a technological misconfiguration in the voting machines in certain precincts; as a result, he alleged that his opponent had been given votes that rightly were intended for Gamza. The trial court found that the machine errors and miscounts had resulted from innocent human error. After failing in state court, Gamza claimed a deprivation of federal voting rights.

In rejecting this claim, the Fifth Circuit acknowledged that the failure to count votes adequately, stated abstractly, could easily sound like a constitutional issue. But the way the legal structure gave content to this abstract right required attending to the functional structure embodied in the Constitution, the nature of the federal court system, the limits of federal jurisdiction, and the role of states in election processes. Because the constitutional framework leaves the conduct of state elections to the states, the Fifth Circuit concluded that federal law must:

> . . . recognize a distinction between state laws and patterns of state action that systematically deny equality in voting, and episodic events that, despite non-discriminatory laws, may result in the dilution of an individual's vote. Unlike systematically discriminatory laws, isolated events that adversely affect individuals are not presumed to be a violation of the equal protection clause. The unlawful administration by state officers of a non-discriminatory state law, "resulting in its unequal application to those who are entitled to be treated alike, is not a denial of equal protection unless there is shown to be present in it an element of intentional or

purposeful discrimination."

If every state election irregularity were considered a federal constitutional deprivation, federal courts would adjudicate every state election dispute, and the elaborate state election contest procedures, designed to assure speedy and orderly disposition of the multitudinous questions that may arise in the electoral process, would be superseded by a section 1983 gloss. [Constitutional law does] not authorize federal courts to be state election monitors.

619 F.2d at 453.

In a similar case, voters claimed constitutional voting rights had been denied because electronic voting machines, which allegedly did not meet state-law standards, had malfunctioned and election officials had failed to respond as state law purportedly required. The Seventh Circuit rejected these claims, noting that not every election irregularity rises to the level of a constitutional violation — and that mere violation of a state statute by an election official was not, in itself, such a violation. *Hennings v. Grafton*, 523 F.2d 861 (7th Cir. 1975). As that court put it: "the work of conducting elections in our society is typically carried on by volunteers and recruits for whom it is at most an avocation and whose experience and intelligence vary widely. Given these conditions, errors and irregularities, including the kind of conduct proved here, are inevitable, and no constitutional guarantee exists to remedy them. Rather, state election laws must be relied upon to provide the proper remedy (citations omitted)." *See also Welch v. McKenzie*, 765 F.2d 1311 (5th Cir. 1985) (despite numerous violations of state election laws, no federal constitutional violation in absence of racially discriminatory intent behind those violations or racial vote dilution occurring); *Pettengill v. Putnam County School district, Unionsville, Missouri*, 472 F. 2d 121 (8th Cir. 1973) (federal courts should not become the "arbiter of disputes" which arise in elections and attempt to "oversee the administrative details of a local election" absent aggravating factors such as denial of the vote on grounds of race or fraudulent interference with a free election by stuffing of the ballot box) (holding no federal violation in alleged improper counting of ballots).

Similarly, in an important dispute over the Alabama Democratic gubernatorial primary, the Eleventh Circuit held that the appropriate forums for election disputes involving state offices were the court system of the affected state and, for primaries, the internal machinery of the political parties themselves. *Curry v. Baker*, 802 F.2d 1302 (11th Cir. 1986) involved a dispute over whether one of the Democratic primary candidates, Graddick, had encouraged voters who had already voted in the earlier Republican primary to turn out and vote in the special run-off primary for the Democratic nominee — despite state law precluding such cross-over voting. State law permitted the parties to resolve such contested primary disputes through internal party machinery. The Democratic Party used this machinery and concluded that Graddick had violated state law and party rules; the Party therefore awarded the nomination to his competitor. Graddick then turned to the federal courts and argued that the Democratic Party decision had violated "the fundamental fairness of the electoral process." According to Graddick and his supporters, the Party decision had diluted and debased the constitutionally protected right to vote. The Eleventh Circuit rejected this argument, holding that state processes, including internal party processes, were adequate to deal with the primary-election contest.

In sum, while "federal courts [will] closely scrutinize state laws whose very design infringes on the rights of voters, federal courts will not intervene to examine the validity of individual ballots or supervise the administrative details of a local election." *Id.*, at 1314. A "federally protected right 'is implicated where the entire election process — including as part thereof the state's administrative and judicial corrective process — fails on its face to afford fundamental fairness." *Id.*, at 1317.

2. SUFFICIENT FEDERAL INTERESTS

At the same time that federal courts seek to avoid becoming enmeshed in election disputes, given that the electoral machinery is overwhelmingly controlled at the state level, federal courts do of course enforce *specific* constitutional and federal statutory guarantees when they are implicated in elections. In addition to those interests — ensuring one-person, one-vote, avoiding impermissible restrictions on the franchise, avoiding certain forms of vote dilution, and the like — the further important question that arises in ongoing election disputes is whether there is any more general federal constitutional interest in ensuring that states resolve election disputes "appropriately."

The most aggressive and intriguing finding of just such a federal constitutional interest, which reached a final judgment in the federal Court of Appeals for the Eleventh Circuit, resulted from a trilogy of cases titled *Roe v. Alabama*. The electoral context involved a statewide general election for Chief Justice of the Alabama Supreme Court and the state Treasurer, among other offices. Particularly for the former office, the initial votes were quite close, with the margin of victory appearing to be between 200 to 300 votes. A massive and lengthy dispute then arose over 1000 to 2000 contested absentee ballots not counted in the initial returns. The critical state-law question was whether those ballots were illegal and not validly to be counted because they were either not properly notarized or witnessed. And the further question, which eventually triggered a federal constitutional decision, was whether the answer the Alabama state courts gave to *that* question — whether these absentee ballots could be counted — was *itself* an answer that was consistent with prior state law and practice on absentee ballots with these defects. If not — if the Alabama courts had changed a clearly established rule of state law and/or longstanding established state practices — did the decision of the state judicial system then amount to a federal constitutional violation? What is the federal interest in state elections in ensuring consistency and regularity? If there is such a federal interest, it would presumably apply with even greater force, would it not, in the context of elections for national office, even if the ground rules for those elections are established in the first instance at the state level?

Particularly noteworthy is the fact that these cases come from the Eleventh Circuit. That is the Court that oversees Florida, among other states, and therefore it is the federal court of appeals that would play a key role — if any federal court of appeals would play any role at all — in the 2000 Presidential election dispute that emerged out of the Florida electoral process. In light of the *Roe* cases, it may be easier to understand why lawyers for the Bush campaign pressed so ardently to draw the Eleventh Circuit into the Florida dispute. We will begin with the crucial substantive holding, in *Roe I*, 43 F.3d 574 (11th Cir.1995), about the nature of the federal substantive interest in state electoral ground rules. After presenting *Roe I*, we will then elaborate upon the procedural interplay between state and federal courts in this contest — returning to the issues of timing of federal intervention discussed in Chapter 5. This procedural aspect of the *Roe* cases will, like the substantive aspect, help explain why the interaction between state and federal courts in the 2000 Presidential election litigation had the structure and sequence of events that it did.

Roe I arose in this context: after the disputed election, absentee voters brought suit in the Alabama Circuit Court in which they sought an order requiring these disqualified absentee ballots to be included in the vote count. The state Circuit Court ordered the Secretary of State to include these ballots in the count. Another group of plaintiffs then turned to the United States District Court with an action that argued the state Circuit Court's order to include the absentee ballots so changed pre-existing state law on absentee ballots as to violate federal constitutional standards under the Fourteenth Amendment. The District Court agreed and issued a preliminary injunction against the state Circuit Court order. *Roe I* addressed whether, at this stage of the litigation, such a claim against state-election decisions by state courts could constitute a federal constitutional violation — and if so, under what circumstances. We include the central holding of *Roe I* on that key point:

Roe v. State of Alabama [Roe I]

43 F.3d 574 (11th Cir. 1995)

■ JUDGES: BEFORE TJOFLAT, CHIEF JUDGE, EDMONDSON AND BIRCH, CIRCUIT JUDGES.

PER CURIAM:

* * * *

II

Appellants contend that the plaintiffs failed to allege, or to demonstrate, the violation of a right "secured by the Constitution" as required under section 1983. We disagree. In this case, Roe, Hooper, and Martin allege that "the actions of the Defendants and the Defendant Class . . . would constitute a retroactive validation of a potentially controlling number of votes in the elections for Chief Justice and Treasurer" that "would result in fundamental unfairness and would violate plaintiffs' right to due process of law" in violation of the Fourteenth Amendment, and that this violation of "the plaintiffs' rights to vote and . . . have their votes properly and honestly counted" constitutes a violation of the First and Fourteenth Amendments.

The right of suffrage is "a fundamental political right, because preservative of all rights." *Yick Wo v. Hopkins*, 118 U.S. 356, 370 (1886). "The right of suffrage can be denied by a debasement or dilution of the weight of a citizen's vote just as effectively as by wholly prohibiting the free exercise of the franchise." *Reynolds v. Sims*, 377 U.S. 533, 554 (1964). Not every state election dispute, however, implicates the Due Process Clause of the Fourteenth Amendment and thus leads to possible federal court intervention. Generally, federal courts do not involve themselves in "'garden variety' election disputes." If, however, "the election process itself reached the point of patent and fundamental unfairness, a violation of the due process clause may be indicated and relief under §1983 therefore in order. Such a situation must go well beyond the ordinary dispute over the counting and marking of ballots." We address, then, whether the plaintiffs have demonstrated fundamental unfairness in the November 8 election. We conclude that they have.

The plaintiffs acknowledge that the State of Alabama is free to place reasonable time, place, and manner restrictions on voting, and that Alabama can require that voters be qualified electors. *See generally Burdick v. Takushi*, 504 U.S. 428, 433 (1992) ("Common sense, as well as constitutional law, compels the conclusion that government must play an active role in structuring elections. . . ."). They argue, however, that section 17-10-7 of the Alabama Election Code clearly requires that affidavits accompanying absentee ballots either be notarized or signed by two witnesses; that the statewide practice in Alabama prior to the November 8 general election was to exclude absentee ballots that did not comply with this rule; and that the circuit court's order requiring the state's election officials to perform the ministerial act of counting the contested absentee ballots, if permitted to stand, will constitute a retroactive change in the election laws that will effectively "stuff the ballot box," implicating fundamental fairness issues.

We agree that failing to exclude the contested absentee ballots will constitute a post-election departure from previous practice in Alabama. *See Griffin v. Burns*, 570 F.2d 1065, 1075 (1st Cir. 1978). This departure would have two effects that implicate fundamental fairness and the propriety of the two elections at issue. First, counting ballots that were not previously counted would dilute the votes of those voters who met the requirements of section 17-10-7 as well as those voters who actually went to the polls on election day. Second, the change in the rules after the election would have the effect of disenfranchising those who would have voted but for the inconvenience imposed by the notarization/witness requirement.

Appellants point out that "[a] judicial construction of a statute is an authoritative statement of what the statute meant before as well as after the decision of the case giving rise to that construction." Thus, appellants urge, the Montgomery County Circuit Court's ruling merely articulated in a clearer way what the law has always been in Alabama. This argument, however, ignores the fact that section 17-10-7, on its face, requires notarization or witnessing, that the Secretary and the Attorney General have acknowledged the requirement and that, as the district court found, the practice of the election officials throughout the state has been to exclude absentee ballots that did not meet this requirement. We consider it unreasonable to expect average voters and candidates to question the Secretary's, the Attorney General's, and the election officials' interpretation and application of the statute, especially in light of its plain language.

Appellants also argue that this case presents a case of enfranchisement of those who cast the contested absentee ballots, rather than a disenfranchisement of qualified voters, and thus does not rise to the level of a constitutional violation. They rely heavily on *Partido Nuevo Progresista v. Barreto Perez,* 639 F.2d 825 (1st Cir. 1980), *cert. denied,* 451 U.S. 985 (1981). In that case, the plaintiffs challenged the tallying of ballots in a local election in Puerto Rico. A section of the Electoral Law of Puerto Rico provided that, if a handwritten ballot was used in an election, the Electoral Commission had to guarantee that the elector was qualified to vote by making a mark in a specific place on the ballot. The section stated that if the mark was not made in the correct space, the ballot would be null and void. After the election, the Administrator of the Election Commission and the Commonwealth's Electoral Review Board held that several ballots were invalid because they were not marked correctly. The Supreme Court of Puerto Rico reversed, holding that, despite the section's clear language, the ballots should be counted. The *Barreto Perez* plaintiffs, citing *Griffin,* alleged that the Puerto Rico Supreme Court's ruling constituted a change in the method of counting ballots after the election and, therefore, violated the Constitution. *Id.* at 826.

The First Circuit did not agree for two reasons. First, the court found it significant that "this case does not involve a state court order that disenfranchises voters; rather it involves a . . . decision that enfranchises them — plaintiffs claim that votes were 'diluted' by the votes of others, not that they themselves were prevented from voting." *Id.* at 828 (emphasis in original). Second, the court found that "no party or person is likely to have acted to their detriment by relying upon the invalidity of [the contested] ballots . . . ." *Id.* Accordingly, the First Circuit found no constitutional injury. We need not address the court's apparent holding that dilution is not a constitutional injury because the facts of this case differ markedly from those of *Barreto Perez.* We believe that, had the candidates and citizens of Alabama known that something less than the signature of two witnesses or a notary attesting to the signature of absentee voters would suffice, campaign strategies would have taken this into account and supporters of Hooper and Martin who did not vote would have voted absentee.

DISSENT:

■ EDMONDSON, Circuit Judge, dissenting:

I know of no other case involving disputed ballots in which a federal court has intervened in a state election where the plaintiff failed to show, in fact, either:

1. that plaintiff had "lost" the election but would have won the election if lawful votes only had been counted (that is, the alleged constitutional error changed the election result); or

2. that it was impossible ever to know that his opponent (the apparent winner) had truly won the election because of the nature of the voting irregularities (that is, the alleged constitutional error placed in everlasting doubt what was the true result of the election).

Nothing is known in this case about whether the alleged illegalities have affected or will affect the outcome of the pertinent elections. Yet today we plow into Alabama's election process and uphold a preliminary injunction that, in effect, overrules a pre-existing state court order which had directed that the contested votes be counted. And, instead, the federal courts (basically, stopping short the state election processes) order that the contested votes be not counted at all. This high level of federal activity seems unnecessary and, therefore, improper. So, I conclude that the district court abused its discretion.

For all we or anyone else knows, if the contested absentee votes in this case were counted, plaintiffs' candidates would win the elections, even taking those contested votes into account. In such event, none of the plaintiffs would be aggrieved by the decision to count absentee ballots not strictly complying with the state's statute. I believe everyone involved in this election dispute would understand that a court's allowing the simple adding up of which of the contested absentee votes went to which candidate would not be the same thing as saying that the' contested votes will have value ultimately, as a matter of law, for deciding the final, official outcome of the elections. But instead of letting the votes be counted as an Alabama court has directed and then seeing if there is even a controversy about the election's outcome, the federal courts have jumped into the process and blocked the very step that might show there is no big problem to be dealt with by federal judges. I would not interfere with the counting of the contested ballots, although I agree that all the ballots and envelopes and other election materials pertinent to the contested ballots should be maintained and protected so that additional judicial review, if needed, would be convenient and possible.

This difference with my colleagues is more than just academic bickering about technicalities. Federal courts are not the bosses in state election disputes unless extraordinary circumstances affecting the integrity of the state's election process are clearly present in a high degree. This well-settled principle — that federal courts interfere in state elections as a last resort — is basic to federalism, and we should take it to heart. . . .

As I understand the law, "only in extraordinary circumstances will a challenge to a state election rise to the level of a constitutional deprivation." *Curry v. Baker*, 802 F.2d 1302, 1314 (11th Cir. 1986). To my way of thinking, the federal courts have acted too aggressively too soon and have, as a result, become entangled in Alabama's state election too much. At a time when we do not know whether the contested votes, in fact, will make any difference at all in the outcome of the elections, it is hard for me to say that I am now facing the kind of extraordinary circumstances — patent and fundamental unfairness tied to concrete harm — that will amount to a constitutional deprivation and that will justify immediate significant federal interference in the election processes of a state.

I would dissolve the district court's injunction except to the extent that the injunction requires all election materials in the defendants' control to be preserved and protected in a way (for example, keeping questionable individual absentee ballots and their envelopes together) that a fair review of the election remains, in fact, possible and convenient. This limited relief should be enough to protect plaintiffs until the Alabama law becomes clear, assuming that there is a live controversy about this election after the contested ballots are counted.

NOTES ON THE PROCEDURAL POSTURE AND AFTERMATH OF THE ROE LITIGATION

The minuet between state and federal judicial movements in the *Roe* litigation reveals much about the general timing of federal judicial intervention in state-regulated electoral processes, a subject we explore in more detail in the Chapter 5. We summarize those steps here to enable readers to appreciate these timing issues. First, after the disputed election results became apparent, certain absentee voters brought an action in the state Circuit Court, in which they sought an order that the contested absentee ballots be counted. That court issued a temporary restraining order (TRO) in which it ordered the Secretary of State to refrain from certifying the election until the county canvassing officials had included the contested absentee ballots in the vote totals they forwarded to the Secretary of State. Second, in response to this decision, other voters and two candidates went to federal District Court to seek an injunction ordering state officials *not* to comply with the state Circuit Court's orders. The federal District Court found from the evidence presented that the state Circuit Court order constituted a "change in the past practice" of Alabama regarding absentee ballots. As a result, the District Court concluded that were state officials to comply with the state Circuit Court's orders, those officials would be in violation of the Fourteenth Amendment to the United States Constitution. The District Court therefore entered a preliminary injunction requiring the Secretary of State to certify the election results *without* the contested absentee ballots.

Roe I was the appeal from the District Court's injunction. As the above excerpts portray, *Roe I* agreed with the District Court's judgment that federal constitutional interests would be implicated were the state courts of Alabama to change the state practice of dealing with the contested ballots in issue. But *Roe I* concluded that it was as yet unclear whether Alabama had indeed changed its pre-existing electoral rules and practices. *Roe I* therefore accommodated the diverse federal and state interests in disputed elections in the following way: having established the relevant substantive constitutional principles, *Roe I* then certified to the Alabama Supreme Court the central question of state law: did Alabama law make the contested absentee ballots legal or illegal votes? At the same time, the Eleventh Circuit ordered the

Secretary of State not to certify any election results for Chief Justice and Treasurer, the two offices in question.

The Alabama Supreme Court responded to the Eleventh Circuit by concluding that the ballots in question were indeed legal votes under Alabama law. The Eleventh Circuit's next move, then, was to remand the proceedings to the federal District Court for extensive findings of fact on 17 specific questions designed to establish whether the state courts had actually changed state election laws that had existed before the fall election. *Roe v. State of Alabama*, 52 F.3d 300 (11th Cir. 1995) (*Roe II*), *cert. denied*, 516 U.S. 908 (1995). After a three-day trial, the District Court then made detailed findings that before the contested election Alabama's practice had "uniformly" been to exclude absentee ballots like those contested. Indeed, the Eleventh Circuit concluded that the facts found in the District Court "were stronger in favor of the Roe class than the prior panel could have expected" and thus that the evidence of a change in state election practices had been firmly established. The District Court had entered a final judgment ordering the Secretary of State to certify the results for the Chief Justice and Treasurer *without* including the contested absentee ballots. In *Roe III*, the 11th Circuit affirmed this final judgment. *Roe v. State of Alabama*, 68 F.3d 404 (11th Cir. 1995). Thus, the federal courts ended up holding that a state court interpretation of state election law, for two state offices, had so changed the pre-existing state law as to constitute impermissible vote dilution under the Due Process clause of the Fourteenth Amendment.

How long did this dance between federal and state courts take? The election was held on November 8, 1994. The state Circuit Court TRO was entered nine days later, on November 17, 1994. The federal district court preliminary injunction was entered on December 5, 1994. *Roe I* was decided January 4, 1995. *Roe III*, which brought the litigation to conclusion, was issued October 13, 1995 — nearly a year after the election. In light of the unique time pressures in resolving disputed Presidential elections, driven by the meeting date of the Electoral College, what does the *Roe* litigation suggest about the capacity of federal and state courts jointly to work out adequate judicial solutions to disputed Presidential contests? Would it have improved the resolution of the Presidential election dispute had any of the federal courts involved, such as the Eleventh Circuit, followed the *Roe* practice of certifying questions of state-election law to the Florida Supreme Court?

NOTES AND QUESTIONS

1. The constitutional violation established in *Roe I* seemingly rests on "two effects" that implicate constitutional due process and equal protection concerns. A crucial question relevant to the *Bush v. Gore* litigation, among others, is whether *both* these effects must be present to generate a federal constitutional violation. The first effect centers on a change in state election law: the conclusion of a federal court that a state-court interpretation of state election laws effectively changes those laws. The second effect focuses on actual detrimental reliance of state voters on what appeared to be existing state election law before the state court interpretation at issue. Is a "change" in state law sufficient to trigger the constitutional violation? Or must it be a "change" that also frustrates concrete and specific reliance interest of voters? Note that in the *Roe* litigation there was not any allegation that state officials had engaged in fraudulent conduct or acted with partisan intent to manipulate outcomes; the claim was that even apparently neutral action could amount to unconstitutional unfairness by its effects on the electoral process.

2. *Vote Dilution and Changes in State Law.* The first effect is unconstitutional vote dilution that occurs when state election rules change in a way to include votes that were previously not treated as legal votes under state law. Those injured would include voters who went to the polls and cast legal votes or who cast legal absentee votes; a change in state law that permits previously illegal votes to be counted then, apparently, dilutes the votes legally cast. Recall that the federal courts must distinguish, as *Roe I* itself recognizes, between ordinary disputes over counting ballots, and state practices that reach the point of "patent and fundamental unfairness." But suppose a federal court simply disagrees with a state court interpretation of the state's election laws, when the consequence of any judicial decision is to include or exclude certain ballots: if the federal court believed state law precluded inclusion of certain ballots, would *Roe I* mean that unconstitutional vote dilution would occur were the state court to interpret state law differently and conclude that those ballots *should* be included? Or, if the state court excludes certain ballots, and the federal courts believe state law requires inclusion of such ballots, is this tantamount to unconstitutional vote dilution against voters whose votes have been excluded? Is there a risk that the principle of *Roe I* would turn every dispute over the interpretation of state election law into a federal constitutional question? Does *Roe I* succeed at its own task of drawing a line between ordinary ballot counting disputes and those that involve patent and fundamental unfairness? Does the answer depend on exactly how overwhelming the evidence must be that a state court interpretation actually changes existing state law? Does the answer also depend on whether detrimental reliance, as well as a change in state law, is required to establish a federal constitutional violation?

3. *Assessing State Judicial Interpretations as Unconstitutional Changes in State Law.* How convinced, and with what evidence, should a federal court be that a state judicial decision changes state election practices, in the midst of an election dispute, so dramatically as to amount to a federal constitutional violation? We can imagine a spectrum of possible contexts. At one end, the prior state law can be embodied not only in written legal texts, but in longstanding judicial and administrative practices consistent with those texts. The more the specific issue has been regularly confronted, particularly in contexts analogous to that at issue, the more possible it becomes to have a firmly anchored set of baseline laws and practices against which federal courts can assess any potential "changes" in state practices. In such a case, a federal court has a wealth of evidence to draw on in assessing whether one particular state judicial ruling is a sharp departure from pre-existing state rules.

That was precisely the situation in the *Roe* litigation. After an extensive trial, the District Court made the following factual findings: (1) every county in Alabama (except one) had consistently and for years excluded absentee ballots like those contested; (2) the Secretary of State had consistently maintained that ballots like those contested were not to be counted and had instructed every voting official in the State to that effect; (3) not one election official testified to the Court that the contested ballots would ordinarily be included; (4) had voters known they could have voted absentee under laxer standards, many more might have voted. In light of this longstanding, unequivocal, consistent state practice, the District Court concluded the state Circuit Court's decision to include the ballots was an "abominable" post-election change of practice that amounted to "ballot-box stuffing" and was hence unconstitutional. *Roe v. Mobile County Appointing Board*, 904 F. Supp. 1315, 1335 (S. D. Ala. 1995).

Now consider the other pole of the spectrum. Suppose a state has an election law on the books that has not been tested or applied with any frequency (if at all) and hence has not been the subject of extensive judicial or administrative elaboration. Indeed, suppose the statute has never been applied to the kind of election context currently before the state courts. When the state courts interpret such a statute in the midst of this kind of election, what possible baseline can the federal courts use to assess whether that state interpretation is a dramatic "change in state law"? If there is no evidence of actual prior state practices on the matter, nor even official positions that the Secretary of State has taken in advance and instructed state officials to follow, what kind of evidence can the federal court possibly look at to determine whether judicial interpretation has become an "abominable" post-election change?

In such a situation, can the federal court possibly be engaging in anything other than simply second-guessing whether the state court has read the statute the same way the federal court would, if the federal court had the power to interpret state law? The only evidence the federal court would have before it would be the text of the state statute itself. Perhaps, in some states, the federal court would also have whatever legislative history was relevant — though the state legislature might well have enacted the statute without any thought at all about its application to the particular kind of election matter now at issue. Yet this set of information, mostly confined to the text of the statute itself, is exactly the same information before the state court. Absent any fuller set of evidence about established state practices implementing the law in question, is not the federal court left with nothing more than the role of deciding whether it, in the first instance, would interpret the bare text of the state law the same way the state court has? If the federal court has no more to draw on than the same state statutory text on which the state court drew, is there a sufficient prior established state-law practice that ought to justify triggering the "extraordinary" federal constitutional intervention that is warranted only when matter of "patent and fundamental unfairness" are involved? Recall that the task of doctrine in this area is to distinguish between ordinary state-election disputes from matters that warrant the extraordinary intervention of constitutional law because some "abominable" or comparable change in law has turned the election. If the situation can only involve differences in view between state and federal courts over how state laws ought to be interpreted, where those differences cannot be grounded in anything other than the words of the particular statute itself — because there is no longstanding state practice one way or the other — how can federal courts conclude a constitutional violation has occurred? In this context, is there not a real danger that federal courts will simply substitute their own judgment about the proper meaning of state law — precisely the massive intrusion on state interests the doctrine is designed to guard against — rather than ensure the state acts consistently with its own prior laws and practices? It is only ensuring that consistency that is supposed to trigger any federal constitutional interest.

4. The Presidential election dispute in Florida arose in this latter context. Florida law provided for the protest and the contest of disputed elections. Fla. Stat. Ann. §§ 102.166 (protest); 102.168 (contest). Yet uncontradicted assertions at oral argument before the Supreme Court stated that the last *statewide* contest of an election had been in 1919 — long before the current statutes had been enacted. Thus, there was simply no state law or administrative practice of significance that bore on the question of how Florida applied these disputed-election statutes to a statewide election contest. In addition, there was no evidence that, when these state laws were designed, any legislator had a Presidential election contest in mind one way or the other. These protest and contest statutes make no reference at all to disputed Presidential elections; yet such elections undoubtedly raise distinct concerns of their own, such as the relevance of the Electoral College meeting date — distinct concerns even as compared to disputed statewide races for offices like Governor, to which the statutes had also not previously been applied.

The Florida courts were thus required to apply state laws never before applied to statewide disputed elections, in the even more remote context of a Presidential election whose resolution the Florida legislature had presumably not considered one way or the other when drafting these protest and contest statutes. When the Florida courts then issued their interpretations of these statutes in the midst of the Presidential election dispute, what role should the federal courts have played in determining whether any of those interpretations so changed pre-existing Florida law as to be an "abominable" change in state practice justifying "extraordinary" federal constitutional intervention to ensure no "patent and fundamental unfairness" that rose to the level of a federal constitutional violation? If the Florida courts permitted amended returns, based on manual recounts, or ordered manual recounts to be conducted in certain ways and under certain conditions, against what baseline would federal courts assess whether these interpretations amounted to "changes in state law practices" akin to those in *Roe I*? In this context, *should* federal courts play any role in overseeing state-election laws? Lacking any firm anchor in a clear set of established prior practices, if the federal courts can do no more than simply issue their own interpretations of how best to read state law, can such a difference of view ever rise to the level of the "patent" unfairness that is required for a federal constitutional interest in the process?

Does or should *Roe I* permit federal courts to find state judicial interpretation an unconstitutional change in law when there is no evidence on which to anchor that judgment other than the very statutes being interpreted? If *Roe I* is extended that far, does the decision succeed in its stated goal of avoiding turning every disputed state election law ruling into a federal constitutional question? Note that in the Presidential election litigation, when decisions of the Florida courts were challenged as having unconstitutionally changed state law, the central evidence of that change was simply the text of the relevant statutes themselves and arguments about how best to interpret them. Thus, the complexity and ferocity of disputes over whether there was any federal constitutional issue posed by the Florida Supreme Court interpretations of state law can be illuminated by recognizing that these disputes arose at one pole of the spectrum of possibilities for federal oversight of state election rulings — the pole at which there is little upon which to base judgment of consistency other than the state statutes themselves whose interpretation is at issue.

5. *Detrimental Reliance, Due Process, and Constitutional Violations.* Recall that *Roe I* identified two constitutional defects that justified constitutional intervention there. Up until now, we have been exploring the first: a profound change in state law in the midst of a disputed election. The second effect rests on detrimental reliance and appears to implicate due process, as opposed to vote dilution, constitutional principles. Here the constitutional question is whether the purportedly "new" state rule — had it been clearly specified in advance — would have led (or might have led) significant numbers of non-voters to vote, had they known that a laxer standard would have been in place. That principle was also implicated in *Roe I* because the disputed judicial interpretation made it easier for voters to cast absentee ballots. Thus, according to the *Roe I* court, the post-election change in interpretation "disenfranchised" those who would have voted but for the more onerous absentee ballot restrictions previous state practice had imposed. Because voters notified in advance of the "new rule" might well have voted, the retroactive adoption of this rule violated the Due Process rights of such potential voters.

As noted above, a key question about *Roe I* is whether both effects — a change in state law and detrimental reliance leading to non-voting by those who might otherwise have voted — are necessary to establish a constitutional violation. Suppose a state judicial decision that arguably changes state law, but not in a way that could plausibly be said to deny due process by effectively disenfranchising voters who would otherwise have voted had they known of the new rule. For further analysis of these issues, see Richard H. Pildes, *Judging "New Law" in Election Disputes*, 28 Fla. St. U. L. Rev. ____ (2001).

An important predecessor to *Roe I*, which rests heavily on the detrimental reliance, due process principal, is *Griffin v. Burns*, 570 F.2d 1065 (1st Cir. 1978). In the primary for a local city council race, the Secretary of State concluded that ordinary absentee and shut-in ballot laws for the general election should also be applied to primaries. The Secretary and other state officials publicized the availability of such ballots, and almost 10% of the total vote in the primary came from these ballots. The candidate who had won the machine vote, McCormick, but lost the total vote due to these absentee ballots then brought and won an action in the Rhode Island Supreme Court. In a 3-2 decision, the state Supreme Court held that state law did not permit these ballots for primary elections, since the relevant laws did not explicitly so authorize. Four days later, the Rhode Island legislature amended the law to permit expressly the use of such ballots in primaries. Meanwhile, the candidate who had won the total vote, Griffin, but lost in light of the state Supreme Court ruling that the absentee ballots that had provided his margin of victory were illegally cast under state law, then brought an action in federal district court (along with voters who had used the absentee ballots that had been tossed out). The district court found that the Rhode Island Supreme Court decision had violated the constitutional rights of these voters; as a remedy, the district court ordered that a new primary election be held.

The First Circuit affirmed. On the substantive federal interest, the First Circuit noted that states are not constitutionally required to provide for absentee or shut-in voting in primary elections. The First Circuit also noted that, despite the constitutional importance of the right to vote, federal courts tended to intervene in state election disputes only in the most limited circumstances: where state laws of general applicability are unconstitutional on their face, or where overt racial discrimination in limiting the ballot was involved. In contrast, "garden variety" election irregularities — errors in election administration, malfunctioning of voting machines, even some claims of official misconduct — do not typically rise to the level of constitutional violations, especially where the state provides adequate corrective processes. "If every election irregularity or contested vote involved a federal violation, the court would 'be thrust into the details of virtually every election, tinkering with the state's election machinery, reviewing petitions, registration cards, vote tallies, and certificates of election for all manner of error and insufficiency under state and federal law.'" *Id.* at 1977 (citation omitted).

Nonetheless, the First Circuit concluded, federal intervention was warranted here. The general principle justifying such intervention was similar to that in *Roe I*: where "broad-gauged unfairness permeates an election, even if derived from apparently neutral action" an election process can reach "the point of patent and fundamental unfairness" that triggers a due process violation. Due process "is implicated where the entire election process — including as part thereof the state's administrative and judicial corrective process — fails on its face to afford fundamental fairness." *Id.*, at 1078. Applying this standard, the First Circuit did *not* hold, as in *Roe I*, that the Rhode Island Supreme Court had unconstitutionally changed state law. Instead, the First Circuit compared the state Supreme Court's decision with longstanding, prior state practice; with the advice the relevant state administrative officials provided before the election; with the actions of the state legislature both before the state Supreme Court decision (acquiescing in regular use of such ballots in primaries) and after the decision (amending the law to expressly permit such ballots in primaries). Thus, the First Circuit concluded that absentee voters had relied reasonably on the advice that they could cast absentee ballots and that the Rhode Island Supreme Court decision had come as such a surprise, that to exclude these ballots — around 10% of those cast — would violate fundamental fairness notions embodied in the Due Process clause. The key fact was the reliance of these voters on longstanding state practice: evidence had been introduced that, had they known absentee balloting was not permitted, at least some of these voters would have gone to the polls and voted in person. The evidence was sufficient to establish that this number could have affected the election outcome. Because Rhode Island's

Supreme Court had ruled these illegal votes, the First Circuit concluded that it ought not to order the votes to be treated as legally cast. Instead, the First Circuit affirmed the District Court's use of its equitable powers to order a new primary election. Note that *Griffin* is a case of (1) detrimental reliance without also being a case of (2) a change in state law that, in and of itself, amounted to an unconstitutional departure. That is, if *Roe I* requires both (1) and (2), *Griffin* is a case that turns on the unfair surprise to individual voters of being disenfranchised by a state Supreme Court interpretation that was inconsistent with longstanding state practice and with official state advice these voters were given in advance of the election.

If detrimental reliance of individual voters is critical to the federal substantive interest in election disputes like those in *Roe I* and *Griffin*, how would that affect what kind of federal substantive interest, if any, existed in the 2000 Presidential election litigation? Recall that one of the key flashpoints for controversy was whether the Florida Supreme Court had changed pre-existing state law through any of that court's important decisions: permitting amended returns from selective hand recounts to be included in the pre-certification vote totals; or permitting a post-certification contest of election which involved extensive hand recounts of "undervoted" ballots across numerous counties. Whatever else might be said about these decisions, if they do constitute a change of law, do they do so in a way that would implicate detrimental reliance on the part of voters comparable to that in *Roe I* and *Griffin*? Would any voters be able to claim, plausibly, that had they known the Florida Supreme Court would authorize hand recounts, those voters would have acted in some different way — somehow changed their voting practices? Wouldn't the claim of detrimental reliance have to amount to voters saying, had they known they could get a vote counted without fulling punching out the chad, they would have done so? For voters who did the work required to punch out the actual chad, can they claim any due process violation in having had to do more work than required, had they only known of the hand recount possibility? For voters who did not vote, could they plausibly claim, as in *Griffin*, that they would have turned out at the polls had they only known a partially punched chad would be treated as a valid vote? All readers can agree, we assume, that these claims of detrimental reliance would be fanciful. It is thus important to notice one way in which any challenge to the Florida Supreme Court decisions as "changed law" necessarily differs from the claims in cases like *Roe I* and *Griffin;* such claims depend on the view that a state court change in election law, in itself, can amount to a constitutional violation, even without that change implicating the Due Process interests of individual voters by retroactively changing the election process in a way to which voters would have self-protectively responded *ex ante* had they had notice of the change in advance. In other words, a challenge to the Florida Supreme Court decisions on "changed law" grounds would depend on federal constitutional law prohibiting such changes, even when they do not implicate specific reliance interests of voters (note that in the litigation, the Bush lawyers did point to other federal sources of such a "general" constraint on changes in state law, beyond the fundamental fairness due process principles invoked in *Roe I* and *Griffin;* the Bush campaign argued that in the distinct context of a presidential election, Art.II of the U.S. Constitution and The Electoral Count Act, 3 U.S.C. § 5, did constitute broad, general barriers against judicial interpretations that changed pre-existing law, without the further need to show detrimental reliance of individual voters on the previous interpretation).

6. *The dissent in Roe I.* To protect the boundary between constitutional law and state-election dispute resolution processes for state elections, including state judicial processes, Judge Edmondson re-asserts that federal intervention requires "extraordinary circumstances affecting the integrity of the state's election processes." Note that he fails to find that in *Roe I* because of the *timing* of federal intervention being sought, not because of disagreement with the underlying substantive constitutional principles. Judge Edmondson therefore disagreed with the District Court's grant of a preliminary injunction and the Eleventh Circuit's affirmance of that injunction. Recall that the injunction precluded the Secretary of State, in reliance on the state Circuit Court's order, from including the contested absentee ballots in the certified vote totals. On Judge Edmondson's view, the state system should be allowed to reach finality in addressing the disputed election; only after that point, should federal courts intervene — "as a last resort" — with any kind of relief.

Thus, Judge Edmondson's dissent argues both that the federal court should not intervene until Alabama law becomes clear, through the Alabama Supreme Court, *and until the contested ballots are counted*, should the Alabama courts require their inclusion. This disagreement about the timing of federal court intervention appears to rest on two principles: (1) until the federal courts learn whether the contested ballots would, in fact, change the election outcome if counted, there is no "concrete harm" to any of the plaintiffs. That is, to justify federal intervention, plaintiffs must be able to show as a matter of actual fact that the election outcome has been altered as a result of the state court decision. In addition, Judge Edmondson believes that the federal courts are capable of providing fully adequate relief at the end of the process; that is, should it turn out that state judicial decisions do admit votes to be counted that change the election outcome, and the state courts commit constitutional error in doing so, the federal courts can fully remedy that violation. How? Simply by holding that the Secretary of State must certify the constitutionally valid "winner" as the actual winner of the election. Thus, if candidate A is certified the Chief Justice of the Alabama Supreme Court because the Alabama courts include the contested ballots, and it was constitutional error to include those ballots — and their inclusion changed the election outcome — then the Eleventh Circuit should intervene at that point and order a change in result. Note, then, the second principle included in Judge Edmondson's position on the timing of federal intervention: (2) there is no irreparable harm in letting disputed ballots be counted in the state system, because the federal courts can always repair any wrong simply by ordering a different candidate validly elected. In contrast, the panel majority specifically enjoined anyone from *opening* the contested absentee ballots (needless to say, without opening them, it would have been quite a feat to count them).

These debates about the timing of federal intervention reach a national audience with the question of whether the United States Supreme Court should have *stayed* the ongoing Florida recounts, undertaken pursuant to Florida Supreme Court orders. Note that the question of a stay is a distinct question from that of the proper constitutional rule on the merits, though the questions are related. Should federal courts enjoin the counting of disputed ballots until those courts pass on the merits of the constitutional claims — as the *Roe I* panel majority does? Or should federal courts permit disputed ballots to be counted, with the assurance that if their inclusion is unconstitutional and changes the election outcome, federal courts can order the proper winner to assume office — as the *Roe I* dissent argues? Should federal courts find it irreparable harm to count disputed ballots, which may for the moment change the "winner" of the election, if those courts believe on the merits the process generating those counts is unconstitutional and makes the results a legal nullity? Or should the release of information, whether legally obtained or not, never be considered irreparable harm if the federal courts can intervene at the end and ensure that the correct "winner" assume the office in question?

B. DISTINCT FEDERAL INTERESTS IN NATIONAL ELECTIONS: U.S. HOUSE AND SENATE ELECTIONS

Thus far, we have focused on defining the substantive federal interests implicated in state election disputes. Those interests typically derive from the U.S. Constitution, although important federal statues, such as the Voting Rights Act, also oversee state electoral practices. When it comes to national offices, the Constitution does assign Congress certain additional powers, or perhaps impose some additional constraints on States, beyond those implicated in state elections. For example, Art. I., Sec. 4 of the Constitution gives Congress a backup power to regulate the time, place, and manner of holding congressional elections. In 1842, Congress first exercised this power to require members of Congress to be elected from single-member districts, rather than at-large. Enforcement of the current version of that federal statute in congressional elections would afford a distinct federal interest for federal court intervention in congressional elections. Additionally, the Seventeenth Amendment provides that states shall have the right to vote directly for senators.

But for the most part, apart from a few discrete federal interventions such as the requirement of single-member districts, state law offers the electoral machinery and regulation that determines the conduct of elections — including resolution of disputed elections — for national as well as state offices. Thus, the discussion thus far on the federal judicial role, both procedurally and substantively, for state-election disputes carries over directly to the resolution of election disputes for the United States House and Senate. With one exception about to be mentioned, there is no distinct national regulatory structure for national elections, nor for resolving disputes over such elections. Typically, the ordinary state laws that regulate state election contests and disputes are simply carried over at the state level to national elections. Unless Congress has distinctly legislated special rules for national elections, those elections are governed by whatever laws individual states choose to adopt. As a result, the regulatory framework for national elections in the United States is radically decentralized, not only with individual states free to adopt different regulations, but with individual states free to delegate to their local governments, such as counties, the discretion to adopt diverse rules — such as the appearance of the ballot, the type of voting technology to employ, and the like. That is why, in the recent 2000 Presidential election dispute, one individual county in Florida — Palm Beach County — was able to design and employ its own distinct ballot, the "Butterfly Ballot," even though the election involved the highest national office. The Constitution has not been thought to require national uniformity in national elections in matters like ballot design, nor has Congress legislated such requirements. Similarly, with one exception, the Constitution also does not impose any uniform procedure for dealing with disputed elections for national office, whether for Congress or the Presidency. To the extent disputes arise, they are left in the first instance to state administrative and judicial processes.

As just suggested, there is one exception, however, when it comes to elections for the House and Senate. The Constitution explicitly makes its each Chamber the exclusive judge of the qualifications of its members. Thus, Art.I, § 5, provides in part: "Each House shall be the Judge of the Elections, Returns and Qualifications of its own Members. . . ." This means that when election disputes arise concerning Senate and House races, the Senate and the House, respectively, are the forums in which such disputes must be resolved. There is no comparable constitutional provision for resolution of disputes over the choice of Presidential electors.

Does Art. I, § 5 therefore oust all ordinary state-law processes for resolving disputed House and Senate elections? Recall that Art. I, § 4 empowers the States to choose the times, places, and manner of holding elections for Senators and Representatives. Put another way, then, what exactly is the line between the state processes through which members of the House and Senate are chosen, and the resolution of any disputes over those choices? When does the "election process" end — the state controlled phase — and a dispute over Elections and Qualifications begin — a process exclusively under the control of the national political branches? That was the question in *Roudebush v. Hartke*, 405 U.S. 15 (1972), the leading case on these issues.

After the closest Senate election in Indiana history in 1970, the Secretary of State certified incumbent Vance Hartke as the winner. The next day, his opponent, Roudebush, filed a petition for a recount in state court. The state court appointed a three-person commission to begin that recount. Hartke then sought an injunction against the recount in federal district court. Hartke argued that any state recount process would interfere with the Senate's Art. I, § 5 powers to judge the qualifications of its own members. While the case was pending in the United States Supreme Court, the Senate administered the oath of office to Hartke, but he was seated without prejudice to the litigation's outcome. The district court had enjoined the recount on the grounds that any judgments about which ballots to count or not could be made only by the Senate, and that permitting any state-run recount might also damage the integrity of the ballots on which the Senate would have to rely.

In a 5-2 decision, the United States Supreme Court reversed and upheld the power of a state to conduct a manual recount, pursuant to ordinary state law, even for disputed Senate elections. The Court held that states had broad powers to regulate elections for national offices, including the use of manual recount processes as the last stage in resolving disputed elections. The Court held that a recount did not prevent the Senate from making an independent evaluation of the election returns any more than the initial count would. The Senate remained free to accept or reject the apparent winner in either count, and to conduct its own recount if it so chose. In response to the concern that a manual recount in the state might compromise the integrity of the ballots, the Court concluded that a court-appointed recount commission could not be supposed to be any less honest or conscientious than the precinct boards that made the initial counts. Thus, *Roudebush* holds that even after the Senate has provisionally seated a member, and even with the Senate's constitutional power to judge the Qualifications of its Members, a state manual recount process does not violate Art. I, § 5.

Given the recent controversies over recounts in Florida, several references to recount procedures in the Court's opinion are perhaps worth noting. Thus, on manual recounts in general, the Supreme Court wrote:

> Indiana has found, along with many other States, that one procedure necessary to guard against irregularity and error in the tabulation of votes is the availability of a recount. Despite the fact that a certificate of election may be issued to the leading candidate within 30 days after the election, the results are not final if a candidate's option to compel a recount is exercised. A recount is an integral part of the Indiana electoral process and is within the ambit of the broad powers delegated to the States by Art. I, § 4.

Id., at 25. The Court also noted that the United States Senate itself had at times engaged in recounts in close elections when state law did not provide a recount procedure. Finally, the Court pointed out that Indiana law required the Secretary of State to certify to the Governor the winning candidate as soon as the Secretary received certified returns from the counties, which meant within 26 days of the election. Yet as the Court pointed out, any recount could almost certainly not be completed before the Governor was obligated by statute to certify a winner based on the initial count. As the Court noted, however, under Indiana law a recount would supersede the initial count even though the Governor had issued the certificate of election. *Id.*, at 25 n.22. The manual recount was then conducted, but did not change the outcome. The disputed election had been on November 17, 1970; the United States Supreme Court decision had been handed down on February 23, 1972; and Hartke was officially seated without reservation on July 24, 1972—close to two years after election day. United States Senate: Election, Expulsion and Censure Cases, 1793-1990, Case 136 (Anne M. Butler and Wendy Wolff, U.S. Senate Historical Office (1995)). Could this same procedure have been followed in a contested elections for the House of Representatives, given that the congressional term of office is two years?

Of perhaps some interest in light of the recent Florida recount debate, the United States Senate itself has recounted disputed ballots in contested Senate elections. The ballots are shipped under guard from the relevant state to Washington, D.C., where any recount is undertaken by the Senate Committee on Privileges and Elections or individuals appointed by that Committee. A few brief examples, designed to illustrate Senate practices for comparison with the recent Florida debate: in the 1924 elections in Iowa, an insurgent Republican, Brookhart, appeared to defeat narrowly his Democratic challenger, Steck. There was a good deal of ballot confusion, because during the campaign, the Republican Party withdrew its support from Brookhart. A Senate subcommittee (two Republicans, two Democrats) had all 900,000 ballots shipped to D.C. for a recount. Each ballot was examined "in an effort to ascertain what the true intent of the voter had been." *Id.*, at Case 105, 313. Interestingly, the disputed ballots included ones that were technically illegal under Iowa law, but that showed a clear intent to vote for Steck. These were ballots that in which voters had attempted to copy exactly a sample newspaper ballot that had shown an arrow pointing to Steck's box; since the arrows were extraneous marks by Iowa law, the ballots had not been counted. The Senate, believing the intent of the voter to vote for Steck was clear, counted these ballots. Under the Senate recount, Steck won and was seated. The Senate has also undertaken only *partial* recounts of the particular ballots put into dispute. Thus, in the closest Senate race in New Hampshire history in 1974, the Democrat, Durkin, seemingly lost to his Republican opponent, Wyman, by 355 votes out of more than 200,000 cast. After a state recount, Durkin was certified the winner by 10 votes, but after a different state body recounted, the Governor certified Wyman the winner by 2 votes. Durkin petitioned the Senate and the relevant Committee agreed to itself recount, but limited to 3,500 disputed ballots. The Committee set up elaborate rules for the counting, but in the end could not resolve internal disagreements about standards and passed the case to the full Senate, which also bogged down and could not reach resolution. In the end, the two candidates agreed to resubmit themselves to the voters in a special election, which Durkin won overwhelmingly by more than 27,000 votes. The process within the Senate took seven months and reached no resolution.

C. DISTINCT FEDERAL INTERESTS IN NATIONAL ELECTIONS: PRESIDENTIAL ELECTIONS

At least three features of the constitutional and federal statutory structure potentially present unique legal issue when it comes to presidential elections and potential disputes over their resolution: (1) the role of the Electoral College in general; (2) the role of Art. II, Sec. 1 of the Constitution, which empowers state legislatures to "direct the manner" of choosing presidential electors; and (3) the Electoral Count Act of 1887, which was passed in an effort to create a mechanism for resolving disputed presidential elections. We will provide historical perspective on the Electoral College here, then briefly note these other potential issues, which will be discussed in detail when we examine the Supreme Court's resolution of the 2000 Presidential election.

1. THE ELECTORAL COLLEGE

There was much debate at the time of the Constitution's adoption over how to select the Nation's Chief Executive. Ultimately, Art. II created the Electoral College, in which each State receives the number of votes equal to its numbers of representatives and Senators; and each State is free to appoint, "in such manner as the Legislature thereof may direct," these electors.

Selection of a President and Vice-President by designated electors from each state was chosen by the delegates the Constitutional Convention as a compromise between congressional election and direct popular election of the chief executive. Those favoring legislative election argued that the President should be accountable to the legislature; they pointed out that the executives of 8 of 13 states were elected by the legislatures in those states. Advocates of a direct vote, who argued that the President should represent the people and not the states, were a minority that included figures such as James Wilson and James Madison. Most striking about the debate was that "it revolved around the relative *disadvantages* of each mode of election, and few delegates displayed great enthusiasm for any particular choice on its merits." Jack N. Rakove, The E-College in the E-Age, forthcoming in The Unfinished Election of 2000 (Jack N. Rakove ed. 2001). Legislative election presented separation of powers problems and raised concerns about a weak executive unable to govern; experience with governors elected by state legislatures in the majority of states was thought to bear out this experience. Direct popular vote, on the other hand, would disadvantage the smaller states and slaveholding states, where a significant portion of the population was disfranchised. The framers were also concerned that no genuinely national figure would emerge after George Washington, and that each state would support only its own candidate. The provision in Art. II explicitly prohibiting both presidential and vice-presidential candidates from residing in the same state was designed to address the latter concern.

The delegates to the Constitutional Convention did not expect that the Electoral College alone — after the inevitable election of George Washington — would often select the President. Instead, the anticipated diffusion of support for Presidential candidates would, it was thought, throw the selection of the President into the House of Representatives. As specified in Art. II, a vote in the House would then take place among the top five candidates (later reduced to three by the Twelfth Amendment). Each state delegation receives one ballot in the case of a House vote for the President. Although both the Electoral College and the House vote clearly favor small states, the combination of the two voting procedures was understood by the Framers as a compromise, in the words of James Madison, "between the larger and smaller states, giving to the latter the advantage of selecting a President from the candidates, in consideration of the former in selecting candidates from the people." Neal R. Peirce and Lawrence D. Longley, The People's President: The Electoral College in American History and the Direct Vote Alternative 17 (1981) (citing Jonathan Elliot, II, *The Debates in the Several State Conventions on the Adoption of the Federal Constitution*, 495, 464 (2nd ed. 1836)).

As originally formulated, each elector chose two persons, and the runner-up in the voting became Vice-President. The deficiencies in this arrangement became apparent after the election of 1800, in which an equal number of ballots were cast for Thomas Jefferson, the Republican presidential candidate, and Aaron Burr, his running mate, throwing the election into the House for the first of two times (the other was in 1824). In response, the Twelfth Amendment was ratified in 1804, mandating separate ballots for President and Vice-President. If no vice-presidential candidate receives a majority of electoral votes, the vice-president will be chosen by the Senate, with each Senator voting individually from among the two top vote-getters.

The method of selection of state electors was left to the discretion of the states. In the first four Presidential elections, state legislatures picked the electors in the majority of states. States using a popular election to determine their electors were about equally divided up until 1820 between districted elections of Presidential electors and a winner-take-all system. After that date, the winner-take-all system came to dominate. It continues to be used today in every state but for Maine and Nebraska. Among the reasons the winner-take-all system prevailed was that it gave ruling state parties the ability to deliver complete electoral vote blocs to the national candidate (advocates of a return to districting in many states face an uphill battle today, since such a move would reduce the impact of any given state in presidential elections, and would therefore diminish the incentive of candidates to lavish attention on that state).

Before the 2000 election, the candidate receiving a majority of electoral votes has only once failed to capture the popular vote as well. In 1888, Grover Cleveland received 48.6% of the popular vote to Benjamin Harrison's 47.8%, but lost the electoral vote by a margin of 233 to 168. Both before and after 1888, reformers have steadily issued calls to overhaul the Electoral College, or to abandon it altogether. For the debates on the Electoral College and further historical reading, see the following sources: Neal R. Peirce and Lawrence D. Longley, The People's President: The Electoral College in American History and the Direct Vote Alternative, (1981); Peirce and Longley, The Electoral College Primer, (1996); Judith Best, The Choice of the People? Debating the Electoral College, (1996); Robert M. Hardaway, The Electoral College and the Constitution: The Case for Preserving Federalism, (1994); After the People Vote: Steps in Choosing the President, (Walter Berns ed. 1983); Alexander M. Bickel, Reform and Continuity: The Electoral College, the Convention, and the Party System, (1971); Jack N. Rakove, "The E-College in the E-Age", (manuscript, 2001); Jack N. Rakove, The Political Presidency: Discovery and Invention (forthcoming 2002); Sanford Levinson, *Presidential Elections and Constitutional Stupidities*, in Constitutional Stupidities, Constitutional Tragedies, (Sanford Levinson and William Eskridge, eds.,1998).

2.   ARTICLE II AND THE ROLE OF STATE LEGISLATURES

Note that Art. II textually commits the manner of choosing presidential electors to the State legislatures. This raises two questions involving the so-called "independent legislature doctrine" under Art. II: (1) when state legislatures enact presidential-elector statutes, are the legislatures freed by virtue of Art. II from any state constitutional limitations to which the legislature would otherwise be bound; (2) when state courts interpret state presidential-elector laws, must state courts treat those statutes differently than other state legislation — in particular, does Art. II require that state courts adhere more closely to the text of the legislative enactments than they otherwise would, were the courts to apply their conventional techniques of statutory interpretation to those laws. Both of these questions became central to the litigation involving the 2000 election; we will discuss these legal issues *infra* when we discuss the litigation itself. The best historical treatment to date of these issues, also discussed *infra*, is Hayward Smith, *A Trifle Light as Air: The Article II Independent Legislature Doctrine*, 28 Fla. St. U. L. Rev. ___ (2001).

3. THE ELECTORAL COUNT ACT OF 1887

The Constitution did not create a mechanism through which potential disputes over who the "real" electors of a State were could be resolved. This was long considered one of the major gaps in the Constitution's original design; a disputed choice for Chief Executive could be one of the most explosive issues the country would confront, yet no legal mechanism for resolving such a dispute was established in the Constitution.

Congress debated the issue for years and considered various legislative solutions. But when various disputes arose about the legitimacy of a state's electors, they were resolved in an ad hoc way. Finally, Congress passed the Electoral Count Act in 1887 to establish a uniform system for resolving contested elections. Eleven years earlier, the most serious conflict over who had won the presidential election in United States history had developed over the dispute between Rutherford B. Hayes and Samuel Tilden. Several states had submitted votes from multiple slates of electors; because Congress was divided, with the Republicans controlling the Senate and the Democrats controlling the House, Congress could not easily resolve the issue of which electoral votes to accept. Congress eventually passed a law creating an Electoral Commission composed of five senators, five representatives, and five justices of the Supreme Court which determined what electoral votes to elect and awarded the election to Hayes in a series of 8-7 party line splits.

By 1887, that ad-hoc device of an specially-created Electoral Commission was viewed by Congress as a "contrivance" that could not be repeated in the future. *See* 17 Cong. Rec. 1024 (1886) (Sen. Ingalls). At the same time, Congress needed a binding rule, because the previous approach of counting electoral votes under a joint procedural rule that could be revoked by either house had led to the rule being revoked whenever one house disapproved of the results it would produce. *See* 17 Cong. Rec. 815 (1886) (Sen. Sherman). The Electoral Count Act was passed to resolve these issues definitively without a current election dispute coloring the debate.

The Electoral Count Act has two major provisions. First, it provides that state law procedures in place prior to the election are binding on Congress if they produce a definitive result at least six days prior to the day when the electors are scheduled to meet. 3 U.S.C. § 5. At the very least then, Congress binds itself to accept electoral votes from States that resolve any internal disputes before this six-day window closes. Second, the Electoral Count Act provides a mechanism for resolving disputes over whether to accept votes of electors. 3 U.S.C. § 15. If only one return has been submitted from a state, then that is accepted unless both Houses of Congress, acting separately, agree that it should be rejected because the votes were not "regularly given." *Id*. If multiple returns were submitted, then Congress is to accept the return that conforms to the state determination under Section 5. If the Houses of Congress agree upon which of several returns is the proper one, it is counted. If the Houses disagree, then whichever return is "certified by the executive of the State" is counted. *Id*. Because of an awareness that in any serious dispute multiple returns are likely, this procedure has the effect of allowing Congressional determinations of which return is proper if both houses agree on which vote is proper. In case of disputes, the slate of electors that the state governor certified wins. These provisions were adopted because of a desire to minimize the circumstances under which a state would be disenfranchised while simultaneously preventing any one house from being able to determine the election. *See* 17 Cong. Rec. 1021 (1886) (Sen. Hoar).

The Electoral Count Act had never been applied or construed by the United States Supreme Court before the *Bush v. Gore* litigation. But the Act came to have critical significance at that point. Section 5, which came to be described as a "safe harbor" provision, was directly involved at several stages of the litigation. Section 15 loomed in the background as the possible final mechanism for resolving the 2000 election, though it never came to be interpreted in the courts or employed in Congress. We explore the specific debates about the meaning and role of the Electoral Count Act *infra* as those debates came up within the actual context of the *Bush v. Gore* litigation.

CHAPTER 2

THE STATE INTEREST IN FEDERAL ELECTIONS

Most states have statutory and administrative machinery for resolving election disputes. This machinery typically involves processes for seeking manual recounts and for contesting elections in judicial proceedings. The process is also often divided into two stages: (1) a recount stage, which is a less formalized, more administrative process that can be triggered automatically in close elections or can be candidate-initiated; (2) a contest phase, which can often take weeks or months and is typically run much like ordinary civil litigation. Generally speaking, the two stages are divided by the legal moment of "certification;" once the vote totals are legally certified, one candidate is the presumptive winner of the election. A contest lawsuit must then be pursued to overcome that presumption. In some states, election contest suits are permitted for certain office, but not for others; typically, it is federal offices that such selective-contest statutes exclude. *See, e.g., Young v. Mikva,* 363 N.E. 2d 851 (S.Ct. Ill. 1977) (general contest-of-election laws do not permit contests of congressional elections in Illinois.)

For a superb, comprehensive summary and analysis of state recount and contest-of-election provisions, see Contested Elections and Recount, Final Report, Volume 2, State Perspective (Prepared for National Clearinghouse on Election Administration, Federal Election Commission 1978).

Florida law, like that of most states, provided for recounts and contests of elections in disputed election contexts. Florida law explicitly provided for the possibility of a manual recount in a pre-certification and administrative process labeled as an election "protest." Post-certification, Florida also provided for a judicial election-contest proceeding. However, nothing in the texts of these laws or their history of adoption indicated that the drafters had given any thought, one way or the other, to how these laws ought to apply to disputed elections for Presidential electors. Indeed, careful research into the history of these laws after the 2000 presidential election could find no reference whatever to presidential elections when the relevant Florida laws or their predecessors were written. *See* Eric Schickler, Terri L. Bimes, and Robert W. Mickey, *Safe at Any Speed: Legislative Intent, The Electoral Count Act of 1887, and* Bush v. Gore, __ J.L. & Pol. __ (2001). In addition, according to a representation of counsel at oral argument, Florida had not had a statewide contest of election since a gubernatorial race in 1919, long before the current statues had been written. Finally, the Florida laws were less specific and offered less guidance concerning the conduct of election recounts and contests than the laws of many other states. For these various reasons, it fell to the Florida courts to attempt to determine how Florida's election-dispute mechanisms should be applied to the novel context of a Presidential election dispute.

Before considering how the courts attempted to resolve these difficulties, consider the text of the four statutes that were at the heart of the litigation. Those texts are reprinted in full in the appendix to this volume. It is worth examining them carefully before reading the Florida Supreme Court's decision, then re-examining them in light of that decision as well as the subsequent United States Supreme Court treatment of these state laws. As a general note, perhaps the least controversial thing that can be said is that the statutory scheme was complex and not easily applied in the context of a dramatically close presidential election.

Efforts to interpret and implement the statutory scheme laid out above began shortly after Election Day, November 7, 2000. One commentator provides a helpful colloquial summary of how the Florida statutory provisions work and describes the first two weeks of the struggle to apply these laws in state administrative and judicial processes in the first two weeks after the election:

> The basic structure of Florida's election code is as follows: Each county canvasses the votes and files returns with the Department of State. A candidate or voter may "protest" a county's returns, but any such protest must be filed with the County Canvassing Board before the Board certifies its results or within five days of the election, "whichever is later." If a protest is filed, the Canvassing Board must do certain things to correct for obvious possible problems. In addition, a candidate "may" request a manual recount — either before the county's results are certified or within 72 hours, again, whichever is later — and the Canvassing Board "may" then authorize a partial recount of three precincts or one percent of the total votes. If this recount indicates "an error in the vote tabulation which could affect the outcome of the election," the Canvassing Board must take appropriate action to identify and correct the error, including a countywide manual recount if necessary.

> After the Canvassing Boards file certified results with the Department of State, the Secretary of State certifies the overall election result. According to Florida election law, the county returns "must" be filed with the Department by 5 p.m. on the seventh day following an election. Members of the Canvassing Boards are subject to fines for filing late returns, and the Secretary "may" ignore these returns and rely solely on the results then on file. A candidate whose protest is denied or who does not file a protest can still challenge the certified election result by bringing an action in state court to "contest" the certification. Grounds for contesting an election include

the "rejection of a number of legal votes sufficient to change or place in doubt the result of the election."

The closeness of the vote in Florida triggered an automatic machine recount, which, together with later-arriving overseas ballots, gave Bush a lead of 930 votes (out of almost 6 million votes cast). The Florida Democratic Party filed protests on Gore's behalf in four counties: Broward, Miami-Dade, Palm Beach, and Volusia. After conducting preliminary manual recounts, the Canvassing Boards in these counties determined that the standard for a full recount was satisfied, *i.e.,* that there had been "an error in the vote tabulation" sufficient to affect the election result. After complicated procedural maneuvering, the following situation emerged: The counties concluded that they could not complete full manual recounts within the seven-day deadline and asked permission to file late returns. Secretary of State Katherine Harris ruled that she would waive the deadline only if the problem requiring a recount consisted of fraud, "substantial noncompliance with statutory election procedures," or an act of God. She therefore indicated that she would not accept late returns from the four counties in question, which submitted what returns they had at the required time; the Secretary then certified Bush the winner in Florida. The Florida Democratic Party and Gore filed a lawsuit seeking to compel the Secretary to accept amended returns to reflect completed recounts. Their claims were denied by the trial court and the Florida Supreme Court accepted an expedited appeal and ruled unanimously on November 21 that the Secretary had abused her discretion by refusing to accept late returns. Invoking its equitable power to fashion a remedy, the court ordered that the four counties be given until November 26 to complete their recounts.

Larry Kramer, The Supreme Court in Politics, in Jack N. Rakove, ed., The Unfinished Election of 2000 ___ (2001).

Consider now the Florida Supreme Court's first decision in the 2000 election dispute, which sought to apply these laws:

Palm Beach County Canvasssing Board v. Harris
772 So. 2d 1220 (Fla. S. Ct. Nov. 21, 2000)

■ PER CURIAM:

We have for review two related trial court orders appealed to the First District Court of Appeal, which certified the orders to be of great public importance requiring immediate resolution by this Court [concerning the Florida presidential election of 2000]. . . . For the reasons set forth in this opinion, we reverse the orders of the trial court.

* * * *

II. GUIDING PRINCIPLES

Twenty-five years ago, this Court commented that the will of the people, not a hyper-technical reliance upon statutory provisions, should be our guiding principle in election cases:

> The real parties in interest here, not in the legal sense but in realistic terms, are the voters. They are possessed of the ultimate interest and it is they whom we must give primary consideration. The contestants have direct interests certainly, but the office they seek is one of high public service and of upmost importance to the people, thus subordinating their interest to that of the people. Ours is a government of, by and for the people. Our federal and state constitutions guarantee the right of the people to take an active part in the process of that government, which for most of our citizens means participation via the election process. The right to vote is the right to participate; it is also the right to speak, but more importantly the right to be heard. We must tread carefully on that right or we risk the unnecessary and unjustified muting of the public voice. By refusing to recognize an otherwise valid exercise of the right of a citizen to vote for the sake of sacred, unyielding adherence to statutory scripture, we would in effect nullify that right.

Boardman v. Esteva, 323 So. 2d 259, 263 (Fla. 1975). We consistently have adhered to the principle that the will of the people is the paramount consideration. Our goal today remains the same as it was a quarter of a century ago, i.e., to reach the result that reflects the will of the voters, whatever that might be. This fundamental principle, and our traditional rules of statutory construction, guide our decision today.

III. ISSUES

The questions before this Court include the following: Under what circumstances may a Board authorize a countywide manual recount pursuant to section 102.166(5); must the Secretary and Commission accept such recounts when the returns are certified and submitted by the Board after the seven day deadline set forth in sections 102.111 and 102.112?

IV. LEGAL OPINION OF THE DIVISION OF ELECTIONS

* * * *

Pursuant to section 102.166(4)(a), a candidate who appears on a ballot, a political committee that supports or opposes an issue that appears on a ballot, or a political party whose candidate's name appeared on the ballot may file a written request with the County Board for a manual recount. This request must be filed with the Board before the Board certifies the election results or within seventy-two hours after the election, whichever occurs later. Upon filing the written request for a manual recount, the canvassing board may authorize a manual recount. The decision whether to conduct a manual recount is vested in the sound discretion of the Board. If the canvassing board decides to authorize the manual recount, the recount must include at least three precincts and at least one percent of the total votes cast for each candidate or issue, with the person who requested the recount choosing the precincts to be recounted. If the manual recount indicates an "error in the vote tabulation which could affect the outcome of the election," the county canvassing board "shall":

(a) Correct the error and recount the remaining precincts with the vote tabulation system;

(b) Request the Department of State to verify the tabulation software; or

(c) Manually recount all ballots.

§ 102.166(5)(a)-(c), Fla. Stat. (2000).

The issue in dispute here is the meaning of the phrase "error in the vote tabulation" found in section 102.166(5). The Division opines that an "error in the vote tabulation" only means a counting error resulting from incorrect election parameters or an error in the vote tabulating software. We disagree.

The plain language of section 102.166(5) refers to an error in the vote tabulation rather than the vote tabulation system. On its face, the statute does not include any words of limitation; rather, it provides a remedy for any type of mistake made in tabulating ballots. The Legislature has utilized the phrase "vote tabulation system" and "automatic tabulating equipment" in section 102.166 when it intended to refer to the voting system rather than the vote count. Equating "vote tabulation" with "vote tabulation system" obliterates the distinction created in section 102.166 by the Legislature.

Sections 101.5614(5) and (6) also support the proposition that the "error in vote tabulation" encompasses more than a mere determination of whether the vote tabulation system is functioning. Section 101.5614(5) provides that "no vote shall be declared invalid or void if there is a clear indication of the intent of the voter as determined by the canvassing board." Conversely, section 101.5614(6) provides that any vote in which the Board cannot discern the intent of the voter must be discarded. Taken together, these sections suggest that "error in the vote tabulation" includes errors in the failure of the voting machinery to read a ballot and not simply errors resulting from the voting machinery.

Moreover, section 102.141(4), which outlines the Board's responsibility in the event of a recount, states that the Board "shall examine the counters on the machines or the tabulation of the ballots cast in each precinct in which the office or issue appeared on the ballot and determine whether the returns correctly reflect the votes cast." § 102.141, Fla. Stat. (2000). Therefore, an "error in the vote tabulation" includes a discrepancy between the number of votes determined by a voter tabulation system and the number of voters determined by a manual count of a sampling of precincts pursuant to section 102.166(4).

Although error cannot be completely eliminated in any tabulation of the ballots, our society has not yet gone so far as to place blind faith in machines. In almost all endeavors, including elections, humans routinely correct the errors of machines. For this very reason Florida law provides a human check on both the malfunction of tabulation equipment and error in failing to accurately count the ballots. Thus, we find that the Division's opinion DE 00-13 regarding the ability of county canvassing boards to authorize a manual recount is contrary to the plain language of the statute.

Having concluded that the county canvassing boards have the authority to order countywide manual recounts, we must now determine whether the Commission must accept a return after the seven-day deadline set forth in sections 102.111 and 102.112 under the circumstances presented.

V. THE APPLICABLE LAW

The abiding principle governing all election law in Florida is set forth in article I, section 1, Florida Constitution:

SECTION 1. Political power. All political power is inherent in the people. The enunciation herein of certain rights shall not be construed to deny or impair others retained by the people. Art. I, § 1, Fla. Const.

The constitution further provides that elections shall be regulated by law:

SECTION 1. Regulation of elections. All elections by the people shall be by direct and secret vote. General elections shall be determined by a plurality of votes cast. Registration and elections shall, and political party functions may, be regulated by law; however, the requirements for a candidate with no party affiliation or for a candidate of a minor party for placement of the candidate's name on the ballot shall be no greater than the requirements for a candidate of the party having the largest number of registered voters. Art. VI, § 1, Fla. Const.

The Florida Election Code ("Code"), contained in chapters 97-106, Florida Statutes (2000), sets forth specific criteria regulating elections. The Florida Secretary of State is the chief election officer of the state and is charged with general oversight of the election system. The Supervisor of Elections ("Supervisor") in each county is an elected official and is charged with appointing two Election Boards for each precinct within the county prior to an election. Each Election Board is composed of inspectors and clerks, all of whom must be residents of the county, and is charged with conducting the voting in the election, counting the votes, and certifying the results to the Supervisor by noon of the day following the election. The County Canvassing Board ("Canvassing Board" or "Board"), which is composed of the Supervisor, a county court judge, and the chair of the board of county commissioners, then canvasses the returns countywide, reviews the certificates, and transmits the returns for state and federal officers to the Florida Department of State ("Department") by 5:00 p.m. of the seventh day following the election. No deadline is set for filing corrected, amended, or supplemental returns.

The Elections Canvassing Commission ("Canvassing Commission" or "Commission"), which is composed of the Governor, the Secretary of State, and the Director of the Division of Elections, canvasses the returns statewide, determines and declares who has been elected for each office, and issues a certificate of election for each office as soon as the results are compiled. If any returns appear to be irregular or false and the Commission is unable to determine the true vote for a particular office, the Commission certifies that fact and does not include those returns in its canvass. In determining the true vote, the Commission has no authority to look beyond the county's returns. A candidate or elector can "protest" the returns of an election as being erroneous by filing a protest with the appropriate County Canvassing Board. And finally, a candidate, elector, or taxpayer can "contest" the certification of election results by filing a post- certification action in circuit court within certain time limits and setting forth specific grounds [citing Sec. 102.168 (3) of Florida law, *supra*].

* * * *

VII. LEGISLATIVE INTENT

Legislative intent — as always — is the polestar that guides a court's inquiry into the provisions of the Florida Election Code. Where the language of the Code is clear and amenable to a reasonable and logical interpretation, courts are without power to diverge from the intent of the Legislature as expressed in the plain language of the Code. As noted above, however, chapter 102 is unclear concerning both the time limits for submitting the results of a manual recount and the penalties that may be assessed by the Secretary. In light of this ambiguity, the Court must resort to traditional rules of statutory construction in an effort to determine legislative intent.

First, it is well-settled that where two statutory provisions are in conflict, the specific statute controls the general statute.

* * * *

Second, it also is well-settled that when two statutes are in conflict, the more recently enacted statute controls the older statute.

[Applying these maxims of statutory construction, the Court concluded that the more permissive language of 102.112 was controlling.]

* * * *

Third, a statutory provision will not be construed in such a way that it renders meaningless or absurd any other statutory provision. In the present case, section 102.112 contains a detailed provision authorizing the assessment of fines against members of a dilatory County Canvassing Board. The fines are personal and substantial, i.e., $200 for each day the returns are not received. If, as the Secretary asserts, the Department were required to ignore all returns received after the statutory date, the fine provision would be meaningless.

* * * *

Under this statutory scheme, the County Canvassing Boards are required to submit their returns to the Department by 5 p.m. of the seventh day following the election. The statutes make no provision for exceptions following a manual recount. If a Board fails to meet the deadline, the Secretary is not required to ignore the county's returns but rather is permitted to ignore the returns within the parameters of this statutory scheme. To determine the circumstances under which the Secretary may lawfully ignore returns filed pursuant to the provisions of section 102.166 for a manual recount, it is necessary to examine the interplay between our statutory and constitutional law at both the state and federal levels.

VIII. THE RIGHT TO VOTE

The text of our Florida Constitution begins with a Declaration of Rights, a series of rights so basic that the founders accorded them a place of special privilege. The Court long ago noted the venerable role the Declaration plays in our tripartite system of government in Florida:

> It is significant that our Constitution thus commences by specifying those things which the state government must not do, before specifying certain things that it may do. These Declarations of Rights . . . have cost much, and breathe the spirit of that sturdy and self-reliant philosophy of individualism which underlies and supports our entire system of government. No race of hothouse plants could ever have produced and compelled the recognition of such a stalwart set of basic principles, and no such race can preserve them. They say to arbitrary and autocratic power, from whatever official quarter it may advance to invade these vital rights of personal liberty and private property, "Thus far shalt thou come, but no farther."

State v. City of Stuart, 120 So. 335, 347 (Fla. 1929). Courts must attend with special vigilance whenever the Declaration of Rights is in issue.

* * * *

To the extent that the Legislature may enact laws regulating the electoral process, those laws are valid only if they impose no "unreasonable or unnecessary" restraints on the right of suffrage:

> The declaration of rights expressly states that "all political power is inherent in the people." Article I, Section 1, Florida Constitution. The right of the people to select their own officers is their sovereign right, and the rule is against imposing unnecessary and unreasonable [restraints on that right]. . . . Unreasonable or unnecessary restraints on the elective process are prohibited.

Treiman v. Malmquist, 342 So. 2d 972, 975 (Fla. 1977). Because election laws are intended to facilitate the right of suffrage, such laws must be liberally construed in favor of the citizens' right to vote:

> Generally, the courts, in construing statutes relating to elections, hold that the same should receive a liberal construction in favor of the citizen whose right to vote they tend to restrict and in so doing to prevent disfranchisement of legal voters and the intention of the voters should prevail when counting ballots . . . . It is the intention of the law to obtain an honest expression of the will or desire of the voter.

State ex rel. Carpenter v. Barber, 198 So. 49, 51 (Fla. 1940). Courts must not lose sight of the fundamental purpose of election laws: The laws are intended to facilitate and safeguard the right of each voter to express his or her will in the context of our representative democracy. Technical statutory requirements must not be exalted over the substance of this right.

Based on the foregoing, we conclude that the authority of the Florida Secretary of State to ignore amended returns submitted by a County Canvassing Board may be lawfully exercised only under limited circumstances as we set forth in this opinion. The clear import of the penalty provision of section 102.112 is to deter Boards from engaging in dilatory conduct contrary to statutory authority that results in the late certification of a county's returns. This deterrent purpose is achieved by the fines in section 102.112, which are substantial and personal and are levied on each member of a Board. The alternative penalty, i.e., ignoring the county's returns, punishes not the Board members themselves but rather the county's electors, for it in effect disenfranchises them.

Ignoring the county's returns is a drastic measure and is appropriate only if the returns are submitted to the Department so late that their inclusion will compromise the integrity of the electoral process in either of two ways: (1) by precluding a candidate, elector, or taxpayer from contesting the certification of an election pursuant to section 102.168; or (2) by precluding Florida voters from participating fully in the federal electoral process.[55] In either case, the Secretary must explain to the Board her reason for ignoring the returns and her action must be adequately supported by the law. To disenfranchise electors in an effort to deter Board members, as the Secretary in the present case proposes, is unreasonable, unnecessary, and violates longstanding law.

Allowing the manual recounts to proceed in an expeditious manner, rather than imposing an arbitrary seven-day deadline, is consistent not only with the statutory scheme but with prior United States Supreme Court pronouncements:

Indiana has found, along with many other States, that one procedure

---

55. *See* 3 U.S.C. § § 1-10 (1994).

necessary to guard against irregularity and error in the tabulation of votes is the availability of a recount. Despite the fact that a certificate of election may be issued to the leading candidate within 30 days after the election, the results are not final if a candidate's option to compel a recount is exercised. A recount is an integral part of the Indiana electoral process and is within the ambit of the broad powers delegated to the States by Art. I, s 4.

Roudebush v. Hartke, 405 U.S. 15, 25 (1972).

In addition, an accurate vote count is one of the essential foundations of our democracy. The words of the Supreme Court of Illinois are particularly apt in this case:

The purpose of our election laws is to obtain a correct expression of the intent of the voters. Our courts have repeatedly held that, where the intention of the voter can be ascertained with reasonable certainty from his ballot, that intention will be given effect even though the ballot is not strictly in conformity with the law. . . . The legislature authorized the use of electronic tabulating equipment to expedite the tabulating process and to eliminate the possibility of human error in the counting process, not to create a technical obstruction which defeats the rights of qualified voters. This court should not, under the appearance of enforcing the election laws, defeat the very object which those law are intended to achieve. To invalidate a ballot which clearly reflects the voter's intent, simply because a machine cannot read it, would subordinate substance to form and promote the means at the expense of the end.

The voters here did everything which the Election Code requires when they punched the appropriate chad with the stylus. These voters should not be disfranchised where their intent may be ascertained with reasonable certainty, simply because the chad they punched did not completely dislodge from the ballot. Such a failure may be attributable to the fault of the election authorities, for failing to provide properly perforated paper, or it may be the result of the voter's disability or inadvertence. Whatever the reason, where the intention of the voter can be fairly and satisfactorily ascertained, that intention should be given effect.

Pullen v. Mulligan, 561 N.E.2d 585, 611 (Ill. 1990).

IX. THE PRESENT CASE

The trial court below properly concluded that the County Canvassing Boards are required to submit their returns to the Department by 5:00 p.m. of the seventh day following the election and that the Department is not required to ignore the amended returns but rather may count them. The court, however, erred in holding that the Secretary acted within her discretion in prematurely rejecting any amended returns that would be the result of ongoing manual recounts. The Secretary's rationale for rejecting the Board's returns was as follows:

> The Board has not alleged any facts or circumstances that suggest
> the existence of voter fraud. The Board has not alleged any facts or
> circumstances that suggest that there has been substantial
> noncompliance with the state's statutory election procedures, coupled
> with reasonable doubt as to whether the certified results expressed
> the will of the voters. The Board has not alleged any facts or
> circumstances that suggest that Palm Beach County has been unable
> to comply with its election duties due to an act of God, or other
> extenuating circumstances that are beyond its control. The Board
> has alleged the possibility that the results of the manual recount
> could affect the outcome of the election if certain results obtain.
> However, absent an assertion that there has been substantial
> noncompliance with the law, I do not believe that the possibility of
> affecting the outcome of the election is enough to justify ignoring the
> statutory deadline.   Furthermore, I find that the facts and
> circumstances alleged, standing alone, do not rise to the level of
> extenuating circumstances that justify a decision on my part to
> ignore the statutory deadline imposed by the Florida Legislature.

Letter from Katherine Harris to Palm Beach Canvassing Board (Nov. 15,
2000).

We conclude that, consistent with the Florida election scheme, the
Secretary may reject a Board's amended returns only if the returns are
submitted so late that their inclusion will preclude a candidate from contesting
the certification or preclude Florida's voters from participating fully in the
federal electoral process. The Secretary in the present case has made no claim
that either of these conditions apply at this point in time.

The above analysis is consistent with *State ex rel. Chappell v. Martinez*,
536 So. 2d 1007 (Fla. 1988), wherein the Court addressed a comparable recount
issue. There, the total votes cast for each of two candidates for a seat in the
United States House of Representatives were separated by less than one-half
of one percent; the county conducted a mandatory recount; the Board's
certification of results was not received by the Department until two days after
the deadline, although the Board had telephoned the results to the Department
prior to the deadline; and the unsuccessful candidate sued to prevent the
Department from counting the late votes. The Court concluded that the will of
the electors supersedes any technical statutory requirements:

> The electorate's effecting its will through its balloting, not the
> hypertechnical compliance with statutes, is the object of holding an
> election. "There is no magic in the statutory requirements. If they are
> complied with to the extent that the duly responsible election officials
> can ascertain that the electors whose votes are being canvassed are
> qualified and registered to vote, and that they do so in a proper
> manner, then who can be heard to complain the statute has not been
> literally and absolutely complied with?"

Chappell, 536 So. 2d at 1008-09 (quoting *Boardman v. Esteva,* 323 So. 2d 259, 267 (Fla. 1975)).

X. CONCLUSION

According to the legislative intent evinced in the Florida Election Code, the permissive language of section 102.112 supersedes the mandatory language of section 102.111. The statutory fines set forth in section 102.112 offer strong incentive to County Canvassing Boards to submit their returns in a timely fashion. However, when a Board certifies its returns after the seven-day period because the Board is acting in conformity with óther provisions of the Code or with administrative rules or for other good cause, the Secretary may impose no fines. It is unlikely that the Legislature would have intended to punish a Board for complying with the dictates of the Code or some other law.

Because the right to vote is the pre-eminent right in the Declaration of Rights of the Florida Constitution, the circumstances under which the Secretary may exercise her authority to ignore a county's returns filed after the initial statutory date are limited. The Secretary may ignore such returns only if their inclusion will compromise the integrity of the electoral process in either of two ways: (1) by precluding a candidate, elector, or taxpayer from contesting the certification of election pursuant to section 102.168; or (2) by precluding Florida voters from participating fully in the federal electoral process. In either such case, this drastic penalty must be both reasonable and necessary. But to allow the Secretary to summarily disenfranchise innocent electors in an effort to punish dilatory Board members, as she proposes in the present case, misses the constitutional mark. The constitution eschews punishment by proxy.

As explained above, the Florida Election Code must be construed as a whole. Section 102.166 governs manual recounts and appears to conflict with sections 102.111 and 102.112, which set a seven day deadline by which County Boards must submit their returns. Further, section 102.111, which provides that the Secretary "shall" ignore late returns, conflicts with section 102.112, which provides that the Secretary "may" ignore late returns. In the present case, we have used traditional rules of statutory construction to resolve these ambiguities to the extent necessary to address the issues presented here. We decline to rule more expansively, for to do so would result in this Court substantially rewriting the Code. We leave that matter to the sound discretion of the body best equipped to address it—the Legislature.

Because of the unique circumstances and extraordinary importance of the present case, wherein the Florida Attorney General and the Florida Secretary of State have issued conflicting advisory opinions concerning the propriety of conducting manual recounts, and because of our reluctance to rewrite the Florida Election Code, we conclude that we must invoke the equitable powers of this Court to fashion a remedy that will allow a fair and expeditious resolution of the questions presented here.

Accordingly, in order to allow maximum time for contests pursuant to section 102.168, amended certifications must be filed with the Elections Canvassing Commission by 5 p.m. on Sunday, November 26, 2000 and the Secretary of State and the Elections Canvassing Commission shall accept any such amended certifications received by 5 p.m. on Sunday, November 26, 2000, provided that the office of the Secretary of State, Division of Elections is open in order to allow receipt thereof. If the office is not open for this special purpose on Sunday, November 26, 2000, then any amended certifications shall be accepted until 9 a.m. on Monday, November 27, 2000. The stay order entered on November 17, 2000, by this Court shall remain in effect until the expiration of the time for accepting amended certifications set forth in this opinion. The certificates made and signed by the Elections Canvassing Commission pursuant to section 102.121 shall include the amended returns accepted through the dates set forth in this opinion.

It is so ordered. No motion for rehearing will be allowed.

WELLS, C.J., and SHAW, HARDING, ANSTEAD, PARIENTE, LEWIS and QUINCE, JJ., concur.

NOTES AND QUESTIONS

1. Normally, questions of the interpretation of state law are to be determined by the relevant state court. We will soon see, however, how that practice might be legally altered in the context of a presidential election. But for now, consider simply as a matter of statutory interpretation the Florida Supreme Court's decision. Much of the ongoing controversy over the litigation traces to judgments about this first opinion. To critics, the decision provides "ample reason to believe" that "under the guise of interpretation, [the Florida Supreme Court created] a scheme for conducting election challenges that deviates markedly from that which the Florida legislature had set out in its statutes." Richard A. Epstein, *"In Such Manner as the Legislature Thereof May Direct":* *The Outcome in* Bush v. Gore *Defended*, 68 U. Chi. L. Rev. 613 (2001). Professor Epstein attempts to document in much specific detail the precise ways in which "the Florida court did violence to the state statutory scheme." *Id.*, at 634. He goes on to defend this view:

To many modern mainstream constitutional scholars that conclusion might seem harsh because they find it hard to accept that weighty matters of constitutional interpretation do have right, and hence wrong, answers that can be gathered from a close examination of text, structure, and function . . . .

But so long as we can maintain the conceptual line between interpretation and legislation, then we must recognize that it is always possible for any court, at any level, to stray over that line so

> that its decrees can be regarded as judicial legislation.

Id., at 634-35. To the same effect is Michael W. McConnell, *Two-and-a-Half Cheers for* Bush v. Gore, 68 U. Chi. L. Rev. 657, 666-67 (2001):

> [The Florida court] disregarded the plain language of the statute and substituted a new deadline entirely of its own making. This was obviously not "interpretation." From its denunciation of "hypertechnical reliance upon statutory provisions" to its fabrication of new deadlines out of whole cloth, the court demonstrated that it would not be bound by the legislature's handiwork. The state court's claim that it was reconciling inconsistent provisions in the statute was specious. To be sure, one statute said that the Secretary of State "shall" ignore late-filed returns, and another statute said she "may" ignore late-filed returns. But that provides no support for interpreting the law to say that she "shall not" ignore them, or to authorize the court to create its own deadline.

In contrast, Professor Larry Kramer argues that the Florida Supreme Court decision should hardly be considered controversial at all and was a relatively routine act of statutory interpretation in line with much of contemporary judicial practice:

> There is, however, another approach to statutory interpretation, one whose principles are different but whose pedigree is just as distinguished. Courts following this approach bring certain *a priori* assumptions about legislative intent into the interpretive process, presuming that lawmakers mean to conform to these assumptions absent a clear statement to the contrary in the language of the statute. Once these presumptions, or "clear statement rules" as they are known in law, have been established, courts will assume the legislature took them into account in the drafting process and so expect their laws to be interpreted accordingly. The U.S. Supreme Court frequently employs this technique. The Court assumes, for example, that federal laws apply only to acts committed on U.S. territory absent unequivocal language to the contrary, and also that Congress does not mean substantive regulation to apply to states (as opposed to private entities) unless Congress says so very explicitly in the wording of a statute . . . .

> Obviously, the Florida Supreme Court adopted this second method in its decision — applying a clear statement rule presuming that, absent unequivocal language to the contrary, the Florida legislature wants every effort made to include each vote cast if at all possible. Hence, the court ruled that manual recounts could be authorized for reasons in addition to mechanical failure, and it made the deadline flexible to accommodate efforts to examine the ballots while construing the Secretary's discretion to limit her authority to ignore returns. Seen in this light, the decision is much less controversial. Indeed, it is hardly controversial at all. The clear statement rule invoked by the court was a matter of well-established Florida law

that had previously been relied on in interpreting election statutes, and the court's interpretations were not inconsistent with the statute's plain language (as opposed to certain implications one might otherwise have assumed would flow from that language). Certainly the state supreme court did less violence to statutory text than did the U.S. Supreme Court in any of the cases mentioned above. All things considered, it was a relatively routine performance for a court relying on clear statement principles . . . .

Larry Kramer, *The Supreme Court in Politics*, in Jack N. Rakove, ed., The Unfinished Election of 2000 ___ (2001).

2. If established academic scholars such as Professors Epstein, McConnell, and Kramer can differ so profoundly on the basic questions of state-law interpretation involved in *Bush v. Gore*, what does that suggest about whether there is a clearly right answer to the relevant questions of interpretation? What does it suggest about whether there is a consistent approach in the American courts to questions of statutory interpretation?

3. The Florida Supreme Court decision and much of the analysis that follows in this casebook focuses on the legal controversies concerning various plans for manual recounts. That focus, however, already leaves in the background what might have been the pivotal moment that initially led the Gore campaign to believe it had legitimately "won" the election and to seek some means of legal redress for establishing that position. Chronologically, the controversy over the election began, not with purported undervotes or overvotes, but with "the butterfly ballot" that had been used in one county and that had appeared to generate an exceptionally large number of invalid ballots or confusing patterns of apparent votes. The manual recount issues came to dominate the national stage for over a month; the most vivid visual memories of the election no doubt involve individual ballots being held up to the light; and the Supreme Court's ultimate decision rested on the constitutional standards for conducting such a recount. But none of these issues had anything to do with what prompted immediate questions about the vote in the first days after the election. Recall that attention at first centered on the "butterfly ballot" that had been used in Palm Beach County and that had produced a staggering 19,000 invalid ballots because voters had voted for two Presidential candidates, and had also generated a difficult to explain 3,407 votes for Patrick Buchanan. At the end of the litigation, the two sides were 537 votes apart and fighting a hand-to-hand war over individual ballots. The votes that were actually fought over in the recount litigation were dwarfed by the nearly 20,000 invalid ballots in Palm Beach County, ballots that were invalid because, it was argued, voters had been confused by the ballot's design into mistakenly voting for two candidates.

Richard Pildes goes on to argue that the recount litigation should be seen as the search for a "surrogate remedy" for these issues over purported confusion and the butterfly ballot, once it became clear the legal system was not going to afford any retrospective remedy for whatever confusion that ballot might have caused:

In the first days after the election, the Gore campaign was able to occupy a kind of moral high ground, with literally tens of thousands of ballots at stake and a badly designed ballot a focal point of blame.

But as the Gore campaign came to discover, the legal system cannot (certainly, it did not) provide any meaningful retrospective remedy in a presidential election for this combination of ballot design and voter confusion.

* * * *

There can be a gap between what we "know" as a matter of common understanding and the knowledge the legal system will let us act upon. And there can be good reasons for the existence of that gap. Put in other terms, in the law of elections, more than in most areas of the law, "wrongs" can occur – ballots can be badly though unintentionally misdesigned – without corresponding remedies being available to undo the wrong. Courts can order the practice changed for future elections, and often do, but that does not change the result of the election at issue. There may be a moral wrong, in that voters should not be forced to confront unduly confusing ballots, but there is no legal remedy. Faced with that legal reality, the Gore campaign's morally most compelling claim dissolved.

The recount litigation was, in a sense, an effort to find a *surrogate* remedy for the "wrong" of the butterfly ballot confusion that could not itself be remedied. Would the recount litigation even have been initiated had there not first been the sense of outrage and unfairness at the thousands of seemingly miscast votes? Perhaps. But once the issue of the butterfly ballot dropped out, the moral high ground became less certain. And we were now fighting over a statistical minuscule number of ballots – a number likely to be smaller than what statisticians would define as the "margin of error" in a process of counting nearly 6 million ballots. This was the context to which the previously existing institutional and legal apparatus had to be applied.

Richard H. Pildes, *Disputing Elections*, in The Longest Night (Arthur Jacobson and Michele Rosenfeld eds. 2001). In a detailed media examination of all the disputed ballots, it was later concluded that, among the "spoiled" butterfly ballots that were not recognized as valid votes by the vote-counting machines, there were a net of approximately 6,500 votes that had been "clearly intended" for Gore – more than Bush's eventual margin of victory. John Mintz and Peter Slevin, *Human Factor Was at Core Of Vote Fiasco*, Wash. Post, June 1, 2001, at A1.

4. In the wake of the Florida Supreme Court decision, and to the surprise of many commentators, the United States Supreme Court exercised its discretionary powers to grant certiorari and quickly heard oral argument and issued an opinion as to whether the Florida court's interpretation of its state elections laws might potentially have violated any distinct and specific federal

interest applicable to presidential elections. Absent such an interest, there would be no basis for Supreme Court oversight of the Florida Supreme Court's decisions regarding the meaning of state law.

CHAPTER 3

THE U.S. SUPREME COURT'S DECISIONS

A. THE FEDERAL INTEREST POTENTIALLY ASSERTED

Bush v. Palm Beach County Canvassing Board *(Bush I)*
530 U.S. 70 (Dec. 4, 2000)

■ PER CURIAM:

The Supreme Court of the State of Florida interpreted its elections statutes in proceedings brought to require manual recounts of ballots, and the certification of the recount results, for votes cast in the quadrennial Presidential election held on November 7, 2000. Governor George W. Bush, Republican candidate for the Presidency, filed a petition for certiorari to review the Florida Supreme Court decision. We granted certiorari on two of the questions presented by petitioner: whether the decision of the Florida Supreme Court, by effectively changing the State's elector appointment procedures after election day, violated the Due Process Clause or 3 U.S.C. § 5, and whether the decision of that court changed the manner in which the State's electors are to be selected, in violation of the legislature's power to designate the manner for selection under Art. II, § 1, cl. 2 of the United States Constitution.

On November 8, 2000, the day following the Presidential election, the Florida Division of Elections reported that Governor Bush had received 2,909,135 votes, and respondent Democrat Vice President Albert Gore, Jr., had received 2,907,351, a margin of 1,784 in Governor Bush's favor. Under Fla. Stat. § 102.141(4) (2000), because the margin of victory was equal to or less than one- half of one percent of the votes cast, an automatic machine recount occurred. The recount resulted in a much smaller margin of victory for Governor Bush. Vice President Gore then exercised his statutory right to submit written requests for manual recounts to the canvassing board of any county. *See* § 102.166. He requested recounts in four counties: Volusia, Palm Beach, Broward, and Miami-Dade.

The parties urged conflicting interpretations of the Florida Election Code respecting the authority of the canvassing boards, the Secretary of State (hereinafter Secretary), and the Elections Canvassing Commission. On November 14, in an action brought by Volusia County, and joined by the Palm Beach County Canvassing Board, Vice President Gore, and the Florida Democratic Party, the Florida Circuit Court ruled that the statutory 7-day deadline was mandatory, but that the Volusia board could amend its returns at a later date. The court further ruled that the Secretary, after "considering all attendant facts and circumstances," could exercise her discretion in deciding whether to include the late amended returns in the statewide certification.

The Secretary responded by issuing a set of criteria by which she would decide whether to allow a late filing. The Secretary ordered that, by 2 p.m. the following day, November 15, any county desiring to forward late returns submit a written statement of the facts and circumstances justifying a later filing. Four counties submitted statements and, after reviewing the submissions, the Secretary determined that none justified an extension of the filing deadline. On November 16, the Florida Democratic Party and Vice President Gore filed an emergency motion in the state court, arguing that the Secretary had acted arbitrarily and in contempt of the court's earlier ruling. The following day, the court denied the motion, ruling that the Secretary had not acted arbitrarily and had exercised her discretion in a reasonable manner consistent with the court's earlier ruling. The Democratic Party and Vice President Gore appealed to the First District Court of Appeal, which certified the matter to the Florida Supreme Court. That court accepted jurisdiction and sua sponte entered an order enjoining the Secretary and the Elections Canvassing Commission from finally certifying the results of the election and declaring a winner until further order of that court.

The Supreme Court, with the expedition requisite for the controversy, issued its decision on November 21. As the court saw the matter, there were two principal questions: whether a discrepancy between an original machine return and a sample manual recount resulting from the way a ballot has been marked or punched is an "error in vote tabulation" justifying a full manual recount; and how to reconcile what it spoke of as two conflicts in Florida's election laws: (a) between the time frame for conducting a manual recount under Fla. Stat. § 102.166 (2000) and the time frame for submitting county returns under §§ 102.111 and 102.112, and (b) between § 102.111, which provides that the Secretary "shall . . . ignor[e]" late election returns, and § 102.112, which provides that she "may . . . ignor[e]" such returns.

With regard to the first issue, the court held that, under the plain text of the statute, a discrepancy between a sample manual recount and machine returns due to the way in which a ballot was punched or marked did constitute an "error in vote tabulation" sufficient to trigger the statutory provisions for a full manual recount.

With regard to the second issue, the court held that the "shall . . . ignor[e]" provision of § 102.111 conflicts with the "may . . . ignor[e]" provision of § 102.112, and that the "may . . . ignor[e]" provision controlled. The court turned to the questions whether and when the Secretary may ignore late manual recounts. The court relied in part upon the right to vote set forth in the Declaration of Rights of the Florida Constitution in concluding that late manual recounts could be rejected only under limited circumstances. The court then stated: "[B]ecause of our reluctance to rewrite the Florida Election Code, we conclude that we must invoke the equitable powers of this Court to fashion a remedy . . . ." The court thus imposed a deadline of November 26, at 5 p.m., for a return of ballot counts. The 7-day deadline of § 102.111, assuming it would have applied, was effectively extended by 12 days. The court further directed the Secretary to accept manual counts submitted prior to that deadline.

As a general rule, this Court defers to a state court's interpretation of a state statute. But in the case of a law enacted by a state legislature applicable not only to elections to state offices, but also to the selection of Presidential electors, the legislature is not acting solely under the authority given it by the people of the State, but by virtue of a direct grant of authority made under Art. II, § 1, cl. 2, of the United States Constitution. That provision reads:

> Each State shall appoint, in such Manner as the Legislature thereof may direct, a Number of Electors, equal to the whole Number of Senators and Representatives to which the State may be entitled in the Congress . . . .

Although we did not address the same question petitioner raises here, in *McPherson v. Blacker*, 146 U.S. 1, 25 (1892), we said:

> [Art. II, § 1, cl. 2] does not read that the people or the citizens shall appoint, but that "each State shall"; and if the words "in such manner as the legislature thereof may direct," had been omitted, it would seem that the legislative power of appointment could not have been successfully questioned in the absence of any provision in the state constitution in that regard. Hence the insertion of those words, while operating as a limitation upon the State in respect of any attempt to circumscribe the legislative power, cannot be held to operate as a limitation on that power itself.

There are expressions in the opinion of the Supreme Court of Florida that may be read to indicate that it construed the Florida Election Code without regard to the extent to which the Florida Constitution could, consistent with Art. II, § 1, cl. 2, "circumscribe the legislative power." The opinion states, for example, that "[t]o the extent that the Legislature may enact laws regulating the electoral process, those laws are valid only if they impose no 'unreasonable or unnecessary' restraints on the right of suffrage" guaranteed by the state constitution. The opinion also states that "[b]ecause election laws are intended to facilitate the right of suffrage, such laws must be liberally construed in favor of the citizens' right to vote . . . ."

In addition, 3 U.S.C. § 5 provides in pertinent part:

> If any State shall have provided, by laws enacted prior to the day

fixed for the appointment of the electors, for its final determination of any controversy or contest concerning the appointment of all or any of the electors of such State, by judicial or other methods or procedures, and such determination shall have been made at least six days before the time fixed for the meeting of the electors, such determination made pursuant to such law so existing on said day, and made at least six days prior to said time of meeting of the electors, shall be conclusive, and shall govern in the counting of the electoral votes as provided in the Constitution, and as hereinafter regulated, so far as the ascertainment of the electors appointed by such State is concerned.

The parties before us agree that whatever else may be the effect of this section, it creates a "safe harbor" for a State insofar as congressional consideration of its electoral votes is concerned. If the state legislature has provided for final determination of contests or controversies by a law made prior to election day, that determination shall be conclusive if made at least six days prior to said time of meeting of the electors. The Florida Supreme Court cited 3 U.S.C. §§ 1-10 in a footnote of its opinion, but did not discuss § 5. Since § 5 contains a principle of federal law that would assure finality of the State's determination if made pursuant to a state law in effect before the election, a legislative wish to take advantage of the "safe harbor" would counsel against any construction of the Election Code that Congress might deem to be a change in the law.

After reviewing the opinion of the Florida Supreme Court, we find "that there is considerable uncertainty as to the precise grounds for the decision." *Minnesota v. National Tea Co.*, 309 U.S. 551, 555 (1940). This is sufficient reason for us to decline at this time to review the federal questions asserted to be present.

It is fundamental that state courts be left free and unfettered by us in interpreting their state constitutions. But it is equally important that ambiguous or obscure adjudications by state courts do not stand as barriers to a determination by this Court of the validity under the federal constitution of state action. Intelligent exercise of our appellate powers compels us to ask for the elimination of the obscurities and ambiguities from the opinions in such cases.

Id. at 557.

Specifically, we are unclear as to the extent to which the Florida Supreme Court saw the Florida Constitution as circumscribing the legislature's authority under Art. II, § 1, cl. 2. We are also unclear as to the consideration the Florida Supreme Court accorded to 3 U.S.C. § 5. The judgment of the Supreme Court of Florida is therefore vacated, and the case is remanded for further proceedings not inconsistent with this opinion.

It is so ordered.

NOTES AND QUESTIONS

1. The U.S. Supreme Court's opinion in *Bush I* addresses some fundamental issues of constitutional and statutory voting law that have gone largely unexplored for the past century, even though *Bush II* quickly superceded *Bush I* in importance.

2. To begin with, the Court places great emphasis on the distinction between the acts of the Florida legislature and the other sources of state law derived either from the State Constitution or the principles of equity. Perhaps not since *Erie v. Tompkins*, 304 U.S. 64 (1938), overruled *Swift v. Tyson,* 41 U.S. (16 Pet.) 1 (1842), has a decision turned so heavily on the question of the source of state law. *Swift* had drawn a sharp distinction between legislative enactments and decisional law of the state courts. For Justice Story, the former were true sources of law that federal courts under the Rules of Decision Act were obligated to follow in construing state law in diversity cases. The latter were merely interpretive guides that could be subsumed under the federal common law without doing violence to state law. *Bush I* suggests that the constitutional delegation of authority in Article II, Section 1 of the Constitution is an exclusive grant of authority to the state legislature to create the procedures for the election of the state's presidential electors. The opinion further raises the possibility that no other state law (including the state constitution) may intercede absent an express delegation of authority from the legislature. If so, the invocation of state constitutional law to cabin the acts of the state legislature would, by extension, violate the supremacy clause of the U.S. Constitution.

3. The most dramatic suggestion in *Bush I* is the possibility that Article II, Section I of the U.S. Constitution might immunize state legislatures, when they enact presidential elector statutes, from the state constitutional limitations that would otherwise channel and circumscribe the state legislature. Some commentators have praised *Bush I* as an act of "judicial minimalism," in the sense that the Court did not actually decide any substantive legal issues but rather remanded for clarification from the Florida Supreme Court. *See* Cass Sunstein, *Order Without Law*, 68 U. Chi. L. Rev. 737 (2001). While it is technically true that the Court did not actually decide that Art. II overrides state constitutional law, every actor after *Bush I* appears to have acted as if the Court *had* decided, as a substantive law matter, that state legislatures could indeed not be constrained by their state constitutions when enacting presidential elector statutes. This position is known as the "independent State legislature" doctrine. As a result of *Bush I* and its subsequent interpretation, it thus becomes critical to explore whether the suggestion — which remains a suggestion, not a holding — that Art. II frees state legislatures from their constitutions is a sound understanding of Art. II

The Court does not point anything in the history of Art. II's adoption or the political practices that emerged in the wake of Art. II's adoption to support the independent state legislature doctrine. The Court points to two sources: (1) the text of Art. II itself and (2) *McPherson v. Blacker*, 146 U.S. 1 (1892), which the Court appears to treat as essentially the final word on the federal interest in state election matters. To explore the important question of the role of State constitutions in the presidential selection process, we therefore begin with *McPherson.*

1. ARTICLE II AND THE "INDEPENDENT STATE LEGISLATURE DOCTRINE"

McPherson v. Blacker
146 U.S. 1 (1892)

[*McPherson* involved a challenge to a statute passed by the Michigan state legislature governing the allocation of Michigan's electoral votes. Previously, Michigan's votes had been distributed on a winner take all, statewide basis. The new legislation required that Michigan electoral votes be awarded on a congressional district basis; the winner in each congressional district in the state would win one elector for that district. The State's remaining two electoral votes (reflecting its two Senate seats) were to go to the winner of the "Eastern" and "Western" halves of the state. Similar district based allocation schemes are used currently in Maine and Nebraska.]

■ CHIEF JUSTICE FULLER delivered the opinion of the Court:

* * * *

[I]t is contended that the act is void because in conflict with (1) clause two of section one of Article II of the Constitution of the United States; (2) the Fourteenth and Fifteenth Amendments to the Constitution; and (3) the act of Congress of February 3, 1887.

The second clause of section one of Article II of the Constitution is in these words: "Each State shall appoint, in such Manner as the Legislature thereof may direct, a Number of Electors, equal to the whole Number of Senators and Representatives to which the State may be entitled in the Congress; but no Senator or Representative, or Person holding an Office of Trust or Profit under the United States, shall be appointed an Elector."

The manner of the appointment of electors directed by the act of Michigan is the election of an elector and an alternate elector in each of the twelve Congressional districts into which the State of Michigan is divided, and of an elector and an alternate elector at large in each of two districts defined by the act. It is insisted that it was not competent for the legislature to direct this manner of appointment because the State is to appoint as a body politic and corporate, and so must act as a unit and cannot delegate the authority to subdivisions created for the purpose; and it is argued that the appointment of electors by districts is not an appointment by the State, because all its citizens otherwise qualified are not permitted to vote for all the presidential electors.

"A State in the ordinary sense of the Constitution," said Chief Justice Chase, *Texas v. White*, 7 Wall. 700, 721, "is a political community of free citizens, occupying a territory of defined boundaries, and organized under a government sanctioned and limited by a written constitution, and established by the consent of the governed." The State does not act by its people in their collective capacity, but through such political agencies as are duly constituted and established. The legislative power is the supreme authority except as limited by the constitution of the State, and the sovereignty of the people is exercised through their representatives in the legislature unless by the fundamental law power is elsewhere reposed. The Constitution of the United States frequently refers to the State as a political community, and also in terms to the people of the several States and the citizens of each State. What is forbidden or required to be done by a State is forbidden or required of the legislative power under state constitutions as they exist. The clause under consideration does not read that the people or the citizens shall appoint, but that "each State shall"; and if the words "in such manner as the legislature thereof may direct," had been omitted, it would seem that the legislative power of appointment could not have been successfully questioned in the absence of any provision in the state constitution in that regard. Hence the insertion of those words, while operating as a limitation upon the State in respect of any attempt to circumscribe the legislative power, cannot be held to operate as a limitation on that power itself.

If the legislature possesses plenary authority to direct the manner of appointment, and might itself exercise the appointing power by joint ballot or concurrence of the two houses, or according to such mode as designated, it is difficult to perceive why, if the legislature prescribes as a method of appointment choice by vote, it must necessarily be by general ticket and not by districts. In other words, the act of appointment is none the less the act of the State in its entirety because arrived at by districts, for the act is the act of political agencies duly authorized to speak for the State, and the combined result is the expression of the voice of the State, a result reached by direction of the legislature, to whom the whole subject is committed.

[To further support the constitutionality of electing presidential electors from individual districts, the Court analogized to the congressional mandate that required individual members of Congress to be elected from single-member districts, rather than at-large. That practice, the Court noted, did not contradict the constitutional imperative of Art. I. Sec. 2 that members of Congress be selected by "the People of the several states." Further, the Court suggested that districting is an implicit element of the Twelfth Amendment, as well as its precursor language in Article II. The Twelfth Amendment grants the House of Representatives the authority to resolve Presidential elections not decided by the Electoral College. The House exercises that authority in voting state by state, with each state voting "as a unit, but that vote is arrived at through the votes of its representatives in Congress elected by districts."]

* * * *

By the first paragraph of section two, Article I, it is provided: "The House of Representatives shall be composed of Members chosen every second year by the people of the several States, and the Electors in each State shall have the Qualifications requisite for Electors of the most numerous Branch of the State Legislature;" and by the third paragraph "when vacancies happen in the

Representation from any State, the Executive Authority thereof shall issue Writs of Election to fill such Vacancies." Section four reads: "The Times, Places and Manner of holding Elections for Senators and Representatives, shall be prescribed in each State by the Legislature thereof; but the Congress may at any time by Law make or alter such Regulations, except as to the Places of choosing Senators."

Although it is thus declared that the people of the several States shall choose the members of Congress, (language which induced the State of New York to insert a salvo as to the power to divide into districts, in its resolutions of ratification,) the state legislatures, prior to 1842, in prescribing the times, places and manner of holding elections for representatives, had usually apportioned the State into districts, and assigned to each a representative; and by act of Congress of June 25, 1842, 5 Stat. 491, c. 47, (carried forward as Sec. 23 of the Revised Statutes), it was provided that where a State was entitled to more than one representative, the election should be by districts. It has never been doubted that representatives in Congress thus chosen represented the entire people of the State acting in their sovereign capacity.

By original clause three of section one of Article II, and by the Twelfth Amendment which superseded that clause, in case of a failure in the election of President by the people, the House of Representatives is to choose the President; and "the vote shall be taken by States, the representation from each State having one vote." The State acts as a unit and its vote is given as a unit, but that vote is arrived at through the votes of its representatives in Congress elected by districts.

The State also acts individually through its electoral college, although, by reason of the power of its legislature over the manner of appointment, the vote of its electors may be divided.

The Constitution does not provide that the appointment of electors shall be by popular vote, nor that the electors shall be voted for upon a general ticket, nor that the majority of those who exercise the elective franchise can alone choose the electors. It recognizes that the people act through their representatives in the legislature, and leaves it to the legislature exclusively to define the method of effecting the object.

* * * *

The Journal of the Convention discloses that propositions that the President should be elected by "the citizens of the United States," or by the "people," or "by electors to be chosen by the people of the several States," instead of by the Congress, were voted down, (Jour. Con. 286, 288; 1 Elliot's Deb. 208, 262,) as was the proposition that the President should be "chosen by electors appointed for that purpose by the legislatures of the States," though at one time adopted. Jour. Con. 190; 1 Elliot's Deb. 208, 211, 217. And a motion to postpone the consideration of the choice "by the national legislature," in order to take up a resolution providing for electors to be elected by the qualified voters in districts, was negatived in Committee of the Whole. Jour. Con. 92; 1 Elliot's Deb. 156. Gerry proposed that the choice should be made by the State executives; Hamilton, that the election be by electors chosen by electors chosen by the people; James Wilson and Gouverneur Morris were strongly in favor of popular vote; Ellsworth and Luther Martin preferred the choice by electors elected by the legislatures; and Roger Sherman, appointment by Congress. The final result seems to have reconciled contrariety of views by leaving it to the state legislatures to appoint directly by joint ballot or concurrent separate action, or through popular election by districts or by general ticket, or as otherwise might be directed.

Therefore, on reference to contemporaneous and subsequent action under the clause, we should expect to find, as we do, that various modes of choosing the electors were pursued, as, by the legislature itself on joint ballot; by the legislature through a concurrent vote of the two houses; by vote of the people for a general ticket; by vote of the people in districts; by choice partly by the people voting in districts and partly by the legislature; by choice by the legislature from candidates voted for by the people in districts; and in other ways, as, notably, by North Carolina in 1792, and Tennessee in 1796 and 1800. No question was raised as to the power of the State to appoint, in any mode its legislature saw fit to adopt, and none that a single method, applicable without exception, must be pursued in the absence of an amendment to the Constitution. The district system was largely considered the most equitable, and Madison wrote that it was that system which was contemplated by the framers of the Constitution, although it was soon seen that its adoption by some States might place them at a disadvantage by a division of their strength, and that a uniform rule was preferable.

[The opinion then goes into an election-by-election summary of the various methods diverse state legislatures used during the 18th and 19th centuries of choosing presidential electors. Among other interesting facts, it notes that Thomas Jefferson advised Virginia for the 1800 election to use the general ticket method "until some uniform mode of choosing a President and Vice-President of the United States shall be prescribed by an amendment to the Constitution." Similarly, the opinion quotes Mr. Justice Story, in the 1st Edition of his Commentaries on the Constitution, as remarking that "it has been thought desirable by many statesmen to have the Constitution amended so as to provide for a uniform mode of choice by the people." The opinion also notes various proposed but failed constitutional amendments requiring that electors be chosen by popular vote on a districted basis.]

* * * *

From this review, in which we have been assisted by the laborious research of counsel, and which might have been greatly expanded, it is seen that from the formation of the government until now the practical construction of the clause has conceded plenary power to the state legislatures in the matter of the appointment of electors.

Even in the heated controversy of 1876-1877 the electoral vote of Colorado cast by electors chosen by the legislature passed unchallenged; and our attention has not been drawn to any previous attempt to submit to the courts the determination of the constitutionality of state action.

In short, the appointment and mode of appointment of electors belong exclusively to the States under the Constitution of the United States. They are, as remarked by Mr. Justice Gray in *In re Green*, 134 U.S. 377, 379 (1890) " no more officers or agents of the United States than are the members of the state legislatures when acting as electors of Federal senators, or the people of the States when acting as the electors of representatives in Congress." Congress is empowered to determine the time of choosing the electors and the day on which they are to give their votes, which is required to be the same day throughout the United States, but otherwise the power and jurisdiction of the State is exclusive, with the exception of the provisions as to the number of electors and the ineligibility of certain persons, so framed that Congressional and Federal influence might be excluded.

* * * *

It is argued that the district mode of choosing electors, while not obnoxious to constitutional objection, if the operation of the electoral system had conformed to its original object and purpose, had become so in view of the practical working of that system. Doubtless it was supposed that the electors would exercise a reasonable independence and fair judgment in the selection of the Chief Executive, but experience soon demonstrated that, whether chosen by the legislatures or by popular suffrage on general ticket or in districts, they were so chosen simply to register the will of the appointing power in respect of a particular candidate. In relation, then, to the independence of the electors the original expectation may be said to have been frustrated. But we can perceive no reason for holding that the power confided to the States by the Constitution has ceased to exist because the operation of the system has not fully realized the hopes of those by whom it was created. Still less can we recognize the doctrine, that because the Constitution has been found in the march of time sufficiently comprehensive to be applicable to conditions not within the minds of its framers, and not arising in their time, it may, therefore, be wrenched from the subjects expressly embraced within it, and amended by judicial decision without action by the designated organs in the mode by which alone amendments can be made.

Nor are we able to discover any conflict between this act and the Fourteenth and Fifteenth Amendments to the Constitution . . . . If presidential electors are appointed by the legislatures, no discrimination is made; if they are elected in districts where each citizen has an equal right to vote the same as any other citizen has, no discrimination is made.

We repeat that the main question arising for consideration is one of power and not of policy, and we are unable to arrive at any other conclusion than that the act of the legislature of Michigan of May 1, 1891, is not void as in contravention of the Constitution of the United States for want of power in its enactment.

The judgment of the Supreme Court of Michigan must be affirmed.

NOTES AND QUESTIONS

1. *McPherson* reaffirmed that there could be Court review of a claim that the state legislature's prerogatives in setting the mechanisms for the selection of electors had been overridden. But *McPherson* stopped at the structural constitutional arrangements governing what body makes the decisions as to how the electors are selected. Much constitutional water has flowed over the dam since *McPherson,* and most of it has addressed an expanded set of constitutional interests in substantive voting rights. It is interesting to speculate how much of the Florida state constitutional doctrine invoked by the Florida Supreme Court could as easily (and unobjectionably) been derived from federal constitutional law found in the breakthrough one-person, one-vote cases and their progeny. Would *Bush I* collapse if the Florida Supreme Court were to turn to federal constitutional authority for the same equitable principles that it derived from state constitutional law? To what extent has the Fourteenth Amendment's guarantee of due process and equal protection impliedly limited the conferral of state legislative authority under Art. II, § 1?

2. The precise issue that concerned the litigants in *McPherson v. Blacker* was the constitutionality of a Michigan statute that had provided that the state's presidential electors were to be selected from congressional districts, with two floterial districts selecting the electors attributable to the state's senate seats. The plaintiffs claimed that the state had to select its electors at large.

The Court disagreed, holding that the state Legislature's decision to enact a statute providing for popular election by districts was a permissible use of the power conferred by Article II, § 1's directive that "[e]ach State shall appoint, in such Manner as the Legislature thereof may direct" the electors to which it was entitled. Given that the Legislature could have rejected popular election altogether, there was no problem with its deciding that each voter could essentially vote for only two of the state's twelve electors — the one from his congressional district and a second from the floterial district — rather than for all twelve, the gravamen of plaintiffs' complaint.

3. The first suggestion that Article II's use of the word "Legislature" somehow limits the *states'* ability, through their constitutions or otherwise, to cabin the legislature's decision about how to appoint electors, apparently arises not at the time of the framing but in 1874, in a Senate report proposing that states be required to select their electors from districts. Given that this report was issued eighty years after Art. II's enactment and accompanied legislation that apparently was never enacted, how much weight ought it to be given?

In particular, in *McPherson*, the Michigan Supreme Court had upheld the challenged statute against federal constitutional attack. Thus, the U.S. Supreme Court was not asked to address the question whether, had the Michigan Supreme Court struck down the statute on state constitutional grounds, the Michigan Supreme Court's judgment would have violated Article II. That was roughly the question that engaged the Court in *Bush I*: Assuming that the Florida Legislature had enacted deadlines for certifying presidential elections that violated Florida constitutional law, would the Florida Supreme Court lack its usual power of judicial review? That question conceals some heroic assumptions. It assumes, for example, that Florida's state legislators knowingly enacted a statute contrary to their state's own constitution, despite the oaths they (like all state elected officials) take to uphold the state, as well as the federal, constitution. Isn't the more reasonable assumption that state legislators act against a background commitment to adhering to their state's constitution as well as the United States Constitution and that, absent a clear statement of state constitutional defiance, their acts should be subject to the normal process of judicial review? What does the *McPherson* Court mean when it says: "The State does not act by its people in their collective capacity, but through such political agencies as are duly constituted and established. The legislative power is the supreme authority except as limited by the constitution of the State, and the sovereignty of the people is exercised through their representatives in the legislature unless by the fundamental law power is elsewhere reposed." Does *Bush I* give appropriate consideration to this passage?

4. *The History of Art. II.* The most detailed historical examination of Art. II and the independent state legislature doctrine is Hayward Smith, *A Trifle Light as Air: The Article II Independent Legislature Doctrine*, 28 Fla .St. U. L. Rev. ___ (2001). In brief, Smith reaches the following conclusions: (1) there was no direct debate one way or the other on whether the Framers or the ratifying conventions meant Art. II to create independent state legislatures for this one unique role; (2) however, some state constitutions did restrain state legislatures in their Art. II role; for example, Massachusetts and New York contained gubernatorial vetoes in their early constitutions and state legislatures submitted presidential election statutes, like all others, to this veto mechanism; (3) and that there appears to be no historical support for the independent state legislature doctrine before the Civil War. During that War, however, a series of "soldier voter" cases arose in which State constitutions appeared to preclude soldiers, who were out of state at the time, from voting in the pending presidential election. State courts strained to read their constitutions to permit such voting, and in doing so, suggested for the first time the possibility that Art. II overrode state constitutions, though these courts did not directly so hold. Thus, in the context of expanding the franchise for soldiers, some judicial basis for the independent state legislature doctrine was recognized for the first time in this era. Some state courts held that Art. II required these soldiers to be enfranchised, notwithstanding the state constitutional provisions. Two state courts had directly affirmed the power of state constitutions to regulate the Art. II powers of state legislatures before *Bush I;* these decisions, like the rest of the history of Art. II, are not mentioned in *Bush I* or *Bush II.*

5. Even the *McPherson* Court recognized that the state legislature's Article II powers are circumscribed by later constitutional provisions, such as the Fourteenth and Fifteenth Amendments, that prohibit discrimination in voting. Thus, for example, although a state legislature might be free to abandon popular voting for electors altogether, it could not deny black citizens the right to vote in a popular election if it should decide to hold one. In light of one-person, one-vote, could Michigan today enact a statute selecting its electors from districts if those districts contained different numbers of people? Indeed, *Bush II's* central holding will rest, as we shall see, on a rejection of any view that Article II might be unconstrained by later U.S. constitutional amendments: *Bush II* held that state statutes for presidential elections must comply with modern voting rights jurisprudence developed under the Fourteenth Amendment.

6. *The Disappearance of the Issue.* On the same day that the U.S. Supreme Court heard oral argument in *Bush v. Gore (Bush II), infra,* the Florida Supreme Court issued its opinion on remand from *Bush I.* In *Palm Beach County Canvassing Board v. Harris,* 772 So. 2d 1273 (Fla. S. Ct., Dec. 11, 2000), the Florida Supreme Court reached precisely the same result: that is, it held that Secretary of State Harris was required to accept, and include in the certified total, late-arriving returns from counties conducting manual recounts pursuant to Fla. Stat. § 102.166(5). But it reached that result in a different manner. Gone from the Court's opinion was Section II — "Guiding Principles" — in which the Court declared that "the will of the people, not a hyper-technical reliance upon statutory provisions, should be our guiding principle in election cases," and the reliance on the state constitution's recognition of the right to vote. Gone, too, was Section VIII — on "The Right to Vote" — which quoted from the Florida Constitution and its Declaration of Rights." The Court re-emphasized in its section on "Legislative Intent" that "[l]egislative intent — as always — is the polestar that guides a court's inquiry into the provisions of the Florida Election Code. *See Florida Birth-Related Neurological Injury Compensation Ass'n v. Florida Div. of Admin. Hearings,* 686 So. 2d 1349 (Fla. 1997)." The Court furthered repeated that because chapter 102 was ambiguous and contradictory, "the Court must resort to traditional rules of statutory construction to determine legislative intent." Throughout the new opinion, and especially in the conclusion, the Florida Supreme Court restricted its citations of authority to legislative materials and wrapped itself in the mantle of statutory interpretation:

> [. . . T]his Court has at all times been faced with a question of the statutory construction of Florida's election laws in accord with the intent of the Florida Legislature. Our examination of that issue has been limited to a determination of legislative intent as informed by the traditional sources and rules of construction we have long accepted as relevant in determining such intent. Not surprisingly, we have identified the right of Florida's citizens to vote and to have elections determined by the will of Florida's voters as important policy concerns of the Florida Legislature in enacting Florida's election code . . . .

> By providing for the popular election of presidential electors, Florida's Legislature has also placed that election under Florida's general statutory election scheme. Hence, there is essentially only one statutory election scheme for all elections whether the elections be for local and state officials or for presidential electors. The Legislature has not chosen to have a separate set of election laws for elections for presidential electors. The Legislature has chosen to have a single election code control all elections. So, we must interpret and apply that single election code here . . . .

It should not be surprising then that this Court's prior opinions that we have relied on for guidance in resolving the pending issue of statutory construction would have little reference to the Legislature's authority in the selecting of presidential electors or the Legislature's decision to grant Florida voters the right to elect presidential electors. In fact, the parties have provided us no citations to court cases in Florida involving disputes over presidential electors under Florida's election laws. This case may be the first.

In sum, Florida's statutory scheme simply makes no provision for applying its rules one way for presidential elector elections and another way for all other elections. That was a legislative decision that we have accepted . . . . We have construed the provisions providing for a time table as directory in light of what we perceive to be a clear legislative policy of the importance of an elector's right to vote and of having each vote counted. Hopefully, our unbroken line of cases identifying and relying on these legislative policies have not missed the mark. Further, if anything, more recent legislative changes have been crafted not only to be consistent with these policies, but also to ensure adherence to them.

Hence, based upon our perception of legislative intent, we have ruled that election returns must be accepted for filing unless it can clearly be determined that the late filing would prevent an election contest or the consideration of Florida's vote in a presidential selection. This statutory construction reflects our view that the Legislature would not wish to endanger Florida's vote not being counted in a presidential election. This ruling is not only consistent with our prior interpretation of the entire statutory election scheme, but also with our identification of the important legislative policies underlying that scheme.

For the reasons stated in this opinion, we reverse the orders of the trial court. Based on this Court's status as the ultimate arbiter of conflicting Florida law, we conclude that our construction of the above statutes results in the formation of no new rules of state law but rather results simply in a narrow reading and clarification of those statutes, which were enacted long before the present election took place. We decline to rule more expansively in the present case, for to do so would result in this Court substantially rewriting the Code. We leave that matter to the sound discretion of the body best equipped to address it, the Legislature.

Does the fact that the Florida Supreme Court reached the same result on remand suggest that state constitutional principles had played a role in informing that court's statutory interpretation, but that those principles had not played a decisive role? Or is it a testament to the plasticity of legal reasoning? Why might the Florida Supreme Court have invoked the state constitution and the right to vote in its first opinion? Note that no party had argued to that court that Art. II precluded it from relying on its State constitution to interpret state election laws. Had the U.S. Supreme Court's decision the next day in *Bush II* not rendered the Florida Supreme Court's decision essentially moot, how would the U.S. Supreme Court have analyzed the Florida Supreme Court's decision? More generally, what does this inter-court dialogue reveal about the entire subject of "adequate and independent state grounds" and the ability of state courts to insulate their judgments from federal review?

2. OF "SAFE HARBORS" AND THE ELECTORAL COUNT ACT

Bush II draws to the center of the dispute the role of 3 U.S.C. § 5, a central provision of the Electoral Count Act of 1887. The history of this Act is provided above. This provision of the U.S. Code speaks to after-the-fact alterations of procedures in state presidential elections. But the Court in *Bush I* appears to accept the argument that 3 U.S.C. § 5 is, in essence, a safe harbor that creates a strong presumption of legitimacy for the state's selection of electors when *Congress* reviews their votes in January. As a general matter, it is difficult to construct out of a safe harbor an obligation that the states must act in conformity with its provisions, as opposed to simply being induced to follow its suggested course of action. Nonetheless, the Court directs the Florida Supreme Court on remand to address what consideration it gave to 3 U.S.C. § 5. This remand set off a chain of invocation of 3 U.S.C. § 5 by every court and every brief filed in the rapidly unfolding Florida cascade. But, if 3 U.S.C. § 5 is truly a guide to congressional evaluation of the credentials of electors from the states, should this statute play any role in judicial oversight of elections? Further, can 3 U.S.C. § 5 be the basis for federal courts overturning the actions of state courts or state legislatures?

Section 5 of Title 3 serves as a "safe harbor" provision for a state determination of who the winning electors are. The design was to ensure that disputes over which electors were the proper electors would always be resolved, but that to the extent possible these determinations would be made by the state government because the Constitution gives responsibility for selecting electors to the states in an effort to isolate Congress from the election of the President. *See* 17 Cong. Rec. 1023 (1886) (Sen. Hoar). At the same time, Congress feared that the process of determining which slate of electors would become too chaotic and subject to state legislatures overturning the will of the people if legislatures were permitted to change the rules for contests after the election. *See* 18 Cong. Rec. 47 (1886) (Rep. Cooper). Consequently, the Act was designed to balance these concerns by making the decisions of the state government binding, but only if the decisions were controlled by state laws "enacted prior to the day fixed for the appointment of the electors" and only if the final determination was made six days prior to the meeting of the electors. 3 U.S.C. § 5.

Under a robust reading of *McPherson*, is the Electoral Count Act itself unconstitutional? That is, doesn't Art. II preclude Congress from intruding into the manner the states have chosen for selecting their presidential electors? Questions about the constitutionality of the Electoral Count Act have been raised but never fully addressed. Various members of Congress argued at the time of passage that the Electoral Count Act was an unconstitutional attempt to remedy "defects in the Constitution . . . by acts of Congress." 17 Cong. Rec. 1058 (1886) (Sen. Wilson). The specifics of the Act were criticized by arguments that the President of the Senate was alone empowered to count the votes of the Electoral College and that both early commentators and the practice of early Congresses showed that Congress's role was purely as witness to the counting by the President of the Senate. *Id.* at 1059.

For example, does Congress actually have the power it asserts in 3 U.S.C. § 15, to give primacy to the set of electors certified by the "state Executive" in a situation where the two houses of Congress cannot resolve an election contest? What if a state would assign priority in such a situation differently — say, to the electors as determined finally in state judicial proceedings? And what about the "safe harbor" provision, 3 U.S.C. § 5, which played such a central role throughout the litigation? Does Art. II preclude Congress from threatening states with the loss of their preferred electors if those electors are not chosen six days before the Electoral College meets? Should not Art. II, under the strongest reading, permit states to act independently of Congress up until the actual meeting of the Electoral College?

Indeed, these and other questions regarding the constitutionality of the Electoral Count Act have been longstanding. For example, seven dissenting members of the House committee that reported the Act constitutionally objected precisely to Congress' assertion of power to impose a "safe harbor" on the States:

> In accord with the principles I have mentioned, seven of the committee are of the opinion that, so far as casting the vote is concerned, the State has all the constitutional power conferred, and that Congress can not prescribe that a State shall make its determination within a limited time prior to the day of casting the vote.

> When the Constitution of the United States says that the day on which the electoral votes shall be cast shall be the same throughout the United States, the Constitutional thereby imposes a limitation upon the appointing power of the States. The appointment must be made, all determinations concerning it must be made, all disputes concerning it must be settled, prior to that day; but Congress has no power, as is attempted here, to put a statute of limitations other than the limitation imposed by the Constitution on the appointing power of the State, by enacting that the determination of such question must be made six days, or at any other period, before the vote is cast. That is our point of difference [with the committee majority].

18 Cong. Rec. 47 (Dec. 8, 1886) (Rep. Dibble).

Why were these constitutional objections to the imposition of a "safe harbor" — tantamount to an earlier deadline than the meeting of the Electoral College — not raised in the *Bush v. Gore* litigation? None of these arguments have been decided upon by a court; given the structure of the Act, the

circumstances under which a court would have the ability to decide whether
the Act is constitutional are unclear. A majority of Congress was persuaded
by the argument that the Act was permitted under the Necessary and Proper
Clause to give substance to the provisions of the Twelfth Amendment.

B. THE FINAL FLORIDA COURT DECISION AND THE UNITED STATES SUPREME COURT STAY

While *Bush* was pending on remand from the U.S. Supreme Court, the
Florida Supreme Court returned to matters of the state's electoral-dispute
resolution laws in a second appeal, *Gore v. Harris,* 773 So. 2d 524 (Fla. S. Ct.,
Dec. 8, 2000). At issue was an appeal from the denial of a recount by a Leon
County trial court. We summarize the result briefly here; the United States
Supreme Court decision in *Bush v. Gore* provides a full account of this decision.

The Florida Supreme Court divided 4-3, with the majority reversing the
trial court and ordering, *inter alia,* an immediate hand recount of all ballots in
the state that were counted by machine and did not register a vote for
president — the "undervote" ballots. Unlike the court's earlier opinion in *Palm
Beach County Canvassing Board,* the opinion in *Gore* eschewed all reliance on
the state constitution in favor of careful invocations of statutory authority for
the ordered recount. Similarly, the dissents took pains to challenge the
statutory construction of the majority opinion and to claim that the majority
had acted beyond the bounds of state legislative action. Although this opinion
was ultimately overturned in *Bush II,* a separate interesting question still
remains on the remedial front. Because of its determination that the trial
court had erred in requiring proof of a "reasonable probability" of an altered
election outcome as a precondition to a recount, the *Gore v. Harris* majority
fashioned a distinct remedy to address the immediate time pressure created
by the rapidly approaching convocation of Electors. This remedy included a
recount process for all counties in the state using machine counting
mechanisms, but only for the undervote ballots. In addition, the Court ordered
that the actions be taken through somewhat altered procedures using, if
necessary, court personnel to conduct the recounts. Finally, the majority
endorsed a standard that all ballots were to be accepted if the will of the voter
could be reasonably ascertained through a visual inspection of the ballot. As
support for these remedial actions, the majority pointed to Section 102.168(8)
of the contest statute, which is reproduced in its entirety in the Appendix. This
provision empowers courts in contest actions to provide "any relief appropriate"
to prevent or correct any electoral wrong recognized Section 102.168.

The dissenting opinions argued that such processes were unprecedented
in Florida, were not statutorily authorized, and would not work. Does *Bush I*
imply anything about the scope of the remedial authority of the Florida
Supreme Court? Is it appropriate for the United States Supreme Court to
"imply" legal principles without actually announcing those principles as matter
of substantive law? It is interesting to note that the Florida Supreme Court

acted in *Gore v. Harris* without having actually addressed this issue on remand from the U.S. Supreme Court in *Bush I*. Assuming that the Florida Supreme Court majority is correct in concluding that Florida statutory law compels a recount under the conditions proven at trial in *Gore,* does *Bush I* raise doubts about the range of remedial authority claimed by the *Gore* majority?

Immediately after this second Florida Supreme Court decision, lawyers for the Bush campaign sought a stay from the United States Supreme Court. For part of a Friday evening and Saturday day, the recount process as ordered that Friday by the Florida Supreme Court began to be set into motion. By midday on Saturday, the United States Supreme Court granted the requested stay on a 5-4 vote, treated the request for a stay as a petition for certiorari, granted that requested writ, and ordered oral argument to take place on the merits on that Monday. In an unusual action, the Court's internal disagreements over whether to grant the stay were publicly aired in separate opinions:

Bush v. Gore
121 S.Ct. 512 (Dec. 9, 2000)

■ PER CURIAM:

The application for stay presented to JUSTICE KENNEDY and by him referred to the Court is granted, and it is ordered that the mandate of the Florida Supreme Court, case No. SCOO-2431, is hereby stayed pending further order of the Court. In addition, the application for stay is treated as a petition for writ of certiorari, and the petition for writ of certiorari granted. . . .

■ JUSTICE SCALIA, concurring.

Though it is not customary for the Court to issue an opinion in connection with its grant of a stay, I believe a brief response is necessary to JUSTICE STEVENS' dissent. I will not address the merits of the case, since they will shortly be before us in the petition for certiorari that we have granted. It suffices to say that the issuance of the stay suggests that a majority of the Court, while not deciding the issues presented, believe that the petitioner has a substantial probability of success.

On the question of irreparable harm, however, a few words are appropriate. The issue is not, as the dissent puts it, whether "[c]ounting every legally cast vote ca[n] constitute irreparable harm." One of the principal issues in the appeal we have accepted is precisely whether the votes that have been ordered to be counted are, under a reasonable interpretation of Florida law, "legally cast vote[s]." The counting of votes that are of questionable legality does in my view threaten irreparable harm to petitioner, and to the country, by casting a cloud upon what he claims to be the legitimacy of his election. Count first, and rule upon legality afterwards, is not a recipe for producing election results that have the public acceptance democratic stability requires. Another issue in the case, moreover, is the propriety, indeed the constitutionality, of letting the standard for determination of voters' intent –

dimpled chads, hanging chads, etc.– vary from county to county, as the Florida Supreme Court opinion, as interpreted by the Circuit Court, permits. If petitioner is correct that counting in this fashion is unlawful, permitting the count to proceed on that erroneous basis will prevent an accurate recount from being conducted on a proper basis later, since it is generally agreed that each manual recount produces a degradation of the ballots, which renders a subsequent recount inaccurate.

For these reasons I have joined the Court's issuance of stay, with a highly accelerated timetable for resolving this case on the merits.

■ JUSTICE STEVENS, with whom JUSTICE SOUTER, JUSTICE GINSBURG, and JUSTICE BREYER join, dissenting.

To stop the counting of legal votes, the majority today departs from three venerable rules of judicial restraint that have guided the Court throughout its history.   On questions of state law, we have consistently respected the opinions of the highest courts of the States. On questions whose resolution is committed at least in large measure to another branch of the Federal Government, we have construed our own jurisdiction narrowly and exercised it cautiously.   On federal constitutional questions that were not fairly presented to the court whose judgment is being reviewed, we have prudently declined to express an opinion. The majority has acted unwisely.

Time does not permit a full discussion of the merits. It is clear, however, that a stay should not be granted unless an applicant makes a substantial showing of a likelihood of irreparable harm. In this case, applicants have failed to carry that heavy burden. Counting every legally cast vote cannot constitute irreparable harm. On the other hand, there is a danger that a stay may cause irreparable harm to the respondents – and, more importantly, the public at large – because of the risk that "the entry of the stay would be tantamount to a decision on the merits in favor of the applicants." *National Socialist Party of America v. Skokie*, 434 U.S. 1327, 1328 (1977) (STEVENS, J., in chambers). Preventing the recount from being completed will inevitably cast a cloud on the legitimacy of the election.

It is certainly not clear that the Florida decision violated federal law. The Florida Code provides elaborate procedures for ensuring that every eligible voter has a full and fair opportunity to cast a ballot and that every ballot so cast is counted. *See, e.g.*, Fla. Stat. §§ 101.5614(5), 102.166 (2000). In fact, the statutory provision relating to damaged and defective ballots states that "[n]o vote shall be declared invalid or void if there is a clear indication of the intent of the voter as determined by the canvassing board." Fla. Stat. § 101.5614(5) (2000).   In its opinion, the Florida Supreme Court gave weight to that legislative command. Its ruling was consistent with earlier Florida cases that have repeatedly described the interest in correctly ascertaining the will of the voters as paramount. *See State ex rel. Chappell v. Martinez*, 536 So.2d 1007 (Fla.1998); *Boardman v. Esteva*, 323 So.2d 259 (Fla.1976); *McAlpin v. State ex rel. Avriett*, 155 Fla. 33, 19 So.2d 420 (1944); *State ex rel. Peacock v. Latham*, 125 Fla. 69, 169 So. 597, 598 (1936); *State ex rel. Carpenter v. Barber*, 144 Fla. 159, 198 So. 49 (1940). Its ruling also appears to be consistent with the prevailing view in other States. *See, e.g., Pullen v. Mulligan*, 138 Ill.2d 21, 149 Ill.Dec. 215, 561 N.E.2d 585, 611 (1990). As a more fundamental matter, the Florida court's ruling reflects the basic principle, inherent in our Constitution and our democracy, that every legal vote should be counted. *See Reynolds v. Sims*, 377 U.S. 533, 544-555 (1964); *cf. Hartke v. Roudebush*, 321 F.Supp. 1370, 1378-1379 (S.D.Ind.1970) (STEVENS, J., dissenting); *accord Roudebush v. Hartke*, 405 U.S. 15 (1972).

Accordingly, I respectfully dissent.

C. THE FEDERAL INTEREST DECISIVELY ASSERTED

Bush v. Gore
531 U.S. 98 (Dec. 12, 2000)

■ PER CURIAM:

On December 8, 2000, the Supreme Court of Florida ordered that the Circuit Court of Leon County tabulate by hand 9,000 ballots in Miami-Dade County. It also ordered the inclusion in the certified vote totals of 215 votes identified in Palm Beach County and 168 votes identified in Miami-Dade County for Vice President Albert Gore, Jr., and Senator Joseph Lieberman, Democratic Candidates for President and Vice President. The Supreme Court noted that petitioner, Governor George W. Bush, asserted that the net gain for Vice President Gore in Palm Beach County was 176 votes, and directed the Circuit Court to resolve that dispute on remand. The court further held that relief would require manual recounts in all Florida counties where so-called "undervotes" had not been subject to manual tabulation. The court ordered all manual recounts to begin at once. Governor Bush and Richard Cheney, Republican Candidates for the Presidency and Vice Presidency, filed an emergency application for a stay of this mandate. On December 9, we granted the application, treated the application as a petition for a writ of certiorari, and granted certiorari.

* * * *

The petition presents the following questions: whether the Florida Supreme Court established new standards for resolving Presidential election contests, thereby violating Art. II, § 1, cl. 2, of the United States Constitution and failing to comply with 3 U.S.C. § 5, and whether the use of standardless manual recounts violates the Equal Protection and Due Process Clauses. With respect to the equal protection question, we find a violation of the Equal Protection Clause.

II

A

The closeness of this election, and the multitude of legal challenges which have followed in its wake, have brought into sharp focus a common, if heretofore unnoticed, phenomenon. Nationwide statistics reveal that an estimated 2% of ballots cast do not register a vote for President for whatever reason, including deliberately choosing no candidate at all or some voter error, such as voting for two candidates or insufficiently marking a ballot. *See* Ho, More Than 2M Ballots Uncounted, AP Online (Nov. 28, 2000); Kelley, Balloting Problems Not Rare But Only In A Very Close Election Do Mistakes And Mismarking Make A Difference, Omaha World-Herald (Nov. 15, 2000). In certifying election results, the votes eligible for inclusion in the certification are the votes meeting the properly established legal requirements.

This case has shown that punch card balloting machines can produce an unfortunate number of ballots which are not punched in a clean, complete way by the voter. After the current counting, it is likely legislative bodies nationwide will examine ways to improve the mechanisms and machinery for voting.

B

The individual citizen has no federal constitutional right to vote for electors for the President of the United States unless and until the state legislature chooses a statewide election as the means to implement its power to appoint members of the Electoral College. U.S. Const., Art. II, § 1. This is the source for the statement in *McPherson v. Blacker*, 146 U.S. 1, 35 (1892), that the State legislature's power to select the manner for appointing electors is plenary; it may, if it so chooses, select the electors itself, which indeed was the manner used by State legislatures in several States for many years after the Framing of our Constitution. *Id.*, at 28-33. History has now favored the voter, and in each of the several States the citizens themselves vote for Presidential electors. When the state legislature vests the right to vote for President in its people, the right to vote as the legislature has prescribed is fundamental; and one source of its fundamental nature lies in the equal weight accorded to each vote and the equal dignity owed to each voter. The State, of course, after granting the franchise in the special context of Article II, can take back the power to appoint electors. *See id.*, at 35 ("[T]here is no doubt of the right of the legislature to resume the power at any time, for it can neither be taken away nor abdicated") (quoting S.Rep. No. 395, 43d Cong., 1st Sess.).

The right to vote is protected in more than the initial allocation of the franchise. Equal protection applies as well to the manner of its exercise. Having once granted the right to vote on equal terms, the State may not, by later arbitrary and disparate treatment, value one person's vote over that of another. *See, e.g., Harper v. Virginia Bd. of Elections*, 383 U.S. 663, 665 (1966) ("[O]nce the franchise is granted to the electorate, lines may not be drawn which are inconsistent with the Equal Protection Clause of the Fourteenth Amendment"). It must be remembered that "the right of suffrage can be denied by a debasement or dilution of the weight of a citizen's vote just as effectively as by wholly prohibiting the free exercise of the franchise." *Reynolds v. Sims*, 377 U.S. 533, 555 (1964).

There is no difference between the two sides of the present controversy on these basic propositions. Respondents say that the very purpose of vindicating the right to vote justifies the recount procedures now at issue. The question before us, however, is whether the recount procedures the Florida Supreme Court has adopted are consistent with its obligation to avoid arbitrary and disparate treatment of the members of its electorate.

Much of the controversy seems to revolve around ballot cards designed to be perforated by a stylus but which, either through error or deliberate omission, have not been perforated with sufficient precision for a machine to count them. In some cases a piece of the card — a chad — is hanging, say by two corners. In other cases there is no separation at all, just an indentation.

The Florida Supreme Court has ordered that the intent of the voter be discerned from such ballots. For purposes of resolving the equal protection challenge, it is not necessary to decide whether the Florida Supreme Court had the authority under the legislative scheme for resolving election disputes to define what a legal vote is and to mandate a manual recount implementing that definition. The recount mechanisms implemented in response to the decisions of the Florida Supreme Court do not satisfy the minimum requirement for non-arbitrary treatment of voters necessary to secure the fundamental right. Florida's basic command for the count of legally cast votes is to consider the "intent of the voter." This is unobjectionable as an abstract proposition and a starting principle. The problem inheres in the absence of specific standards to ensure its equal application. The formulation of uniform rules to determine intent based on these recurring circumstances is practicable and, we conclude, necessary.

The law does not refrain from searching for the intent of the actor in a multitude of circumstances; and in some cases the general command to ascertain intent is not susceptible to much further refinement. In this instance, however, the question is not whether to believe a witness but how to interpret the marks or holes or scratches on an inanimate object, a piece of cardboard or paper which, it is said, might not have registered as a vote during the machine count. The factfinder confronts a thing, not a person. The search for intent can be confined by specific rules designed to ensure uniform treatment.

The want of those rules here has led to unequal evaluation of ballots in various respects. *See Gore v. Harris*, 772 So.2d, at 1267; (Wells, J., dissenting) ("Should a county canvassing board count or not count a 'dimpled chad' where the voter is able to successfully dislodge the chad in every other contest on that ballot? Here, the county canvassing boards disagree"). As seems to have been acknowledged at oral argument, the standards for accepting or rejecting contested ballots might vary not only from county to county but indeed within a single county from one recount team to another.

* * * *

An early case in our one person, one vote jurisprudence arose when a State accorded arbitrary and disparate treatment to voters in its different counties. *Gray v. Sanders*, 372 U.S. 368 (1963). The Court found a constitutional violation. We relied on these principles in the context of the Presidential selection process in *Moore v. Ogilvie*, 394 U.S. 814 (1969), where we invalidated a county-based procedure that diluted the influence of citizens in larger counties in the nominating process. There we observed that "[t]he idea that one group can be granted greater voting strength than another is hostile to the one man, one vote basis of our representative government." *Id.*, at 819.

The State Supreme Court ratified this uneven treatment. It mandated that the recount totals from two counties, Miami-Dade and Palm Beach, be included in the certified total. The court also appeared to hold sub silentio that the recount totals from Broward County, which were not completed until after the original November 14 certification by the Secretary of State, were to be considered part of the new certified vote totals even though the county certification was not contested by Vice President Gore. Yet each of the counties used varying standards to determine what was a legal vote. Broward County used a more forgiving standard than Palm Beach County, and uncovered almost three times as many new votes, a result markedly disproportionate to the difference in population between the counties.

In addition, the recounts in these three counties were not limited to so-called undervotes but extended to all of the ballots. The distinction has real consequences. A manual recount of all ballots identifies not only those ballots which show no vote but also those which contain more than one, the so- called overvotes. Neither category will be counted by the machine. This is not a trivial concern. At oral argument, respondents estimated there are as many as 110,000 overvotes statewide. As a result, the citizen whose ballot was not read by a machine because he failed to vote for a candidate in a way readable by a machine may still have his vote counted in a manual recount; on the other hand, the citizen who marks two candidates in a way discernable by the machine will not have the same opportunity to have his vote count, even if a manual examination of the ballot would reveal the requisite indicia of intent. Furthermore, the citizen who marks two candidates, only one of which is discernable by the machine, will have his vote counted even though it should have been read as an invalid ballot. The State Supreme Court's inclusion of vote counts based on these variant standards exemplifies concerns with the remedial processes that were under way.

That brings the analysis to yet a further equal protection problem. The votes certified by the court included a partial total from one county, Miami-Dade. The Florida Supreme Court's decision thus gives no assurance that the recounts included in a final certification must be complete. Indeed, it is respondent's submission that it would be consistent with the rules of the recount procedures to include whatever partial counts are done by the time of final certification, and we interpret the Florida Supreme Court's decision to permit this. *See* 772 So.2d, at 1261, n. 21, (noting "practical difficulties" may control outcome of election, but certifying partial Miami-Dade total nonetheless). This accommodation no doubt results from the truncated contest period established by the Florida Supreme Court in *Bush I*, at respondents' own urging. The press of time does not diminish the constitutional concern. A desire for speed is not a general excuse for ignoring equal protection guarantees.

In addition to these difficulties the actual process by which the votes were to be counted under the Florida Supreme Court's decision raises further concerns. That order did not specify who would recount the ballots. The county canvassing boards were forced to pull together ad hoc teams comprised of judges from various Circuits who had no previous training in handling and interpreting ballots. Furthermore, while others were permitted to observe, they were prohibited from objecting during the recount.

The recount process, in its features here described, is inconsistent with the minimum procedures necessary to protect the fundamental right of each voter in the special instance of a statewide recount under the authority of a single state judicial officer. Our consideration is limited to the present circumstances, for the problem of equal protection in election processes generally presents many complexities.

The question before the Court is not whether local entities, in the exercise of their expertise, may develop different systems for implementing elections. Instead, we are presented with a situation where a state court with the power to assure uniformity has ordered a statewide recount with minimal procedural safeguards. When a court orders a statewide remedy, there must be at least some assurance that the rudimentary requirements of equal treatment and fundamental fairness are satisfied.

Given the Court's assessment that the recount process underway was probably being conducted in an unconstitutional manner, the Court stayed the order directing the recount so it could hear this case and render an expedited decision. The contest provision, as it was mandated by the State Supreme Court, is not well calculated to sustain the confidence that all citizens must have in the outcome of elections. The State has not shown that its procedures include the necessary safeguards. The problem, for instance, of the estimated 110,000 overvotes has not been addressed, although Chief Justice Wells called attention to the concern in his dissenting opinion.

Upon due consideration of the difficulties identified to this point, it is obvious that the recount cannot be conducted in compliance with the requirements of equal protection and due process without substantial additional work. It would require not only the adoption (after opportunity for argument) of adequate statewide standards for determining what is a legal vote, and practicable procedures to implement them, but also orderly judicial review of any disputed matters that might arise. In addition, the Secretary of State has advised that the recount of only a portion of the ballots requires that the vote tabulation equipment be used to screen out undervotes, a function for which the machines were not designed. If a recount of overvotes were also required, perhaps even a second screening would be necessary. Use of the equipment for this purpose, and any new software developed for it, would have to be evaluated for accuracy by the Secretary of State, as required by Fla. Stat. § 101.015 (2000).

The Supreme Court of Florida has said that the legislature intended the State's electors to "participat[e] fully in the federal electoral process," as provided in 3 U.S.C. § 5. 772 So.2d, at 1254; *see also Palm Beach Canvassing Bd. v. Harris*, 772 So.2d 1220, (Fla. 2000). That statute, in turn, requires that any controversy or contest that is designed to lead to a conclusive selection of electors be completed by December 12. That date is upon us, and there is no recount procedure in place under the State Supreme Court's order that comports with minimal constitutional standards. Because it is evident that any recount seeking to meet the December 12 date will be unconstitutional for the reasons we have discussed, we reverse the judgment of the Supreme Court of Florida ordering a recount to proceed.

Seven Justices of the Court agree that there are constitutional problems with the recount ordered by the Florida Supreme Court that demand a remedy. *See post*, at 545 (SOUTER, J., dissenting); post, at 551, 557-558 (BREYER, J., dissenting). The only disagreement is as to the remedy. Because the Florida Supreme Court has said that the Florida Legislature intended to obtain the safe-harbor benefits of 3 U.S.C. § 5, Justice BREYER's proposed remedy-- remanding to the Florida Supreme Court for its ordering of a constitutionally proper contest until December 18-contemplates action in violation of the Florida election code, and hence could not be part of an "appropriate" order authorized by Fla. Stat. § 102.168(8) (2000).

* * * *

None are more conscious of the vital limits on judicial authority than are the members of this Court, and none stand more in admiration of the Constitution's design to leave the selection of the President to the people, through their legislatures, and to the political sphere. When contending parties invoke the process of the courts, however, it becomes our unsought responsibility to resolve the federal and constitutional issues the judicial system has been forced to confront.

The judgment of the Supreme Court of Florida is reversed, and the case is remanded for further proceedings not inconsistent with this opinion.

It is so ordered.

* * * *

■ CHIEF JUSTICE REHNQUIST, with whom Justice SCALIA and Justice THOMAS join, concurring.

We join the per curiam opinion. We write separately because we believe there are additional grounds that require us to reverse the Florida Supreme Court's decision.

I

We deal here not with an ordinary election, but with an election for the President of the United States. In *Burroughs v. United States*, 290 U.S. 534,

545 (1934), we said:

> While presidential electors are not officers or agents of the federal
> government (*In re Green*, 134 U.S. 377, 379), they exercise federal
> functions under, and discharge duties in virtue of authority conferred
> by, the Constitution of the United States. The President is vested
> with the executive power of the nation. The importance of his
> election and the vital character of its relationship to and effect upon
> the welfare and safety of the whole people cannot be too strongly
> stated.

Likewise, in *Anderson v. Celebrezze*, 460 U.S. 780, 794-795 (1983) (footnote
omitted), we said: "[I]n the context of a Presidential election, state-imposed
restrictions implicate a uniquely important national interest. For the
President and the Vice President of the United States are the only elected
officials who represent all the voters in the Nation."

In most cases, comity and respect for federalism compel us to defer to the
decisions of state courts on issues of state law. That practice reflects our
understanding that the decisions of state courts are definitive pronouncements
of the will of the States as sovereigns. *Cf. Erie R. Co. v. Tompkins*, 304 U.S.
64 (1938). Of course, in ordinary cases, the distribution of powers among the
branches of a State's government raises no questions of federal constitutional
law, subject to the requirement that the government be republican in
character. *See* U.S. Const., Art. IV, § 4. But there are a few exceptional cases
in which the Constitution imposes a duty or confers a power on a particular
branch of a State's government. This is one of them. Article II, § 1, cl. 2,
provides that "[e]ach State shall appoint, in such Manner as the Legislature
thereof may direct," electors for President and Vice President. Thus, the text
of the election law itself, and not just its interpretation by the courts of the
States, takes on independent significance.

In *McPherson* v. Blacker, 146 U.S. 1 (1892), we explained that Art. II, § 1,
cl. 2, "convey[s] the broadest power of determination" and "leaves it to the
legislature exclusively to define the method" of appointment. Id., at 27. A
significant departure from the legislative scheme for appointing Presidential
electors presents a federal constitutional question.

3 U.S.C. § 5 informs our application of Art. II, § 1, cl. 2, to the Florida
statutory scheme, which, as the Florida Supreme Court acknowledged, took
that statute into account. Section 5 provides that the State's selection of
electors "shall be conclusive, and shall govern in the counting of the electoral
votes" if the electors are chosen under laws enacted prior to election day, and
if the selection process is completed six days prior to the meeting of the
electoral college. As we noted in *Bush v. Palm Beach County Canvassing Bd,*

> Since § 5 contains a principle of federal law that would assure finality
> of the State's determination if made pursuant to a state law in effect
> before the election, a legislative wish to take advantage of the 'safe
> harbor' would counsel against any construction of the Election Code
> that Congress might deem to be a change in the law.

If we are to respect the legislature's Article II powers, therefore, we must ensure that postelection state-court actions do not frustrate the legislative desire to attain the "safe harbor" provided by § 5.

* * * *

In order to determine whether a state court has infringed upon the legislature's authority, we necessarily must examine the law of the State as it existed prior to the action of the court. Though we generally defer to state courts on the interpretation of state law — *see, e.g., Mullaney v. Wilbur*, 421 U.S. 684 (1975) — there are of course areas in which the Constitution requires this Court to undertake an independent, if still deferential, analysis of state law.

For example, in *NAACP v. Alabama ex rel. Patterson*, 357 U.S. 449, (1958), it was argued that we were without jurisdiction because the petitioner had not pursued the correct appellate remedy in Alabama's state courts. Petitioners had sought a state-law writ of certiorari in the Alabama Supreme Court when a writ of mandamus, according to that court, was proper. We found this state-law ground inadequate to defeat our jurisdiction because we were "unable to reconcile the procedural holding of the Alabama Supreme Court" with prior Alabama precedent. *Id.*, at 456. The purported state-law ground was so novel, in our independent estimation, that "petitioner could not fairly be deemed to have been apprised of its existence." *Id.*, at 457.

Six years later we decided *Bouie v. City of Columbia*, 378 U.S. 347 (1964), in which the state court had held, contrary to precedent, that the state trespass law applied to black sit-in demonstrators who had consent to enter private property but were then asked to leave. Relying upon NAACP, we concluded that the South Carolina Supreme Court's interpretation of a state penal statute had impermissibly broadened the scope of that statute beyond what a fair reading provided, in violation of due process. *See* 378 U.S., at 361-362. What we would do in the present case is precisely parallel: Hold that the Florida Supreme Court's interpretation of the Florida election laws impermissibly distorted them beyond what a fair reading required, in violation of Article II.

This inquiry does not imply a disrespect for state courts but rather a respect for the constitutionally prescribed role of state legislatures. To attach definitive weight to the pronouncement of a state court, when the very question at issue is whether the court has actually departed from the statutory meaning, would be to abdicate our responsibility to enforce the explicit requirements of Article II.

II

* * * *

In its first decision, the Florida Supreme Court extended the 7-day statutory certification deadline established by the legislature. This modification of the code, by lengthening the protest period, necessarily shortened the contest period for Presidential elections. Underlying the extension of the certification deadline and the shortchanging of the contest period was, presumably, the clear implication that certification was a matter of significance: The certified winner would enjoy presumptive validity, making a contest proceeding by the losing candidate an uphill battle. In its latest opinion, however, the court empties certification of virtually all legal consequence during the contest, and in doing so departs from the provisions enacted by the Florida Legislature.

The court determined that canvassing boards' decisions regarding whether to recount ballots past the certification deadline (even the certification deadline established by *Harris I*) are to be reviewed de novo, although the election code clearly vests discretion whether to recount in the boards, and sets strict deadlines subject to the Secretary's rejection of late tallies and monetary fines for tardiness. *See* Fla. Stat. § 102.112 (2000). Moreover, the Florida court held that all late vote tallies arriving during the contest period should be automatically included in the certification regardless of the certification deadline (even the certification deadline established by *Harris I*), thus virtually eliminating both the deadline and the Secretary's discretion to disregard recounts that violate it.

Moreover, the court's interpretation of "legal vote," and hence its decision to order a contest-period recount, plainly departed from the legislative scheme. Florida statutory law cannot reasonably be thought to require the counting of improperly marked ballots. Each Florida precinct before election day provides instructions on how properly to cast a vote, § 101.46; each polling place on election day contains a working model of the voting machine it uses, § 101.5611; and each voting booth contains a sample ballot, § 101.46. In precincts using punch-card ballots, voters are instructed to punch out the ballot cleanly:

> AFTER VOTING, CHECK YOUR BALLOT CARD TO BE SURE YOUR VOTING SELECTIONS ARE CLEARLY AND CLEANLY PUNCHED AND THERE ARE NO CHIPS LEFT HANGING ON THE BACK OF THE CARD.

Instructions to Voters, quoted in *Touchston v. McDermott*, 234 F.3d 1133 (11th Cir. 2000) (Tjoflat, J., dissenting). No reasonable person would call it "an error in the vote tabulation," Fla. Stat. §

166(5), or a "rejection of legal votes," Fla. Stat. § 102.168(3)(c),[4] when electronic or electromechanical equipment performs precisely in the manner designed,

---

4. It is inconceivable that what constitutes a vote that must be counted under the "error in the vote tabulation" language of the protest phase different from what constitutes a vote that must be counted under the "legal votes" language of the contest phase.

and fails to count those ballots that are not marked in the manner that these voting instructions explicitly and prominently specify. The scheme that the Florida Supreme Court's opinion attributes to the legislature is one in which machines are required to be "capable of correctly counting votes," § 101.5606(4), but which nonetheless regularly produces elections in which legal votes are predictably not tabulated, so that in close elections manual recounts are regularly required. This is of course absurd. The Secretary of State, who is authorized by law to issue binding interpretations of the election code, §§ 97.012, 106.23, rejected this peculiar reading of the statutes. See DE 00-13 (opinion of the Division of Elections). The Florida Supreme Court, although it must defer to the Secretary's interpretations, *see Krivanek v. Take Back Tampa Political Committee*, 625 So.2d 840, 844 (Fla. 1993), rejected her reasonable interpretation and embraced the peculiar one. *See Palm Beach County Canvassing Board v. Harris*, 772 So.2d 1273, (Dec. 11, 2000) (*Harris III*).

But as we indicated in our remand of the earlier case, in a Presidential election the clearly expressed intent of the legislature must prevail. And there is no basis for reading the Florida statutes as requiring the counting of improperly marked ballots, as an examination of the Florida Supreme Court's textual analysis shows. We will not parse that analysis here, except to note that the principal provision of the election code on which it relied, § 101.5614(5), was, as THE CHIEF JUSTICE pointed out in his dissent from Harris II, entirely irrelevant. June 18, 2001 *See Gore v. Harris*, 772 So.2d 1243, (Dec. 8, 2000). The State's Attorney General (who was supporting the Gore challenge) confirmed in oral argument here that never before the present election had a manual recount been conducted on the basis of the contention that "undervotes" should have been examined to determine voter intent. Tr. of Oral Arg. in *Bush v. Palm Beach County Canvassing Bd.*, 2000 WL 1763666, at *39-*40 (Dec. 1, 2000); *cf. Broward County Canvassing Board v. Hogan*, 607 So.2d 508, 509 (Fla.Ct.App.1992) (denial of recount for failure to count ballots with "hanging paper chads"). For the court to step away from this established practice, prescribed by the Secretary of State, the state official charged by the legislature with "responsibility to . . . [o]btain and maintain uniformity in the application, operation, and interpretation of the election laws," § 97.012(1), was to depart from the legislative scheme.

III

The scope and nature of the remedy ordered by the Florida Supreme Court jeopardizes the "legislative wish" to take advantage of the safe harbor provided by 3 U.S.C. § 5. *Bush v. Palm Beach County Canvassing Bd., ante.* December 12, 2000, is the last date for a final determination of the Florida electors that will satisfy § 5. Yet in the late afternoon of December 8th — four days before this deadline — the Supreme Court of Florida ordered recounts of tens of thousands of so-called "undervotes" spread through 64 of the State's 67 counties. This was done in a search for elusive — perhaps delusive — certainty as to the exact count of 6 million votes. But no one claims that these ballots have not previously been tabulated; they were initially read by voting machines at the time of the election, and thereafter reread by virtue of Florida's automatic recount provision. No one claims there was any fraud in the election. The Supreme Court of Florida ordered this additional recount under the provision of the election code giving the circuit judge the authority to provide relief that is "appropriate under such circumstances." Fla. Stat. § 102.168(8) (2000).

Surely when the Florida Legislature empowered the courts of the State to grant "appropriate" relief, it must have meant relief that would have become final by the cut-off date of 3 U.S.C. § 5. In light of the inevitable legal challenges and ensuing appeals to the Supreme Court of Florida and petitions for certiorari to this Court, the entire recounting process could not possibly be completed by that date. Whereas the majority in the Supreme Court of Florida stated its confidence that "the remaining undervotes in these counties can be [counted] within the required time frame," 772 So.2d. at 1262, n. 22, it made no assertion that the seemingly inevitable appeals could be disposed of in that time.

* * * *

Given all these factors, and in light of the legislative intent identified by the Florida Supreme Court to bring Florida within the "safe harbor" provision of 3 U.S.C. § 5, the remedy prescribed by the Supreme Court of Florida cannot be deemed an "appropriate" one as of December 8. It significantly departed from the statutory framework in place on November 7, and authorized open-ended further proceedings which could not be completed by December 12, thereby preventing a final determination by that date.

For these reasons, in addition to those given in the per curiam, we would reverse.

* * * *

■ Justice STEVENS, with whom Justice GINSBURG and Justice BREYER join, dissenting.

The Constitution assigns to the States the primary responsibility for determining the manner of selecting the Presidential electors. *See* Art. II, § 1, cl. 2. When questions arise about the meaning of state laws, including election laws, it is our settled practice to accept the opinions of the highest courts of the States as providing the final answers. On rare occasions, however, either federal statutes or the Federal Constitution may require federal judicial intervention in state elections. This is not such an occasion.

The federal questions that ultimately emerged in this case are not substantial. Article II provides that "[e]ach State shall appoint, in such Manner as the Legislature thereof may direct, a Number of Electors." *Id.* It does not create state legislatures out of whole cloth, but rather takes them as they come — as creatures born of, and constrained by, their state constitutions. Lest there be any doubt, we stated over 100 years ago in *McPherson* v. Blacker, 146 U.S. 1, 25 (1892), that "[w]hat is forbidden or required to be done by a State" in the Article II context "is forbidden or required of the legislative power under state constitutions as they exist." In the same vein, we also observed that "[t]he [State's] legislative power is the supreme authority except as limited by the constitution of the State." *Id.; cf. Smiley v. Holm*, 285 U.S. 355, 367 (1932). The legislative power in Florida is subject to judicial review pursuant to Article V of the Florida Constitution, and nothing in Article II of the Federal Constitution frees the state legislature from the constraints in the state constitution that created it. Moreover, the Florida Legislature's own decision to employ a unitary code for all elections indicates that it intended the Florida Supreme Court to play the same role in Presidential elections that it has historically played in resolving electoral disputes. The Florida Supreme Court's exercise of appellate jurisdiction therefore was wholly consistent with, and indeed contemplated by, the grant of authority in Article II.

It hardly needs stating that Congress, pursuant to 3 U.S.C. § 5, did not impose any affirmative duties upon the States that their governmental branches could "violate." Rather, § 5 provides a safe harbor for States to select electors in contested elections "by judicial or other methods" established by laws prior to the election day. Section 5, like Article II, assumes the involvement of the state judiciary in interpreting state election laws and resolving election disputes under those laws. Neither § 5 nor Article II grants federal judges any special authority to substitute their views for those of the state judiciary on matters of state law.

Nor are petitioners correct in asserting that the failure of the Florida Supreme Court to specify in detail the precise manner in which the "intent of the voter," Fla. Stat. § 101.5614(5) (Supp.2001), is to be determined rises to the level of a constitutional violation.[2] We found such a violation when individual votes within the same State were weighted unequally, *see, e.g., Reynolds v. Sims*, 377 U.S. 533 (1964), but we have never before called into question the substantive standard by which a State determines that a vote has been legally cast. And there is no reason to think that the guidance provided to the factfinders, specifically the various canvassing boards, by the "intent of the voter" standard is any less sufficient — or will lead to results any less uniform — than, for example, the "beyond a reasonable doubt" standard employed everyday by ordinary citizens in courtrooms across this country.

Admittedly, the use of differing substandards for determining voter intent in different counties employing similar voting systems may raise serious concerns. Those concerns are alleviated — if not eliminated — by the fact that a single impartial magistrate will ultimately adjudicate all objections arising from the recount process. Of course, as a general matter, "[t]he interpretation of constitutional principles must not be too literal. We must remember that the machinery of government would not work if it were not allowed a little play in its joints." *Bain Peanut Co. of Tex. v. Pinson*, 282 U.S. 499, 501 (1931)

---

2. The Florida statutory standard is consistent with the practice of the majority of States, which apply either an "intent of the voter" standard or an "impossible to determine the elector's choice" standard in ballot recounts. [The footnote goes on to list those states.]

(Holmes, J.).   If it were otherwise, Florida's decision to leave to each county the determination of what balloting system to employ — despite enormous differences in accuracy[4] — might run afoul of equal protection. So, too, might the similar decisions of the vast majority of state legislatures to delegate to local authorities certain decisions with respect to voting systems and ballot design.

* * * *

In the interest of finality, however, the majority effectively orders the disenfranchisement of an unknown number of voters whose ballots reveal their intent — and are therefore legal votes under state law — but were for some reason rejected by ballot-counting machines.   It does so on the basis of the deadlines set forth in Title 3 of the United States Code. *Ante*, at 532. But, as I have already noted, those provisions merely provide rules of decision for Congress to follow when selecting among conflicting slates of electors. They do not prohibit a State from counting what the majority concedes to be legal votes until a bona fide winner is determined.

Indeed, in 1960, Hawaii appointed two slates of electors and Congress chose to count the one appointed on January 4, 1961, well after the Title 3 deadlines. *See* Josephson & Ross, Repairing the Electoral College, 22 J. Legis. 145, 166, n. 154 (1996). Thus, nothing prevents the majority, even if it properly found an equal protection violation, from ordering relief appropriate to remedy that violation without depriving Florida voters of their right to have their votes counted.   As the majority notes, "[a] desire for speed is not a general excuse for ignoring equal protection guarantees."

Finally, neither in this case, nor in its earlier opinion in *Palm Beach County Canvassing Bd. v. Harris*, 772 So.2d 1220 (2000), did the Florida Supreme Court make any substantive change in Florida electoral law. Its decisions were rooted in long-established precedent and were consistent with the relevant statutory provisions, taken as a whole. It did what courts do — it decided the case before it in light of the legislature's intent to leave no legally cast vote uncounted.   In so doing, it relied on the sufficiency of the general "intent of the voter" standard articulated by the state legislature, coupled with a procedure for ultimate review by an impartial judge, to resolve the concern about disparate evaluations of contested ballots. If we assume — as I do — that the members of that court and the judges who would have carried out its mandate are impartial, its decision does not even raise a colorable federal

---

4. The percentage of nonvotes in this election in counties using a punch-card system was 3.92%; in contrast, the rate of error under the more modern optical-scan systems was only 1.43%. *Siegel v. LePore*, 234 F.3d 1163, (charts C and F) (11th Cir., Dec. 6, 2000). Put in other terms, for every 10,000 votes cast, punch-card systems result in 250 more nonvotes than optical-scan systems. A total of 3,718,305 votes were cast under punch- card systems, and 2,353,811 votes were cast under optical-scan systems.   *Id.*

question.

What must underlie petitioners' entire federal assault on the Florida election procedures is an unstated lack of confidence in the impartiality and capacity of the state judges who would make the critical decisions if the vote count were to proceed. Otherwise, their position is wholly without merit. The endorsement of that position by the majority of this Court can only lend credence to the most cynical appraisal of the work of judges throughout the land. It is confidence in the men and women who administer the judicial system that is the true backbone of the rule of law. Time will one day heal the wound to that confidence that will be inflicted by today's decision. One thing, however, is certain. Although we may never know with complete certainty the identity of the winner of this year's Presidential election, the identity of the loser is perfectly clear. It is the Nation's confidence in the judge as an impartial guardian of the rule of law.

I respectfully dissent.

* * * *

■ Justice SOUTER, with whom Justice BREYER joins and with whom Justice STEVENS and Justice GINSBURG join with regard to all but Part C, dissenting.

The Court should not have reviewed either *Bush v. Palm Beach County Canvassing Bd.*, or this case, and should not have stopped Florida's attempt to recount all undervote ballots, by issuing a stay of the Florida Supreme Court's orders during the period of this review. If this Court had allowed the State to follow the course indicated by the opinions of its own Supreme Court, it is entirely possible that there would ultimately have been no issue requiring our review, and political tension could have worked itself out in the Congress following the procedure provided in 3 U.S.C. § 15. The case being before us, however, its resolution by the majority is another erroneous decision.

* * * *

C

It is only on the third issue before us [the equal protection claim] that there is a meritorious argument for relief, as this Court's Per Curiam opinion recognizes. It is an issue that might well have been dealt with adequately by the Florida courts if the state proceedings had not been interrupted, and if not disposed of at the state level it could have been considered by the Congress in any electoral vote dispute. But because the course of state proceedings has been interrupted, time is short, and the issue is before us, I think it sensible for the Court to address it.

Petitioners have raised an equal protection claim (or, alternatively, a due process claim), in the charge that unjustifiably disparate standards are applied in different electoral jurisdictions to otherwise identical facts. It is true that the Equal Protection Clause does not forbid the use of a variety of voting mechanisms within a jurisdiction, even though different mechanisms will have different levels of effectiveness in recording voters' intentions; local variety can be justified by concerns about cost, the potential value of innovation, and so on. But evidence in the record here suggests that a different order of disparity obtains under rules for determining a voter's intent that have been applied (and could continue to be applied) to identical types of ballots used in identical brands of machines and exhibiting identical physical characteristics (such as "hanging" or "dimpled" chads). I can conceive of no legitimate state interest served by these differing treatments of the expressions of voters' fundamental rights. The differences appear wholly arbitrary.

In deciding what to do about this, we should take account of the fact that electoral votes are due to be cast in six days. I would therefore remand the case to the courts of Florida with instructions to establish uniform standards for evaluating the several types of ballots that have prompted differing treatments, to be applied within and among counties when passing on such identical ballots in any further recounting (or successive recounting) that the courts might order.

Unlike the majority, I see no warrant for this Court to assume that Florida could not possibly comply with this requirement before the date set for the meeting of electors, December 18.

* * * *

To recount these manually would be a tall order, but before this Court stayed the effort to do that the courts of Florida were ready to do their best to get that job done. There is no justification for denying the State the opportunity to try to count all disputed ballots now.

I respectfully dissent.

■ Justice GINSBURG, with whom Justice STEVENS joins, and with whom Justice SOUTER and Justice BREYER join as to Part I, dissenting.

I

THE CHIEF JUSTICE acknowledges that provisions of Florida's Election Code "may well admit of more than one interpretation." *Ante*, at 534. But instead of respecting the state high court's province to say what the State's Election Code means, THE CHIEF JUSTICE maintains that Florida's Supreme Court has veered so far from the ordinary practice of judicial review that what it did cannot properly be called judging. My colleagues have offered a reasonable construction of Florida's law. Their construction coincides with the view of one of Florida's seven Supreme Court justices. *Gore v. Harris*, 772 So.2d 1243, 1262, (Fla.2000) (Wells, C. J., dissenting); *Palm Beach County Canvassing Bd. v. Harris*, 772 So.2d 1220 (Fla.2000) (on remand) (confirming, 6-1, the construction of Florida law advanced in Gore). I might join THE CHIEF JUSTICE were it my commission to interpret Florida law. But disagreement with the Florida court's interpretation of its own State's law does not warrant the conclusion that the justices of that court have legislated.

There is no cause here to believe that the members of Florida's high court have done less than "their mortal best to discharge their oath of office," *Sumner v. Mata*, 449 U.S. 539, 549 (1981), and no cause to upset their reasoned interpretation of Florida law.

* * * *

Rarely has this Court rejected outright an interpretation of state law by a state high court. *Fairfax's Devisee v. Hunter's Lessee*, 7 Cranch 603 (1813), *NAACP v. Alabama ex rel. Patterson*, 357 U.S. 449 (1958), and *Bouie v. City of Columbia*, 378 U.S. 347 (1964), cited by THE CHIEF JUSTICE, are three such rare instances. But those cases are embedded in historical contexts hardly comparable to the situation here. *Fairfax's Devisee*, which held that the Virginia Court of Appeals had misconstrued its own forfeiture laws to deprive a British subject of lands secured to him by federal treaties, occurred amidst vociferous States' rights attacks on the Marshall Court. The Virginia court refused to obey this Court's Fairfax's Devisee mandate to enter judgment for the British subject's successor in interest. That refusal led to the Court's pathmarking decision in *Martin v. Hunter's Lessee*, 1 Wheat. 304 (1816). *Patterson*, a case decided three months after *Cooper v. Aaron*, 358 U.S. 1 (1958), in the face of Southern resistance to the civil rights movement, held that the Alabama Supreme Court had irregularly applied its own procedural rules to deny review of a contempt order against the NAACP arising from its refusal to disclose membership lists. We said that "our jurisdiction is not defeated if the nonfederal ground relied on by the state court is without any fair or substantial support." 357 U.S. at 455. *Bouie*, stemming from a lunch counter "sit-in" at the height of the civil rights movement, held that the South Carolina Supreme Court's construction of its trespass laws — criminalizing conduct not covered by the text of an otherwise clear statute — was "unforeseeable" and thus violated due process when applied retroactively to the petitioners. 378 U.S. at 350.

THE CHIEF JUSTICE's casual citation of these cases might lead one to believe they are part of a larger collection of cases in which we said that the Constitution impelled us to train a skeptical eye on a state court's portrayal of state law. But one would be hard pressed, I think, to find additional cases that fit the mold. As JUSTICE BREYER convincingly explains, this case involves nothing close to the kind of recalcitrance by a state high court that warrants extraordinary action by this Court. The Florida Supreme Court concluded that counting every legal vote was the overriding concern of the Florida Legislature when it enacted the State's Election Code. The court surely should not be bracketed with state high courts of the Jim Crow South.

THE CHIEF JUSTICE says that Article II, by providing that state legislatures shall direct the manner of appointing electors, authorizes federal superintendence over the relationship between state courts and state legislatures, and licenses a departure from the usual deference we give to state court interpretations of state law. The Framers of our Constitution, however, understood that in a republican government, the judiciary would construe the legislature's enactments. *See* U.S. Const., Art. III; *The Federalist* No. 78 (A. Hamilton). In light of the constitutional guarantee to States of a "Republican

Form of Government," U.S. Const., Art. IV, § 4, Article II can hardly be read to invite this Court to disrupt a State's republican regime. Yet THE CHIEF JUSTICE today would reach out to do just that. By holding that Article II requires our revision of a state court's construction of state laws in order to protect one organ of the State from another, THE CHIEF JUSTICE contradicts the basic principle that a State may organize itself as it sees fit. *See, e.g., Gregory v. Ashcroft*, 501 U.S. 452, 460 (1991) ("Through the structure of its government, and the character of those who exercise government authority, a State defines itself as a sovereign."); *Highland Farms Dairy v. Agnew*, 300 U.S. 608, 612 (1937) ("How power shall be distributed by a state among its governmental organs is commonly, if not always, a question for the state itself.").[2] Article II does not call for the scrutiny undertaken by this Court.

The extraordinary setting of this case has obscured the ordinary principle that dictates its proper resolution: Federal courts defer to state high courts' interpretations of their state's own law. This principle reflects the core of federalism, on which all agree. "The Framers split the atom of sovereignty. It was the genius of their idea that our citizens would have two political capacities, one state and one federal, each protected from incursion by the other." *Saenz v. Roe*, 526 U.S. 489, 504, n. 17 (1999) (*citing U.S. Term Limits, Inc. v. Thornton*, 514 U.S. 779, 838 (1995) (KENNEDY, J., concurring)). THE CHIEF JUSTICE's solicitude for the Florida Legislature comes at the expense of the more fundamental solicitude we owe to the legislature's sovereign. U.S. Const., Art. II, § 1, cl. 2 ("Each State shall appoint, in such Manner as the Legislature thereof may direct," the electors for President and Vice President) (emphasis added). Were the other members of this Court as mindful as they generally are of our system of dual sovereignty, they would affirm the judgment of the Florida Supreme Court.

II

I agree with Justice STEVENS that petitioners have not presented a substantial equal protection claim. Ideally, perfection would be the appropriate standard for judging the recount. But we live in an imperfect world, one in which thousands of votes have not been counted. I cannot agree that the recount adopted by the Florida court, flawed as it may be, would yield a result any less fair or precise than the certification that preceded that recount.

Even if there were an equal protection violation, I would agree with Justice STEVENS, Justice SOUTER, and Justice BREYER that the Court's concern about "the December 12 deadline" is misplaced. Time is short in part because of the Court's entry of a stay on December 9, several hours after an able circuit

---

2. Even in the rare case in which a State's "manner" of making and construing laws might implicate a structural constraint, Congress, not this Court, is likely the proper governmental entity to enforce that constraint. *See* U.S. Const., amend. XII; 3 U.S.C. §§ 1-15; *cf. Ohio ex rel. Davis v. Hildebrant*, 241 U.S. 565, 569 (1916) (treating as a nonjusticiable political question whether use of a referendum to override a congressional districting plan enacted by the state legislature violates Art. I, § 4); *Luther v. Borden*, 7 How. 1, 42 (1849).

judge in Leon County had begun to superintend the recount process. More fundamentally, the Court's reluctance to let the recount go forward — despite its suggestion that "[t]he search for intent can be confined by specific rules designed to ensure uniform treatment" ultimately turns on its own judgment about the practical realities of implementing a recount, not the judgment of those much closer to the process.

Equally important, as Justice BREYER explains, *post*, at 556 (dissenting opinion), the December 12 "deadline" for bringing Florida's electoral votes into 3 U.S.C. § 5's safe harbor lacks the significance the Court assigns it. Were that date to pass, Florida would still be entitled to deliver electoral votes Congress must count unless both Houses find that the votes "ha [d] not been . . . regularly given." 3 U.S.C. § 15. The statute identifies other significant dates. *See, e.g.,* § 7 (specifying December 18 as the date electors "shall meet and give their votes"); § 12 (specifying "the fourth Wednesday in December" — this year, December 27 — as the date on which Congress, if it has not received a State's electoral votes, shall request the state secretary of state to send a certified return immediately). But none of these dates has ultimate significance in light of Congress' detailed provisions for determining, on "the sixth day of January," the validity of electoral votes. § 15.

The Court assumes that time will not permit "orderly judicial review of any disputed matters that might arise." *Ante*, at 533. But no one has doubted the good faith and diligence with which Florida election officials, attorneys for all sides of this controversy, and the courts of law have performed their duties. Notably, the Florida Supreme Court has produced two substantial opinions within 29 hours of oral argument. In sum, the Court's conclusion that a constitutionally adequate recount is impractical is a prophecy the Court's own judgment will not allow to be tested. Such an untested prophecy should not decide the Presidency of the United States.

I dissent.

■ Justice BREYER, with whom Justice STEVENS and Justice GINSBURG join except as to Part I-A-1, and with whom Justice SOUTER joins as to Part I, dissenting.

The Court was wrong to take this case. It was wrong to grant a stay. It should now vacate that stay and permit the Florida Supreme Court to decide whether the recount should resume.

I

* * * *

A

1

The majority raises three Equal Protection problems with the Florida Supreme Court's recount order: first, the failure to include overvotes in the manual recount; second, the fact that all ballots, rather than simply the undervotes, were recounted in some, but not all, counties; and third, the absence of a uniform, specific standard to guide the recounts. As far as the first issue is concerned, petitioners presented no evidence, to this Court or to any Florida court, that a manual recount of overvotes would identify additional legal votes. The same is true of the second, and, in addition, the majority's reasoning would seem to invalidate any state provision for a manual recount of individual counties in a statewide election.

The majority's third concern does implicate principles of fundamental fairness. The majority concludes that the Equal Protection Clause requires that a manual recount be governed not only by the uniform general standard of the "clear intent of the voter," but also by uniform subsidiary standards (for example, a uniform determination whether indented, but not perforated, "undervotes" should count). The opinion points out that the Florida Supreme Court ordered the inclusion of Broward County's undercounted "legal votes" even though those votes included ballots that were not perforated but simply "dimpled," while newly recounted ballots from other counties will likely include only votes determined to be "legal" on the basis of a stricter standard. In light of our previous remand, the Florida Supreme Court may have been reluctant to adopt a more specific standard than that provided for by the legislature for fear of exceeding its authority under Article II. However, since the use of different standards could favor one or the other of the candidates, since time was, and is, too short to permit the lower courts to iron out significant differences through ordinary judicial review, and since the relevant distinction was embodied in the order of the State's highest court, I agree that, in these very special circumstances, basic principles of fairness may well have counseled the adoption of a uniform standard to address the problem. In light of the majority's disposition, I need not decide whether, or the extent to which, as a remedial matter, the Constitution would place limits upon the content of the uniform standard.

2

Nonetheless, there is no justification for the majority's remedy, which is simply to reverse the lower court and halt the recount entirely.   An appropriate remedy would be, instead, to remand this case with instructions that, even at this late date, would permit the Florida Supreme Court to require recounting all undercounted votes in Florida, including those from Broward, Volusia, Palm Beach, and Miami-Dade Counties, whether or not previously recounted prior to the end of the protest period, and to do so in accordance with a single-uniform substandard.

* * * *

B

The remainder of petitioners' claims, which are the focus of THE CHIEF JUSTICE's concurrence, raise no significant federal questions. I cannot agree that THE CHIEF JUSTICE's unusual review of state law in this case, see ante, at 548-550 (GINSBURG, J., dissenting opinion), is justified by reference either to

Art. II, § 1, or to 3 U.S.C. § 5. Moreover, even were such review proper, the conclusion that the Florida Supreme Court's decision contravenes federal law is untenable.

* * * *

II

Despite the reminder that this case involves "an election for the President of the United States," *ante*, at 533 (REHNQUIST, C. J., concurring), no preeminent legal concern, or practical concern related to legal questions, required this Court to hear this case, let alone to issue a stay that stopped Florida's recount process in its tracks. With one exception, petitioners' claims do not ask us to vindicate a constitutional provision designed to protect a basic human right. *See, e.g., Brown v. Board of Education*, 347 U.S. 483 (1954). Petitioners invoke fundamental fairness, namely, the need for procedural fairness, including finality. But with the one "equal protection" exception, they rely upon law that focuses, not upon that basic need, but upon the constitutional allocation of power. Respondents invoke a competing fundamental consideration — the need to determine the voter's true intent. But they look to state law, not to federal constitutional law, to protect that interest. Neither side claims electoral fraud, dishonesty, or the like. And the more fundamental equal protection claim might have been left to the state court to resolve if and when it was discovered to have mattered. It could still be resolved through a remand conditioned upon issuance of a uniform standard; it does not require reversing the Florida Supreme Court.

Of course, the selection of the President is of fundamental national importance. But that importance is political, not legal. And this Court should resist the temptation unnecessarily to resolve tangential legal disputes, where doing so threatens to determine the outcome of the election.

The Constitution and federal statutes themselves make clear that restraint is appropriate. They set forth a road map of how to resolve disputes about electors, even after an election as close as this one. That road map foresees resolution of electoral disputes by state courts. *See* 3 U.S.C. § 5 (providing that, where a "State shall have provided, by laws enacted prior to [election day], for its final determination of any controversy or contest concerning the appointment of . . . electors . . . by judicial or other methods," the subsequently chosen electors enter a safe harbor free from congressional challenge). But it nowhere provides for involvement by the United States Supreme Court.

To the contrary, the Twelfth Amendment commits to Congress the authority and responsibility to count electoral votes. A federal statute, the Electoral Count Act, enacted after the close 1876 Hayes-Tilden Presidential election, specifies that, after States have tried to resolve disputes (through "judicial" or other means), Congress is the body primarily authorized to resolve remaining disputes. *See* Electoral Count Act of 1887, 24 Stat. 373, 3 U.S.C. §§ 5, 6, and 15.

The legislative history of the Act makes clear its intent to commit the power to resolve such disputes to Congress, rather than the courts:

> "The two Houses are, by the Constitution, authorized to make the count of electoral votes. They can only count legal votes, and in doing so must determine, from the best evidence to be had, what are legal votes .... The power to determine rests with the two Houses, and there is no other constitutional tribunal." H. Rep. No. 1638, 49th Cong., 1st Sess., 2 (1886) (report submitted by Rep. Caldwell, Select Committee on the Election of President and Vice-President).

* * * *

The Act goes on to set out rules for the congressional determination of disputes about those votes. If, for example, a state submits a single slate of electors, Congress must count those votes unless both Houses agree that the votes "have not been . . . regularly given." 3 U.S.C. § 15. If, as occurred in 1876, one or more states submits two sets of electors, then Congress must determine whether a slate has entered the safe harbor of § 5, in which case its votes will have "conclusive" effect. *Id.* If, as also occurred in 1876, there is controversy about "which of two or more of such State authorities . . . is the lawful tribunal" authorized to appoint electors, then each House shall determine separately which votes are "supported by the decision of such State so authorized by its law." *Id.* If the two Houses of Congress agree, the votes they have approved will be counted. If they disagree, then "the votes of the electors whose appointment shall have been certified by the executive of the State, under the seal thereof, shall be counted." *Id.*

Given this detailed, comprehensive scheme for counting electoral votes, there is no reason to believe that federal law either foresees or requires resolution of such a political issue by this Court. Nor, for that matter, is there any reason to that think the Constitution's Framers would have reached a different conclusion. Madison, at least, believed that allowing the judiciary to choose the presidential electors "was out of the question." Madison, July 25, 1787 (reprinted in 5 Elliot's Debates on the Federal Constitution 363 (2d ed. 1876)).

The decision by both the Constitution's Framers and the 1886 Congress to minimize this Court's role in resolving close federal presidential elections is as wise as it is clear. However awkward or difficult it may be for Congress to resolve difficult electoral disputes, Congress, being a political body, expresses the people's will far more accurately than does an unelected Court. And the people's will is what elections are about.

Moreover, Congress was fully aware of the danger that would arise should it ask judges, unarmed with appropriate legal standards, to resolve a hotly contested Presidential election contest. Just after the 1876 Presidential election, Florida, South Carolina, and Louisiana each sent two slates of electors to Washington. Without these States, Tilden, the Democrat, had 184 electoral votes, one short of the number required to win the Presidency. With those States, Hayes, his Republican opponent, would have had 185. In order to choose between the two slates of electors, Congress decided to appoint an electoral commission composed of five Senators, five Representatives, and five Supreme Court Justices. Initially the Commission was to be evenly divided between Republicans and Democrats, with Justice David Davis, an Independent, to possess the decisive vote. However, when at the last minute the Illinois Legislature elected Justice Davis to the United States Senate, the final position on the Commission was filled by Supreme Court Justice Joseph P. Bradley.

The Commission divided along partisan lines, and the responsibility to cast the deciding vote fell to Justice Bradley. He decided to accept the votes by the Republican electors, and thereby awarded the Presidency to Hayes.

Justice Bradley immediately became the subject of vociferous attacks. Bradley was accused of accepting bribes, of being captured by railroad interests, and of an eleventh-hour change in position after a night in which his house "was surrounded by the carriages" of Republican partisans and railroad officials. C. Woodward, Reunion and Reaction 159-160 (1966). Many years later, Professor Bickel concluded that Bradley was honest and impartial. He thought that " 'the great question' for Bradley was, in fact, whether Congress was entitled to go behind election returns or had to accept them as certified by state authorities," an "issue of principle." The Least Dangerous Branch 185 (1962). Nonetheless, Bickel points out, the legal question upon which Justice Bradley's decision turned was not very important in the contemporaneous political context. He says that "in the circumstances the issue of principle was trivial, it was overwhelmed by all that hung in the balance, and it should not have been decisive." *Id.*

For present purposes, the relevance of this history lies in the fact that the participation in the work of the electoral commission by five Justices, including Justice Bradley, did not lend that process legitimacy. Nor did it assure the public that the process had worked fairly, guided by the law. Rather, it simply embroiled Members of the Court in partisan conflict, thereby undermining respect for the judicial process. And the Congress that later enacted the Electoral Count Act knew it.

This history may help to explain why I think it not only legally wrong, but also most unfortunate, for the Court simply to have terminated the Florida recount. Those who caution judicial restraint in resolving political disputes have described the quintessential case for that restraint as a case marked, among other things, by the "strangeness of the issue," its "intractability to principled resolution," its "sheer momentousness, ... which tends to unbalance judicial judgment," and "the inner vulnerability, the self-doubt of an institution which is electorally irresponsible and has no earth to draw strength from." Bickel, *supra*, at 184. Those characteristics mark this case.

At the same time, as I have said, the Court is not acting to vindicate a fundamental constitutional principle, such as the need to protect a basic human liberty. No other strong reason to act is present. Congressional statutes tend to obviate the need. And, above all, in this highly politicized matter, the appearance of a split decision runs the risk of undermining the public's confidence in the Court itself. That confidence is a public treasure. It has been built slowly over many years, some of which were marked by a Civil War and the tragedy of segregation. It is a vitally necessary ingredient of any successful effort to protect basic liberty and, indeed, the rule of law itself. We run no risk of returning to the days when a President (responding to this Court's efforts to protect the Cherokee Indians) might have said, "John Marshall has made his decision; now let him enforce it!" Loth, Chief Justice John Marshall and The Growth of the American Republic 365 (1948). But we do risk a self-inflicted wound — a wound that may harm not just the Court, but the Nation.

I fear that in order to bring this agonizingly long election process to a definitive conclusion, we have not adequately attended to that necessary "check upon our own exercise of power," "our own sense of self-restraint." *United States v. Butler*, 297 U.S. 1, 79 (1936) (Stone, J., dissenting). Justice Brandeis once said of the Court, "The most important thing we do is not doing." Bickel, *supra*, at 71. What it does today, the Court should have left undone. I would repair the damage done as best we now can, by permitting the Florida recount to continue under uniform standards.

I respectfully dissent.

NOTES AND QUESTIONS

1. *The constitutional right to vote and the Equal Protection clause.*

Bush v. Gore refers back to the evolution of the right to vote in American constitutional law. As the Court notes, the constitutional structure does not create an affirmative right to vote for electors of the President — although the last time any state legislature directly chose the electors appears to have been 1860 in South Carolina (Colorado, on the eve of statehood, chose its electors for the 1876 Presidential election by direct action of the territorial legislature). The only office for which the Constitution directly contemplated a popular election was for Representatives in the United States House; even here, the right to participate in House elections was completely determined by the content of State law, for Art. I, § 2 makes eligibility to participate wholly derivative of those qualifications that state legislatures have imposed for election to the most numerous branch of the State legislature. In cases decided in the aftermath of the Fourteenth Amendment's adoption, the Court also concluded that the Fourteenth Amendment itself did not acknowledge or protect the right to vote as a national constitutional matter. Even after adoption of this Amendment, the vote was a privilege to be bestowed as a matter of state law, but was not a constitutional entailment of citizenship. That this legal structure correctly describes the original understanding of the Framers of both the original Constitution and the Fourteenth Amendment is not seriously disputed.

Not until the 1960s, in the pathbreaking cases that *Bush v. Gore* cites, was this original structure overturned. At the height of the Warren Court's power, the Supreme Court decided the two central cases that *Bush v. Gore* cites and completely revolutionized American constitutional doctrine with respect to the right to vote. In *Harper v. Virginia Bd. Of Elections*, 383 U.S. 663 (1966), the Court recognized the right to vote as a fundamental right under the Equal Protection clause. Because voting was to be treated as a fundamental constitutional right, any restrictions on exercise of the franchise had henceforth to be subjected to strict scrutiny and could not survive unless narrowly tailored and justified by the strongest of state interests. *Harper* involved Virginia state elections, eligibility for which depended on payment of a poll tax — a longstanding requirement of Virginia law. Despite the long tradition of state-imposed poll taxes, and the original intent of the Fourteenth Amendment, the Court held that such taxes were unconstitutional interferences with the right to vote. And because *Harper* recognized voting as a fundamental right, the Court protected this right by judging the extent to which state laws had the effect of burdening the right — without any further requirement that those burdens emanate from a constitutionally impermissible purpose. Thus, the *Harper* Court did not inquire into the motivations or purposes behind Virginia's poll tax (although there was good reason to think it had, indeed, been racially motivated). Instead, the Court struck the poll tax down because the State had insufficient justification for it, given the demands of strict scrutiny. *Harper* did not hold that there was an affirmative right to get to vote in any particular decision-making process; instead, its theory was that once the legislature had chosen to hold an election for certain offices, then legislative decisions about access to participation in that election — the qualifications as to who could participate under what conditions — had to meet the demanding standards of strict scrutiny. *Harper* addressed access to the ballot box itself, or what we call "first generation" voting rights claims: the conditions under which the right to participate itself is legislatively meted out. Its principals were soon extended to elective offices at all levels of government, from school board elections to — as we see in *Bush v. Gore* — the selection of presidential electors.

The other pathbreaking case *Bush* invokes is *Reynolds v. Sims*, 377 U.S. 533 (1964). In terms of practical legal effects, *Reynolds* was one of the most dramatically destabilizing decisions in the Court's history. *Reynolds* required the massive and immediate restructuring of virtually every State legislature in the country. Overturning decades of familiar practices, *Reynolds* held that the Equal Protection clause embodied a principle of political equality; that principle came to be distilled in legal and popular formulation as "one person, one vote." As applied in *Reynolds* and subsequent cases, this principle required that representative bodies at all levels of government be composed of members elected from districts that had roughly equal numbers of residents (the exact baseline against which one person, one vote must be measured — residents, citizens, eligible voters — remains in some legal uncertainty). *Reynolds* applied political equality to what we call the "second generation" of voting rights claims: even after access to the ballot box is nearly universal, the Equal Protection clause can impose limits on the ways in which those votes are *aggregated* to produce the actual electoral outcome. What *Reynolds* condemned was the historic practice of basing political representation in legislative bodies on units of political geography — such as counties, towns, and the like — even if those units had vastly differing populations. Much as the United States Senate bases representation on political units — the States — many state legislatures had based representation on political units, such as local governments, of widely varying numbers of actual voters. *Reynolds* held that the structure of the United States Senate was, uniquely, constitutionally required, but that that structure could not be copied or followed at any other level of government. To weight the political power of voters differently depending on where they happened to live, such as in county A or county B within the same state, was unconstitutionally to "dilute the weight of a citizen's vote." As with *Harper*, this requirement of equally weighting of all votes for the same representative body was to be enforced as an effects-based doctrine; that is, regardless of the intent with which the enacting body created a representative institution that departed from equally weighted votes, that departure would be unconstitutional (except in exceptional circumstances not relevant here). Also, as with *Harper*, the constitutional conception of the right to vote here is necessarily a comparative one: *Reynolds* does not require that there *be* a vote for any particular public office or representative body, but it does hold that once a body is elective, the franchise must be extended on equal terms that avoids diluting the voting power of individual voters on the basis of constitutionally-irrelevant factors such as where they happen to reside within the jurisdiction that is choosing the officeholders.

Harper and *Reynolds* were extremely controversial when decided. They provoked strong dissents from respected Justices, such as Justice Harlan. The decisions rejected years of longstanding political practices. They invoked constitutional doctrine to address problems that were, in some cases, in the process of being addressed through political processes (the Twenty Fourth Amendment had banned poll taxes for national elections, but *Harper* went on and banned them for all elections). They overturned the original understandings of the relevant constitutional provisions. They required immediate and massive restructuring of State institutions. In essence, the decisions held that the original constitutional structures had to be synthesized with emerging conceptions of democracy that required political equality among all voters, a conception that the Court read back into the Fourteenth Amendment.

Bush v. Gore builds on these precedents and follows the same structure. Art. II of the Constitution, which sets up the Electoral College process, does not bestow the right to vote on anyone. Art. II permits state legislatures to appoint presidential electors or to choose other manners of choosing electors, such as various forms of popular election (the electors can be elected on a winner-take-all popular vote, as they are in 48 states today, or the legislature can choose to have the electors chosen congressional district by congressional district, as they are in Maine and Nebraska). But once the state legislature chooses popular election for the selection, the Constitution constrains the kind of voting system the State can employ. The principles of *Harper* and *Reynolds* apply to require that any system of electing presidential electors meet the standards of Equal Protection, including that all votes be weighted equally and that the fundamental rights nature of the right to vote be protected through appropriate procedural and substantive guarantees.

2. *The Application of the Right to Vote and Equal Protection in Bush v. Gore.*

A. *Bush v. Gore* extends to new terrain the Warren Court's constitutionalization of the right to vote. Six members of the Court agreed with this extension, and Justice Breyer agreed that "basic principles of fairness" were implicated by non-uniform recount rules. The first generation cases dealt with the structures of state statutes and the formal conditions on access to the ballot box those statutes — on their face — imposed. The second generation cases dealt with the statutory design of democratic institutions; again, these cases required the Supreme Court to assess state statutes on their face for consistency with Equal Protection principles. Even then, at the time of *Reynolds* important concerns were expressed about the administrability of the Court's newly announced Equal Protection principles: what exactly did an undiluted, equally weighted vote mean? But in the *Reynolds* line of cases, the Supreme Court quickly developed a simple and easily administered answer (albeit one some critics consider *too* simple): one person, one vote. *Bush v. Gore* now extends these doctrines to the micro-level of the actual operation of the electoral machinery, literally as well as figuratively, including the ballot-by-ballot counting of votes. What precisely is the content of the Equal Protection principles that *Bush* announces? How far do or should those principles extend? And as the constitutional ban against unequally weighted votes gets extended to the administration of the voting system, how will or should the courts deal with the administrability concerns that this extension of *Harper* and *Reynolds* inevitably will raise? If the full electoral machinery of the highly decentralized electoral process we currently have must ensure that all votes are, at the end of the day, weighted equally, what precisely does a non-diluted or equally weighted vote mean? Is there any rule-like principle, comparable to that of one vote, one person, looming on the horizon that would provide an answer to these administrability concerns? Note that there is nothing in the Court's opinion that suggests any reason the Equal Protection concerns it announces are limited to Presidential elections, nor is there any reason to think these concerns should be limited to that one electoral context.

B. Critics of the majority's Equal Protection holding argued that the Court had focused on one stage of the vote tabulation process — the manual recounts — in isolation from the other stages that had preceded these recounts. In particular, fact finding during the litigation had revealed great disparities in the rates of recorded "undervotes" for the Presidential election depending upon the type of voting technology different counties used to count votes. In Florida, three of every 1,000 optically scanned ballots recorded no presidential vote, while 15 of every 1,000 punch-card ballots were recorded as showing no presidential vote. *See Bush v. Gore* (Stevens, J., dissenting) (findings of fact on differential undercount rate). Under *Bush v. Gore*, does Florida's use of different technologies, with such dramatically different rates of recording votes, violate the Equal Protection clause? Indeed, can one argue that *Bush v. Gore*'s principles suggest that manual recounts might be constitutionally *required* as a remedy for a voting-rights violation that would otherwise occur were voters in different counties to have differential opportunities of having their "attempted" votes validly counted? If strict scrutiny is the constitutionally required standard, in light of the fundamental right at stake, does a state have a sufficiently compelling justification for permitting such diverse technologies when they have such different consequences for recording votes? Note that the question of the substantive scope of the Equal Protection doctrine announced in *Bush v. Gore* is a distinct question from the legal significance, under Florida or federal law, of the December 12th and 18th dates for the Electoral College process. That is, there are important questions of Equal Protection and the right to vote that *Bush v. Gore* now opens up; in that particular case, the Court majority did not pursue the implications of these questions, given the majority's understanding of the finality of the Dec.12th date. But those questions will remain in future cases where similar cutoff dates do not truncate the power of federal courts to provide remedies for Equal Protection violations.

C. Can one argue that an important constitutional difference exists between differential vote counting that results from different machine technology versus from different human actors applying different standards to evaluate votes in a manual recount? In terms of perceptions of procedural fairness and the legitimacy of election processes, is there a difference between inconsistent technology and inconsistent human judgments about what counts as a vote? Can one argue that the perceived integrity of the electoral process is more compromised when human actors exercise highly discretionary judgments as to what counts as a vote, when those actors know in advance the likely effect on an election outcome? If technology differences do not involve these kind of discretionary and potentially partisan influences, should the Equal Protection clause be less concerned with technological rather than human differences in vote counting? Should it matter to the Equal Protection analysis what reasons lie behind different counties in Florida choosing different technologies? Suppose, for example, the choice of machinery reflects variables such as the time at which different counties upgraded their technologies. Suppose, instead, election officials intentionally located less efficient vote-recording technologies in particular precincts or counties for reasons of anticipated partisan advantage. Should intent be crucial here? Or should differential effects alone be enough?

D. Subsequent investigation long after the litigation was complete revealed that the disparities between Florida's counties was greater, with respect to more issues, than had been realized at the time. For example, while there was a threefold difference in rate at which ballots were treated as undervoted between optical-scan and punch-card machines, there was great variation even within those counties that used optical scanners. Optical-scan machines can be programmed to let voters know their ballot is invalid and to give them a second chance to cast a valid vote; that is why the rate of error tends to be lower with optical-scan machines than with punch-card systems. But not all Florida counties with optical scanners had this aspect of the technology available; and not all those that had the equipment used it. Indeed, two counties had the second-chance capabilities on their machines but chose to deactivate it. Thus, there were 24 optical-scan counties that gave voters a second chance; there only 0.6% of ballots were invalidated. But in 15 optical-scan counties in which the technology was not set up to give voters a second chance, the invalidation rate was 5.7%. This compares with an invalidation rate in the 24 punch-card counties of 3.9%. If optical-scan machines that informed voters that their initial ballot was not valid had been used throughout the State, as many as 120,000 invalidated ballots would, in theory, have been validly corrected and cast.

Other differences across counties also emerged. Voters sometimes filled in an oval — on an optical-scan ballot — or punched a hole — on a punchcard ballot and then also write in the same candidate's name on that ballot. Twenty-six counties did not count these ballots; but 34 counties apparently did. Similarly, Florida law requires an automatic recount when the margin of error between candidates in the initial count is less than 0.5%; the 2000 Presidential election triggered this automatic recount process. A 1999 opinion letter from the Division of Elections states that this requires an actual recounting of the ballots. But 18 counties apparently did no recount and instead merely checked the counting mechanisms of their machines to see whether the numbers previously registered matched the numbers they had turned in. The general picture that emerges is that of a radically decentralized electoral system in Florida, with individual county election supervisors exercising a great deal of discretion and little overriding authority or consistency provided through statewide offices, such as the Secretary of State. The information in this note is taken from the detailed investigation reported in John Mintz and Peter Slevin, *Human Factor Was at Core Of Vote Fiasco*, Wash. Post, June 1, 2001, at A1.

Apparently, the more scrutiny applied to Florida's 2000 election processes, the more differing treatment of ballots across counties at all stages of the process comes to be revealed. What light, if any, does this shed on the Court's Equal Protection holding? What are the implications of that holding for these various other inconsistencies across counties?

E. Were identifiable groups of voters systematically required, in Florida or nationwide, to use punch-card balloting systems rather than more modern technologies, such as optical-scan voting? Although much of the contemporary coverage suggested that black voters or poor voters more often are required to use the less reliable punch-card balloting system, systematic analysis establishes that the punch-card system is not nationally concentrated in counties where such voters reside. Nationwide, punch-card systems are used disproportionately in counties that are white, non-poor, and dominated by Republican voters. The proportion of each of these groups that reside in counties employing punch card balloting nationwide are as follows: 31.4% of African-Americans and 31.9% of whites, 33.4% of those below the poverty level and 31.8% of those above that line, and 31.2% of Dole voters versus 31.0% of Clinton voters from the 1996 Presidential election. Stephen Knack and Martha Kropf, *Who Uses Inferior Voting Technology* (manuscript 2001). In Florida, there was a slight disproportionate use of punch-card technology in counties of black, poor, or Democratic voters, but the differences were not dramatic: 63.1% of black voters and 60.4% of whites lived in punch-card balloting counties, 63.1% of those living below the poverty line compared with 61.5% of those above the poverty line, and 63.8% of 1996 Clinton voters as compared with 55.6% of Dole voters.

However, when it comes to the actual use of these technologies, the picture changes. In a regression analysis of 52 of Florida's 67 counties, Judge Richard Posner concludes that when it comes to "overvotes" — ballots that are marked twice for the same race, as when a voter punches a chad or fills in a circle for a candidate and then also writes that candidate's name in — race of the voter was the only variable statistically significant at the 5% level of confidence in explaining non-counted overvotes. When it comes to undervotes, Judge Posner's analysis concludes that both race and rate of literacy are significant. Judge Posner therefore concludes:

> Black voters are more likely to cast overvotes, and since we know that black voters heavily favored Gore, recovered overvotes would probably favor Gore. It is curious, therefore, that the Democratic recount efforts were focused entirely on undervotes, leaving Republicans to argue that overvotes should be recounted as well.

Richard A. Posner, *Florida 2000: A Legal and Statistical Analysis of the Election Deadlock and the Ensuing Litigation*, 2000 Sup. Ct. Rev. 1. After noting the role that illiteracy rates played in non-counted ballots, Judge Posner also goes on to make the following observation: "Illiterates are permitted to vote, but some conservatives may think it rather an excess of democracy for illiterates to hold the electoral balance of power."

F. One possibility is that *Bush v. Gore* will impel, through litigation or legislative reforms, greater uniformity in voting standards and technologies. Consider the following view: The constitutional obligations *Bush v. Gore* establishes "obviously cannot be limited to the recount process alone. The court condemns the fact that 'standards for accepting or rejecting contested ballots might vary not only from county to county but indeed within a single county.' That criticism would surely apply to the variations in voting machines across Florida, and, for that matter, to similar variations in all other states. That court's new standard may create a more robust constitutional examination of voting practices." Samuel Issacharoff, "The Court's Legacy for Voting Rights," N.Y. Times A39 (Dec. 14, 2000).

Indeed, Florida enacted substantial electoral reform legislation on May 9, 2001. Among other things, that legislation eliminates punch-card machines in the State and requires second-chance technology, such as touch-screen voting systems, throughout the State. The new legislation also requires the State to issue uniform rules regarding the design of ballots. As this book goes to press, lawsuits seeking to apply *Bush v. Gore*, are pending in several other states, and the Florida reforms continue to be challenged in court as not going far enough to remedy the defects of that system. In Illinois, lawsuits have been filed seeking the elimination of punch-card machines and the elimination of a state law that bans local governments from notifying voters at the voting machine if they have erred in marking their ballots. In California, a lawsuit has been filed seeking the elimination of punch-card machines and the setting of uniform standards for vote tabulation and vote recounting. Many of the suits are based on the Voting Rights Act as well as *Bush v. Gore*; these suits, following *Roberts v. Wamser, infra*, allege that punch-card systems disproportionately disadvantage black, Latino, and Asian voters because voters in those groups cast non-counted "undervotes" at a higher rate than members of other groups when punch-card systems are used. Similar lawsuits have been filed in Georgia, with a partial legislative response having been adopted. The Georgia legislature has required uniform voting technology, but not until 2004, and the legislation has no accompanying funding. B. J. Palermo, *Rights*

Groups Latch Onto Bush v. Gore, The National Law Journal A1 (May 21, 2001).

G. *Policing Voting Technology Through the Voting Rights Act.* In *Bush v. Gore*, the Supreme Court observed that "[t]his case has shown that punch card balloting machines can produce an unfortunate number of ballots which are not punched in a clean, complete way by the voter. After the current counting, it is likely legislative bodies nationwide will examine ways to improve the mechanisms and machinery for voting." Is there also a role for courts in policing voting technologies, both before and after *Bush v. Gore*?

Before *Bush v. Gore*, certain of the voting technologies at issue in the 2000 election had been successfully challenged at the district court level as a violation of the Voting Rights Act. The result in *Roberts v. Wamser*, 679 F. Supp. 1513 (E.D. Mo, 1987), *rev'd*, 883 F.2d 617 (8th Cir. 1989), was an extensive set of factual findings on the disproportionate effects punch-card voting systems had on ensuring accurate tabulation of the votes of black voters in the city of St. Louis. Roberts was a black candidate who lost an extremely close election in the Democratic primary for president of the city's board of aldermen. St. Louis is closely divided demographically; black residents make up 46% of the population. Not seeking to overturn the election, but attempting to remedy problems in the vote counting and recounting system that had emerged during the contest, Roberts brought a prospective action seeking reform of the city's voting technology. Under the Voting Rights Act — which requires only proof that voting practices result in racial disparities in the opportunity to elect candidates, regardless of the intent with which those practices were adopted — Roberts argued that uncounted ballots ("over-and-undervoting") occurred in disproportionately greater numbers among blacks and that the ballot casting and counting procedures adopted and implemented by the elections board (i.e., punch-card voting and computerized tabulation) were to blame. The court found that throughout the 1980s, primary elections had routinely resulted in about 3,000 cast ballots not being counted. Relying on expert witness testimony, the court also found that to a statistically significant degree, votes cast in "black" wards were much more likely not to be counted than those cast in "white wards: 7.22 % of the ballots cast by black voters were not counted, whereas only 1.77 % of ballots cast by white voters were not counted in certain elections analyzed.

The court found that city elections were characterized by racially polarized voting and racial appeals. The court also found that black residents were of lower socioeconomic status than white residents and bore the effects of past discrimination in education, employment, and housing. The court then concluded:

> In light of the present record, the Court sustains plaintiff's challenge to the Board's failure manually to review cast ballots rejected by the tabulating equipment and finds, under the circumstances, that that failure constitutes a violation of the Voting Rights Act. The record shows the Board's failure to review and, if appropriate, count such ballots has resulted in the City's black voters having less opportunity than other members of the City's electorate to participate in the

political process and to elect representatives of their choice. It is not the use of the punch card voting system and automated tabulating equipment alone, but the Board's blanket failure to review rejected ballots, that resulted in the disenfranchisement of City voters.

The court therefore ordered the following remedial actions: (1) that the election board take steps manually to count all ballots validly cast but rejected by the tabulating equipment; (2) that the board target for voter education proper use of the punch card voting system in those wards from which the Board receives over a reasonable period of time a relatively high number of uncounted ballots (five percent of the total ballots cast in such wards); and (3) that the elections board offer to voters at the polling places explanations and demonstrations of the proper use of the punch card voting system. Most litigation under the Voting Rights Act has concentrated on rules for aggregating votes — such as the use of at-large elections or the choice among district boundaries in reapportionment plans — rather than on the nuts and bolts of the actual voting process. In part, this may be a function of a general lack of awareness about problems with electoral technology before *Bush v. Gore*.

On appeal, however, a divided panel of the Eighth Circuit reversed the district court. *Roberts v. Wamser*, 883 F.2d 617 (8th Cir. 1989). The majority did not address on the merits the application of the Act to punch-card balloting technology. Instead, it held that Roberts, as a candidate, lacked standing to raise these issues; only voters had such standing, in the view of the Court of Appeals. Suppose Roberts had sued in part on the basis of his being a voter who is a member of a racial minority group. (Many voting rights cases involve plaintiffs who allege their status as registered voters to obtain standing, but whose real motivation for suing stems from their desire to be elected to office.) Could he then have alleged that the group of which he was a member was politically cohesive and that, as a result of their votes being undercounted, they were less able to participate and elect their preferred candidate? Does the termination of the case without a binding decision on the merits simply reflect a failure of pleading?

3. *Substantive Due Process and the Right to Vote*

In addition to constitutional concerns for uniformity in the weighing of votes, *Bush v. Gore* also concludes that the Constitution requires *substantive specificity* as to what counts as an actual vote (at least in the manual recount context). This constitutional principle appears grounded in procedural and substantive due process requirements that attach to the right to vote by virtue of its status as a fundamental constitutional right.

Bush v. Gore's requirement that "intent of the voter" is constitutionally too imprecise raises important constitutional questions about the nature of legal specificity. What does it mean for a legal norm to be sufficiently precise? From what sources and processes does the Constitution permit this specificity to be drawn? Although *Bush v. Gore* addresses the right to vote, the same questions it raises may be relevant to other fundamental constitutional rights.

Specificity of a legal norm can be provided by two alternative sources. The most obvious is the relevant legal text itself; in theory a norm can always be made more precise by the enacting legislature anticipating and specifying in advance how that norm is to be applied in a broad range of contexts. Does *Bush v. Gore* require this kind of specificity? If so, *Bush v. Gore* would hold that the "intent of the voter" standard was unconstitutional on its face. The question of how specific is specific enough to adequately protect the relevant right, cannot itself, of course, admit of any — we hesitate to say it — specific answer.

A second source through which legal norms can gain precision and specificity is through institutional structures and procedures designed to enforce the norm in a clear and reproducible way. Would an "intent of the voter" standard be sufficiently precise if it were clear that the standard were to be administered through a *process* the Supreme Court believed would ensure consistent results? Suppose the standard were not to be administered by multiple county canvassing boards, each with discretion to apply the standard in its own way, but by a single judge or panel of judges who would review all the ballots — and would do so in the first instance, rather than as a last check on the process? Is the defect in the Florida system, according to *Bush v. Gore,* the institutional failure to ensure sufficiently reliable structures for giving content to the "intent of the voter" standard? In that event, perhaps *Bush v. Gore* should be viewed as invalidating the Florida system *as applied*, rather than on its face.

Another important way of raising these questions is to ask whether *Bush v. Gore* requires that the *legislature* have specified *in advance* greater substantive content for voter intent. Or, if the Florida Supreme Court had developed more specific substantive content to the "voter intent" standard — for example, by specifying that only chads with at least two corners removed constituted sufficient evidence of voter intent — would that have been sufficient to meet the specificity requirements *Bush v. Gore* demands? Are all "intent of voter" statutes unconstitutional on their face? Or does *Bush v. Gore* demand something less?

For comparison with Florida law, consider the following provision in Indiana state law that specifies the substantive standard statewide for counting votes in a punch-card balloting system:

3-12-1-9.5 Ballot Card Votes; Chad Irregularities

(a) This section applies to counting votes cast on ballot cards.

(b) As used in this section, "chad" means the part of a ballot card that indicates a vote on the card when entirely punched out by the voter.

(c) A chad that has been pierced, but not entirely punched out of the card, shall be counted as a vote for the indicated candidate or for the indicated response to a public question.

(d) A chad that has been indented, but not in any way separated from the remainder of the card, may not be counted as a vote for a candidate or on a public question.

(e) Whenever:

(1) a ballot card contains a numbered box indicating which chad should be punched out by the voter to cast a vote for a candidate or on a public question;

(2) the indicated chad has not been punched out; and

(3) a hole has been made in the card that touches any part of the numbered box;

the hole shall be counted as a vote for the candidate or on the public question as if the indicated chad had been punched out. However, if a hole has been made in the ballot that does not touch a numbered box or punch out a chad, the hole may not be counted as a vote for a candidate or on a public question.

(f) Whenever:

(1) a chad has been punched out of a ballot card;

(2) a numbered box indicates that another chad may be punched out to cast a vote for:

(A) a different candidate for the same office as the candidate for whom a vote was cast under subdivision (1); or

(B) a different response to the same public question on which a vote was cast under subdivision (1); and

(3) a hole has been punched in the card that touches the numbered box described in subdivision (2);

neither the chad described in subdivision (1) nor the hole described in subdivision (3) may be counted as a vote for a candidate or on a public question.

(g) This subsection applies to a ballot card that:

(1) has been cast in a precinct whose votes are being recounted by a local recount commission or the state recount commission;

(2) is damaged or defective so that it cannot properly be counted by automated tabulating machines; and

(3) cannot be counted for the office subject to the recount due to the damage or defect.

The ballot card shall be remade only if the conditions in subdivisions

(1) through (3) exist.

4. *The Federal Interest in State Judicial Interpretation of State Laws Regulating Presidential Elector Selection*

Chief Justice Rehnquist's concurrence holds various decisions of the Florida Supreme Court to be unconstitutional violations of Art. II of the U.S. Constitution. At various points, that concurrence describes the Florida Supreme Court as "wholly chang[ing]" the pre-existing statutory scheme; as having "plainly departed" from the legislative scheme; as reaching interpretations that "cannot reasonably be thought" correct; or even as rendering "absurd" readings of state law that "no reasonable person" could reach. Although federal courts normally do not oversee state interpretations of state law, the Chief Justice concluded that the distinct federal interests reflected in Art. II warranted this role in presidential elections.

If there is a federal constitutional interest in avoiding dramatic changes in state election laws rendered by state courts, is Art. II necessary to reach such a conclusion? Recall that in the *Roe v. Alabama* litigation, discussed extensively above, the Eleventh Circuit in a *state* election reached essentially the same conclusion as the *Bush v. Gore* concurrence through a different constitutional route. *Roe* held that dramatic changes in state election practices, including judicial interpretations of state laws, could violate the Fourteenth Amendment. Such changes could constitute impermissible vote dilution and/or violate due process by compromising the fundamental integrity of the electoral process. Is the *Roe* approach different from that of Chief Justice Rehnquist's concurrence in any important way, either in terms of consequences or doctrinal justification?

Recall also that in the notes after *Roe*, we discussed the complexities of federal court judgments regarding whether state courts had so "changed" state law as to violate the U.S. Constitution. We noted that there was a spectrum of contexts in which such claims might arise; at one end, typified by *Roe* itself, are cases in which the pre-existing state practice is deeply established through administrative rulings, past decisions, and the like. At the other end are cases in which the only prior state "practice" is the text of the statute itself; in such cases, federal court judgments of "changes" in state law necessarily become much closer to bare disputes over how to read state law. At what point on this spectrum are the issues presented by the Chief Justice's concurrence?

Roe's constitutional principle might also require that voters have detrimentally relied on the prior state law in some concrete way. Should a similar requirement be necessary under Art. II? How about under the *Bush II* equal protection standard? Was that kind of reliance present among Florida voters?

Finally, note that Art. I, Sec. 4 empowers "the Legislature" in each State to prescribe the "manner of holding elections" for members of Congress. This language appears identical to that of Art. II's provisions on State legislative control over the manner of selecting presidential electors. Does Chief Justice

Rehnquist's concurrence therefore permit federal courts to play the same role in overseeing state statutes involving congressional elections? No Supreme Court decision before *Bush II*'s concurrence suggested such a principle under Art. I, Sec. 4.

5. Consider the following argument put forward by Senator Sherman as the primary speaker in 1886 in support of the proposed Electoral Count Act:

> Another plan which has been proposed in the debates at different times and I think also in the constitutional convention, was to allow questions of this kind to be certified at once to the Supreme Court for its decisions in case of a division between the two Houses. If the House should be one way and the Senate the other, then it was proposed to let the case referred directly to the prompt and summary decision of the Supreme Court. But there is a feeling in this country that we ought not to mingle our great judicial tribunal with political questions, and therefore this proposition has not met with much favor. It would be a very grave fault indeed and a very serious objection to refer a political question in which the people of the country were aroused, about which their feelings were excited, to this great tribunal, which after all has to sit upon the life and property of all the people of the United States. It would tend to bring that court into public odium of one or the other of the two great parties. Therefore that plan may probably be rejected as an unwise provision. I believe, however, that it is the provision made in other countries.

7 Cong. Rec. 817-18 (1886)(Sen. Sherman). How does this view appear from the vantage point of the post-2000 election controversy?

6. Finally, consider the actions of the Florida State Legislature in the wake of the uncertainty in Election 2000. Even if Florida could have abandoned popular election of electors prior to Election Day, does the legislature retain the power to appoint electors even after a statutorily authorized popular vote? Does that act run afoul of 3 U.S.C. § 5? Does Congress have any authority to reject such a slate? For further arguments regarding the power of the Florida Legislature, see, e.g., its brief filed in *Bush I*. (See the on-line materials at: http://election2000.stanford.edu/.) That brief takes a strong position not only on legislative authority but also on questions of justiciability.

CHAPTER 4

EIGHT VIEWS OF THE CATHEDRAL

Bush v. Gore is surely among the most momentous decisions in the history of the United States Supreme Court. The decisions raises questions to be debated for years to come, questions about the uses of judicial power, about the relationship of constitutional law to democratic politics, about whether the decision was correctly reached and on what basis. Here we explore some of the range of positions that have emerged in the wake of the decision:

1. If *Bush v. Gore* is not convincing as a doctrinal matter, are there any other grounds on which the decision might nonetheless be justified? David Strauss argues that *Bush v. Gore* was not a "legal" decision in the conventional sense of a decision based on application of existing legal principles. Instead, he argues that the Court acted as if it believed the Florida Supreme Court was acting lawlessly and had to be stopped. Only this justification, in Strauss' view, can explain the various interventions of the Supreme Court, including its opinions in *Bush v. Gore*. If this is right, consider whether *Bush v. Gore* should be seen as an act of judicial "civil disobedience" — and whether, if so, the Supreme Court acted appropriately:

> The conclusion that emerges, in my view, is that several members of the Court — perhaps a majority — were determined to overturn any ruling of the Florida Supreme Court that was favorable to Vice President Gore, at least if that ruling significantly enhanced the Vice President's chances of winning the election. They acted on the basis of strong intuitions — which, as I said, is by no means necessarily inappropriate in itself — but the intuitions were intuitions about the outcome, not about the law. The specific legal questions presented in the litigation were shifting, complex, and esoteric. It is hard to see how the justices could have strong legal intuitions about any of those specific questions. To the extent those questions raised familiar broad issues — like federalism and the relationship between the courts and the political process — the majority's reaction in this litigation contradicted their normal inclinations. During the litigation, the justices in the majority appear to have accepted, at one time or another, four different arguments offered by Governor Bush's lawyers, all of which were questionable — one of which, based on 3 USC § 5, even the majority subsequently abandoned — but which had one common element: they required that the Florida Supreme Court be reversed. On the crucial remedial question that ensured

Governor Bush's election, the majority's decision appears to be simply indefensible. And the majority opinion insisted that its rationale was to be applied, essentially, only in this case — basically conceding that the result, not the legal principle, dictated the outcome.

What explains this extraordinary behavior by the Supreme Court? The most plausible hypothesis, I believe, is that several members of the United States Supreme Court were convinced that the Florida Supreme Court would try to give the election to Vice President Gore and would act improperly if necessary to accomplish that objective. The governing intuition was that the Florida Supreme Court had to be stopped from doing this. The majority's actions in the litigation show a relentless search for some reason that could be put forward to justify a decision reversing the Florida Supreme Court. The outcome was a foregone conclusion.

* * * *

The Equal Protection Clause was the ultimate basis for the decision, but the majority essentially admitted (what was obvious in any event) that it was not basing its conclusion on any general view of what equal protection requires. The decision in *Bush v. Gore* was not dictated by the law in any sense — either the law found through research, or the law as reflected in the kind of intuitive sense that comes from immersion in the legal culture.

* * * *

The argument in defense of the United States Supreme Court would have to be that it engaged in a kind of morally justified civil disobedience. It deliberately acted in a way that could not be legally justified in order to prevent some greater harm. I do not think that argument can be sustained. But it would be enough of a breakthrough if it were generally accepted that the United States Supreme Court's decision has to be justified, if at all, in those terms . . . .

David Strauss, *Bush v Gore: What Were They Thinking?*, 68 U. Chi. L. Rev. 737, 737-39 (2001).

2. Should the Court have been more willing to permit democratic institutions, such as the United States Congress, to resolve the election? Or does *Bush v. Gore* reflect distrust of the capacity of democratic institutions to find appropriate resolutions to controversial political issues? Richard Pildes argues that *Bush v. Gore* was driven by a fear that the democratic institutions that otherwise would have resolved the election – Congress, in particular – were viewed as too chaotic, tumultuous, and partisan by the Court. In this general distrust of democratic institutions, Pildes views *Bush v. Gore* as part of a broader pattern in which the current Court increasingly resists the use of democratic processes to address issues of democracy itself.

Whether democracy requires order, stability, and channeled, constrained forms of engagement, or whether it requires and even celebrates relatively wide-open competition that may appear tumultuous, partisan, or worse, has long been a struggle in democratic thought and practice (indeed, historically it was one of the defining set of oppositions in arguments about the desirability of democracy itself). Of course, the answer is that democracy requires a mix of both order (law, structure, and constraint) and openness (politics, fluidity, and receptivity to novel forms). But people, including judges and political actors, regularly seem to group themselves into characteristic and recurring patterns of response to new challenges that arise. These patterned responses suggest that it is something beyond law, or facts, or narrow partisan politics in particular cases, that determine outcomes; it is, perhaps, cultural assumptions and historical interpretations, conscious or not, that inform or even determine these judgments. Whatever the analytical truth about the necessity of both order and openness to democracy, the cultural question is, from which direction do particular actors, such as judges, tend to perceive the greatest threat. Is the democratic order fragile and potentially destabilized easily? Or is the democratic order threatened by undue rigidity, in need of more robust competition and challenge? Does democratic politics contain within itself sufficient resources to be self-correcting? Or must legal institutions carefully oversee political processes to ensure their continued vitality?

Bush v. Gore can be assessed legally, politically, or as I prefer to here, culturally. I cannot purport to separate the contributing role each of these dimensions might have played in the decision, particularly when *Bush v. Gore* is analyzed as an isolated single event. But when we examine the decision in the full tapestry of the Supreme Court's emerging and increasingly active role in the constitutionalization of democratic politics — a role initiated forty years ago in *Baker v. Carr* — we can see images, metaphors, and assumptions about democracy that consistently recur. These images of the relationship of law and order — constitutional law and judicially-structured order — to democracy are aspects of a broader jurisprudential culture. They emerge most revealingly in cases in which the partisan political consequences are non-existent, or certainly not obvious.

* * * *

The suggestion here is that, whatever role law and conventional politics might be debated to have played in Bush v Gore, a cultural dimension must be considered as well. Because this cultural orientation toward democracy transcends law and narrow partisan politics, and because it itself is not determined by "facts," but leads facts to be understood in particular ways, this cultural dimension plays a powerful role in judicial responses to cases involving democratic politics. When the Court envisioned a political resolution of *Bush v. Gore*, the election, how much was it moved by a cultural view, not a narrowly partisan preference, that "democracy" required judicially-ensured order, stability, and certainty, rather than judicial acceptance of the "crisis" that partisan political resolution might be feared by some to have entailed? If the Court were so moved-by the country's perceived need for what Frank Michelman calls "judicial salvation" — *Bush v. Gore* would be of a piece with the current Court's general vision of democratic politics and the role of constitutional law.

Richard Pildes, *Democracy and Disorder*, 68 U. Chi. L. Rev. 695, 714-15 (2001).

3. What does general consideration of the Court's jurisprudence of democracy suggest about whether the Court should have intervened in the context of an electoral dispute? Professor Issacharoff argues that whether it is was appropriate for the Court to intervene in Election 2000 should be assessed in terms of the larger theoretical framework that justified the Court's initial forays into the law of democracy in cases like *Baker v. Carr*:

Comparing the Court's response to Election 2000 to prior interventions into the political arena actually illuminates an unexplored problem in *Bush v. Gore*. Invariably, the process of judicial review in the electoral arena gives rise in a particularly acute form to the concern over the countermajoritarian difficulty. After all, every time a court strikes down an election statute, or every time it calls into question electoral processes, the unelected judiciary substitutes its judgment for that of the democratically elected branches.

* * * *

What emerges from these rationales, paradoxical as it may sound, is greater legitimacy to judicial intervention in the political process for countermajoritarian purposes than when the Court seeks to invoke the role of protector of majority preferences. The premise of both *Carolene Products* and the political process theories that followed is that intervention is required because an electoral lock on power has made the system unresponsive to permanent electoral minorities — even if the protected minority happens to be a numerical majority of the population, as in *Baker* and *Reynolds*. The unexplored flip-side of this rationale is that there is correspondingly less justification for judicial intervention into the political process for majoritarian aims. This rationale dovetails with the second part of the Court's response to the political question demand for abstention from election controversies. As formulated by Justice Clark in his concurrence in *Baker*, the predicate for judicial intervention had to be the absence of alternative institutional actors capable of repairing the claimed harm. In the case of discrete and insular minorities, or in the case of locked-in political power structures, presumably no other actor could fit the bill because of the unresponsiveness of the governing coalition to the claims of injustice by those on the outs politically. But that rationale extends poorly to electoral majorities, particularly those that control alternative political institutional actors. For such politically engaged majorities, the presumption should be quite the contrary and should begin with the premise that vindication lies in the political arena.

Samuel Issacharoff, Bush v. Gore: *Political Judgments*, 68 U. Chi. L. Rev. 637, 654-55 (2001).

4. With respect to the Court's equal protection holding, Professor Karlan argues that the Court's reliance on previous voting rights cases has a formal appeal, but misses the underlying functional justification that supported those earlier cases:

> The Court analogized these disparities to the disparities condemned in cases such as *Gray v. Sanders* and *Reynolds v. Sims*, identifying the constitutional vice in those cases as different treatment of voters based on where they lived.
>
> On one level, the analogy holds. If, for example, Florida had enacted a statute providing that "punchcard ballots where the chad is only partially detached shall count as valid votes if cast in Broward County but shall not count as valid votes if cast in Palm Beach County," that statute would face grave constitutional difficulty. It would be hard to see any justification, let alone a compelling one, for treating two physically identifiable ballots differently based on the residence of the voter who cast them. Similarly, a statute providing that manual recounts in one category of counties shall reexamine all ballots while recounts in the remaining counties shall reexamine only undervotes would also seem to draw an arbitrary distinction among voters depending on where they lived.
>
> * * * *
>
> And on a deeper level, the analogy to the one-person, one-vote cases breaks down. The problem in *Gray* and *Reynolds* was not the random, one-time-only differential weighting of individuals' votes, but the systematic degradation of identifiable blocs of citizens' voting strength. Malapportionment froze the existing political order into place, and undermined the possibility of truly representative government. That's why the Warren Court repeatedly pointed to the fact that the challenged system allowed a small numerical minority to control the outcome of a statewide election or the composition of the state legislature. By contrast, whatever the vices of the recount ordered by the Florida Supreme Court, it neither produced a systematic, repetitive dilution of any citizens' vote nor did it risk enabling a numerical minority to tie up the political process.

Pamela S. Karlan, *Equal Protection:* Bush v. Gore *and the Making of a Precedent, in* The Unfinished Election of 2000 (Jack Rakove ed., forthcoming 2001).

5. Once the Court majority established constitutional standards for the recount process, should it instead have remanded to enable that process to go forward under the supervision of the Florida courts? Professor Charles Fried argues that a major target of the Court's critics — the Court's decision to terminate the election rather than remand for the Florida courts to decide whether to oversee a Constitutional recount — is misguided:

But [critics] and the two Justices who dissented from the Court's remedy take it as a given that a recount on those terms would in any event have to have been completed by December 18, the day on which by federal law the electoral votes must be reported. But such a recount could not be completed in six days any more than in twenty-four hours. That is because that recount would go forward under the contest provisions of Florida law, and those envisage not a simple tally, but a full-blown legal process, complete with briefing, oral argument, and a full recourse to appellate process. Such contests in Florida have been known to require sixteen months. So imagine what would have happened if Dworkin's and Breyer's solution had been adopted. There would have been further arguments in the Florida Supreme Court on remand, followed by an opinion from that court —which may have occasioned further review in the Supreme Court of the United States. Then the recount would have taken place and there would have to have been still more process about that. If miraculously all this had been compressed into six days that fact itself would have occasioned a complaint to the Supreme Court that the Florida court had once again failed to comply with the preexisting standards of Florida law. Would such a continuation of the legal proceedings, inevitably leading to an indeterminate outcome, really have been more a satisfactory course? Surely if that was the alternative, the Court did well to shut the thing down then and there.

Charles Fried, `A Badly Flawed Election': An Exchange, The New York Review of Books, Feb. 22, 2001.

6. Frank Michelman suggests that the Supreme Court is perhaps best understood as acting not for legal reasons, but out of its perceived belief that its institutional responsibility was to save the country from a continuing "crisis" — although Michelman does not share the view that there was such a crisis in fact. Because the Court did not disclose the justification publicly, Michelman suggested that the Court acted in a Machiavellian fashion– and, more dramatically, that this is perhaps how much of the country expects and wants the court to behave:

It is entirely reasonable to believe that the equal protection complaint succeeded in *Bush v. Gore* only because the following additional factors were present in that case: first, alarm and anger on the part of some justices at what they saw as outrageous and dangerously provocative conduct by the Supreme Court of Florida; second, a general distaste on the part of some justices for the relatively, shall we say, energetic aspects — or we could say the relatively tumultuous or disorderly aspects — of democracy in action;

third, on the part of some justices, a lack of belief in the ability of Congress, if and when the Florida imbroglio were to fall into its lap, to see the affair through to a conclusion that the country could respect; and, perhaps, fourth — a kind of summation to all of the above — a fear that the country was headed for a catastrophe if someone in a position did not act very soon to bring the election to a clean and decisive end.

Frank I. Michelman, *Machiavelli in Robes? The Court in the Election*, in The Longest Night (Arthur Jacobson and Michele Rosenfeld eds., forthcoming, 2001).

7. Is the Court's decision best seen as merely an act of partisan will? Alan Dershowitz argues that the only explanation for *Bush v. Gore* is that the decisive five member majority was explicitly motivated by partisan political calculations: the desire of that majority to see a Republican President elected. He seeks to demonstrate this motivation by comparing the principles on which *Bush v. Gore* rests with other cases in which the same Justices have allegedly rejected those very principles. Moreover, Dershowitz argues that the only legitimate academic response to *Bush v. Gore* is to expose that partisanship. Is his view of the decision more convincing than others offered here? Is his challenge to academics correct?

It is important to note that a number of prominent academics have come forward to defend the majority justices. Several have offered creative, intelligent, and cogent defenses of some of the arguments, especially the ones related to Article II. As is evident from what I have written, I disagree with the merits of these arguments. But I also have a different kind of disagreement with some of these defenders. I believe it is morally wrong for scholars to defend the majority justices, even if they think their arguments are theoretically defensible, unless they honestly believe that the justices themselves would have offered these arguments on behalf of Gore if the shoe had been on the other foot.

For brilliant academics, clever arguments are easy to come by. But to publicly defend an argument that was presented only as a rationalization for a decision based on partisan political grounds rather than nonpartisan legal grounds, is to become complicit in an intellectual fraud perpetrated by the Supreme Court majority on the nation, and to encourage its emulation in future cases. Dishonest justices should not be encouraged by smart academics to concoct arguments — plausible as they may be as an abstract matter — and then invoke them for partisan purposes, expecting that they will be defended by credible scholars. Academics who defend such arguments play right into the hands of dishonest justices.

I cannot conceive of any responsible academic writing an article seeking to justify the decision of a judge who took a bribe.

Alan M. Dershowitz, Supreme Injustice 108-09 (2001).

8. How should judicial power be used in freighted political contexts? How do other judges view the performance of the Supreme Court? Judge Richard Posner, defending the result in *Bush v. Gore*, offers provocative views about the uses of judicial power. He does not believe the Court's decision is doctrinally convincing, but he goes on to argue "[t]here is such a thing as judgment in advance of doctrine. Experienced judges may have a strong intuition about how a case should be decided yet have difficulty matching the intuition to existing doctrine." He finds a reconstructed version of the Art. II argument the most appropriate for ending the election, and he defends the Court for intervening in the following terms:

> [I]f I am right that the Florida Supreme Court may well have been violating the Constitution, and if, as seems likely, without the Court's intervention the deadlock would have mushroomed into a genuine crisis, the Court's refusal to intervene might have prompted the question: what exactly is the Supreme Court good for if it refuses to examine a likely constitutional error that if uncorrected will engender a national crisis? We might call this the reverse political-questions doctrine. Political considerations in a broad, nonpartisan sense will sometimes counsel the Court to abstain, but sometimes to intervene. It is not an ordinary court, however much it may pretend to be one in an effort to insulate itself from political criticism.
>
> Judges worry about expending their political capital, which is to say narrowing the margin of protection from other branches of government that they obtain by being thought by the public to personify the judicial virtues and thus, of distinct relevance in an election case, to be "above" politics. Judges seem not to worry *that* much about spending down their capital, judging from the frequency with which they accuse each other of being "result-oriented," tendentious, and downright lawless. Still, it is a concern, particularly at the highest level of the judiciary. But before criticizing a judge for an expenditure of his political capital, or more crudely for deliberately courting a loss of prestige, we should ask what he bought with his expenditure. (We should also ask whether it isn't a natural tendency of judges to exaggerate the value of their prestige to society.) *Bush v. Gore* may have done less harm to the nation by reducing the Supreme Court's prestige than it did good for the nation by averting a significant probability of a Presidential selection process that would have undermined the Presidency and embittered American politics far more than the decision itself did or is likely to do. Judges unwilling to sacrifice some of their prestige for the greater good of the nation might be thought selfish. The tradeoffs become particularly favorable to intervention if one believes that, had the Court abstained in December, it might well have been dragged back into the Presidential selection process in January, facing multiple appeals from rulings in the Title III proceedings that might have followed a completed recount. If it had ducked *then*, it might have invited comparison to Nero fiddling while Rome burned.

Judge Posner does not find the Court's equal protection holding persuasive. But against the charge that Justices who voted for this holding, yet are not typically receptive to equal protection arguments, must have done so for partisan reasons (as in Professor Dershowitz's charge), Judge Posner offers the following defense: "In a case so politically fraught, a bit of *Realpolitik* affecting only the ground of decision and not the decision itself should be tolerable to anyone who takes a pragmatic approach to adjudication. *Fiat justicia ruat caelum* is not a workable motto for the U.S. Supreme Court." Richard A. Posner, *Florida 2000: A Legal and Statistical Analysis of the Election Deadlock and the Ensuing Litigation*, 2000 S. Ct. Rev. 1 (2001).

CHAPTER 5

THE TIMING OF FEDERAL COURT INTERVENTION

In addition to the substantive issue of what federal interests are sufficiently strong to justify a role for federal law—constitutional and statutory—in resolving state and national issues involving democratic processes, there is an important procedural question about the proper timing of federal court intervention, if such intervention is to occur. As has been stressed in earlier Chapters, the actual conduct of elections is a matter reserved primarily to state law. Nonetheless, there are significant federal interests in the orderly conduct of elections, particularly when the elections in question concern federal office. This tension manifests itself not only in the substantive role of state versus federal law, but in the procedural question of *when* the federal interest arises. Absent a claim of exclusion from the franchise, race discrimination, or an abridgment of some other distinct federal right, the federal interest is primarily in insuring that state procedures are fairly and consistently applied. As a result, the invocation of federal court oversight almost invariably implicates federal review of matters generally thought to be the province of state authority, again reinforcing the importance of the timing question.

To date, the relation of federal and state courts has been most clearly developed in the context of redistricting. There is a distinct federal constitutional interest in guaranteeing equality of voting strength, as reflected in the one-person, one-vote rule of apportionment. However, the cases governing redistricting also point to the right of the states to conduct their own districting practices, subject to the limitations imposed by federal law. An immediate question as to the propriety of federal court action is posed whenever redistricting challenges are filed in both federal and state courts. Such challenges clearly present a constitutionally viable federal claim, but also implicate significant federalism and comity concerns in federal court intervention in ongoing state processes. Although federal court "abstention" doctrines generally dictate caution in invoking federal oversight powers, the fact that there are distinct federal rights at play puts the application of these doctrines in considerable doubt.

Growe v. Emison
507 U.S. 25 (1993)

■ JUSTICE SCALIA delivered the opinion of the Court.

This case raises important issues regarding the propriety of the District Court's pursuing reapportionment of Minnesota's state legislative and federal congressional districts in the face of Minnesota state-court litigation seeking similar relief, and regarding the District Court's conclusion that the state court's legislative plan violated § 2 of the Voting Rights Act of 1965, 42 U.S.C. § 1973.

I

In January 1991, a group of Minnesota voters filed a state-court action against the Minnesota Secretary of State and other officials responsible for administering elections, claiming that the State's congressional and legislative districts were malapportioned, in violation of the Fourteenth Amendment of the Federal Constitution and Article 4, § 2, of the Minnesota Constitution. *Cotlow v. Growe*, [622 N.W. 2d. 561 (Minn. 2001)] The plaintiffs asserted that the 1990 federal census results revealed a significant change in the distribution of the state population, and requested that the court declare the current districts unlawful and draw new districts if the legislature failed to do so. In February, the parties stipulated that, in light of the new census, the challenged districting plans were unconstitutional. The Minnesota Supreme Court appointed a Special Redistricting Panel (composed of one appellate judge and two district judges) to preside over the case.

In March, a second group of plaintiffs filed an action in federal court against essentially the same defendants, raising similar challenges to the congressional and legislative districts. *Emison v. Growe.* The Emison plaintiffs (who include members of various racial minorities) in addition raised objections to the legislative districts under § 2 of the Voting Rights Act, 42 U.S.C. § 1973, alleging that those districts needlessly fragmented two Indian reservations and divided the minority population of Minneapolis. The suit sought declaratory relief and continuing federal jurisdiction over any legislative efforts to develop new districts. A three-judge panel was appointed pursuant to 28 U.S.C. § 2284(a).

While the federal and state actions were getting underway, the Minnesota Legislature was holding public hearings on, and designing, new legislative districts. In May, it adopted a new legislative districting plan, Chapter 246, Minn.Stat. §§ 2.403-2.703 (Supp.1991), and repealed the prior 1983 apportionment. It was soon recognized that Chapter 246 contained many technical errors — mistaken compass directions, incorrect street names, noncontiguous districts, and a few instances of double representation. By August, committees of the legislature had prepared curative legislation, Senate File 1596 and House File 1726 (collectively, Senate File 1596), but the legislature, which had adjourned in late May, was not due to reconvene until January 6, 1992.

* * * *

In early December, before the state court issued its final plan, the District Court stayed all proceedings in the Cotlow case, and enjoined parties to that action from "attempting to enforce or implement any order of the . . . Minnesota Special Redistricting Panel which has proposed adoption of a reapportionment plan relating to state redistricting or Congressional redistricting." The court explained its action as necessary to prevent the state court from interfering with the legislature's efforts to redistrict and with the District Court's jurisdiction.   It mentioned the Emison Voting Rights Act allegations as grounds for issuing the injunction, which it found necessary in aid of its jurisdiction, see 28 U.S.C. § 1651.   One judge dissented.

* * * *

When the legislature reconvened in January, both Houses approved the corrections to Chapter 246 contained in Senate File 1596 and also adopted a congressional redistricting plan that legislative committees had drafted the previous October.   The Governor, however, vetoed the legislation.   On January 30, the state court issued a final order adopting its legislative plan and requiring that plan to be used for the 1992 primary and general elections. By February 6, pursuant to an order issued shortly after this Court vacated the injunction, the parties had submitted their proposals for congressional redistricting, and on February 17 the state court held hearings on the competing plans.

Two days later, the District Court issued an order adopting its own legislative and congressional districting plans and permanently enjoining interference with state implementation of those plans. . . .

In early March, the state court indicated that it was "fully prepared to release a congressional plan" but that the federal injunction prevented it from doing so.   In its view, the federal plan reached population equality "without sufficient regard for the preservation of municipal and county boundaries."

* * * *

II

In their challenge to both of the District Court's redistricting plans, appellants contend that, under the principles of *Scott v. Germano*, 381 U.S. 407 (1965) (per curiam), the court erred in not deferring to the Minnesota Special Redistricting Panel's proceedings.   We agree.

The parties do not dispute that both courts had jurisdiction to consider the complaints before them.   Of course federal courts and state courts often find themselves exercising concurrent jurisdiction over the same subject matter, and when that happens a federal court generally need neither abstain (i.e., dismiss the case before it) nor defer to the state proceedings (i.e., withhold action until the state proceedings have concluded).   *See McClellan v. Carland*, 217 U.S. 268, 282 (1910).   In rare circumstances, however, principles of federalism and comity dictate otherwise. We have found abstention necessary, for example, when the federal action raises difficult questions of state law bearing on important matters of state policy, or when federal jurisdiction has been invoked to restrain ongoing state criminal proceedings. *See Colorado River Water Conservation Dist. v. United States*, 424 U.S. 800 (1976). We have required deferral, causing a federal court to "sta[y] its hands," when a constitutional issue in the federal action will be mooted or presented in a different posture following conclusion of the state-court case. *Railroad Comm'n of Texas v. Pullman Co.*, 312 U.S. 496, 501.[7]

In the reapportionment context, the Court has required federal judges to defer consideration of disputes involving redistricting where the State, through its legislative or judicial branch, has begun to address that highly political task itself. In *Germano*, a Federal District Court invalidated Illinois' Senate districts and entered an order requiring the State to submit to the court any revised Senate districting scheme it might adopt. An action had previously been filed in state court attacking the same districting scheme. In that case the Illinois Supreme Court held (subsequent to the federal court's order) that the Senate districting scheme was invalid, but expressed confidence that the General Assembly would enact a lawful plan during its then current session, scheduled to end in July 1965. The Illinois Supreme Court retained jurisdiction to ensure that the upcoming 1966 general elections would be conducted pursuant to a constitutionally valid plan.

This Court disapproved the District Court's action. The District Court "should have stayed its hand," we said, and in failing to do so overlooked this Court's teaching that state courts have a significant role in redistricting. . . .

Today we renew our adherence to the principles expressed in *Germano*, which derive from the recognition that the Constitution leaves with the States primary responsibility for apportionment of their federal congressional and state legislative districts. *See* U.S. Const., Art. I, § 2. "We say once again what has been said on many occasions: reapportionment is primarily the duty and responsibility of the State through its legislature or other body, rather than of a federal court." *Chapman v. Meier*, 420 U.S. 1, 27 (1975). Absent evidence that these state branches will fail timely to perform that duty, a federal court must neither affirmatively obstruct state reapportionment nor permit federal litigation to be used to impede it.

Judged by these principles, the District Court's December injunction of state-court proceedings, vacated by this Court in January, was clear error. It

---

7. We have referred to the *Pullman* doctrine as a form of "abstention," *see* 312 U.S., at 501-502. To bring out more clearly, however, the distinction between those circumstances that require dismissal of a suit and those that require postponing consideration of its merits, it would be preferable to speak of *Pullman* "deferral." *Pullman* deferral recognizes that federal courts should not prematurely resolve the constitutionality of a state statute, just as *Germano* deferral recognizes that federal courts should not prematurely involve themselves in redistricting.

seems to have been based upon the mistaken view that federal judges need defer only to the Minnesota Legislature and not at all to the State's courts. Thus, the January 20 deadline the District Court established was described as a deadline for the legislature, ignoring the possibility and legitimacy of state judicial redistricting. And the injunction itself treated the state court's provisional legislative redistricting plan as "interfering" in the reapportionment process. But the doctrine of *Germano* prefers both state branches to federal courts as agents of apportionment. The Minnesota Special Redistricting Panel's issuance of its plan (conditioned on the legislature's failure to enact a constitutionally acceptable plan in January), far from being a federally enjoinable "interference," was precisely the sort of state judicial supervision of redistricting we have encouraged.

Nor do the reasons offered by the District Court for its actions in December and February support departure from the *Germano* principles. It is true that the Emison plaintiffs alleged that the 1983 legislative districting scheme violated the Voting Rights Act, while the Cotlow complaint never invoked that statute. *Germano*, however, does not require that the federal and state-court complaints be identical; it instead focuses on the nature of the relief requested: reapportionment of election districts. Minnesota can have only one set of legislative districts, and the primacy of the State in designing those districts compels a federal court to defer.

The District Court also expressed concern over the lack of time for orderly appeal, prior to the State's primaries, of any judgment that might issue from the state court, noting that Minnesota allows the losing party 90 days to appeal. We fail to see the relevance of the speed of appellate review. *Germano* requires only that the state agencies adopt a constitutional plan "within ample time ... to be utilized in the [upcoming] election." It does not require appellate review of the plan prior to the election, and such a requirement would ignore the reality that States must often redistrict in the most exigent circumstances — during the brief interval between completion of the decennial federal census and the primary season for the general elections in the next even-numbered year. Our consideration of this appeal, long after the Minnesota primary and final elections have been held, itself reflects the improbability of completing judicial review before the necessary deadline for a new redistricting scheme.

* * * *

The judgment is reversed, and the case is remanded with instructions to dismiss.

So ordered.

NOTES AND QUESTIONS

1. The *Pullman* abstention doctrine identified by the Court in *Growe* is a doctrine that emerges from concern that there should not be premature federal court intervention when ongoing state proceedings might obviate the need for the federal court to act. As a general matter, *Pullman* abstention has been thought a jurisdictional barrier to federal intervention, hence the requirement that federal courts actually abstain from further involvement. Note that in footnote one of *Growe*, the Court recasts the doctrine to dictate "deferral" rather than absention. Presumably the difference is that the presence of ongoing state proceedings should caution federal courts to wait until there is a clear indication that federal interests require immediate action, rather then to dismiss the federal action as essentially preempted by the presence of the state action. Thus, one federal appellate decision has recast *Pullman* abstention as something that "may be a matter of discretion." Under this view, the *Pullman* doctrine should not force federal court abstention when the "timing, outcome and consequences of the state-court proceedings are uncertain" and where there are circumstances requiring immediate determination of the issues before the court. *Public Service of New Hampshire v. Patch*, 167 F.3d 15, 24 (1st Cir. 1998).

2. Federal courts have also refused to defer consideration of overlapping federal and state issues when further state adjudication is unlikely to alter the way in which the federal issues are to be resolved. Thus, the Fifth Circuit has concluded that "deference to state court adjudication only be made where the issue of state law is uncertain. If the state statute in question, although never interpreted by a state tribunal, is not fairly subject to an interpretation which will render unnecessary or substantially modify the federal constitutional question, it is the duty of the federal court to exercise its properly invoked jurisdiction." *Louisiana Debating & Literary Ass'n v. City of New Orleans*, 42 F.3d 1483, 1491-1492 (5th Cir. 1995). *See also Marks v. Stinson*, 19 F.3d 873, 883 n.6 (3d Cir. 1994) (declining to abstain because there the statutes in question were "neither ambiguous nor material to the federal issues presented in this case"); *S & S Pawn Shop Inc. v. City of Del City*, 947 F.2d 432, 442 (10th Cir. 1991) (abstaining because the state law was uncertain and ambiguous and subject to reasonable interpretation by the state court). The Fifth Circuit has further concluded that "abstention is the exception, not the rule." *Louisiana Debating*, 42 F.3d at 1491.

3. Alternatively, courts have interpreted *Growe* to recognize concurrent jurisdiction between state and federal courts. For example:

> The United States Supreme Court in *Growe* made clear that federal courts and state courts have *concurrent jurisdiction* to entertain challenges to redistricting plans and that, as a result, both courts are open to such claims. *Growe* stands only for the proposition that the federal court must 'defer' to any state-court redistricting effort; it does not say that the federal court must dismiss its own proceedings.
>
> Indeed, in *Growe*, the Supreme Court acknowledged that, after the state court had completed its proceeding, the federal court later rightfully took up the remaining claim under § 2 of the Voting Rights Act of 1965; *Growe* did not require that the plaintiffs there pursue their § 2 claim in state court as well.

Thompson v. Smith, 52 F. Supp. 2d 1364 (M.D. Ala. 1999). On the other hand, federal courts need not be dissuaded from acting by *Pullman* considerations when no state court actions have been filed or are likely to resolve the disputed matters within the relevant period of time. "Once it is apparent that a state court, through no fault of the district court, will not develop a redistricting plan in time for an upcoming election, *Growe* authorizes a federal district court to go ahead and develop a redistricting plan." *Wesch v. Folsom*, 6 F.3d 1465, 1473 (11th Cir. 1993).

4. Once the *Pullman* doctrine is held to require deferral rather than abstention, further options present themselves to the federal courts. In those states that permit federal courts to certify issues of unresolved state law to the highest court of that state, the *Pullman* doctrine may properly be seen as a mechanism to allow further state elaboration of disputed issues of state law, even while the federal courts retain jurisdiction. In *Tunick v. Safir*, 209 F.3d 67 (2d Cir. 2000) Judge Calabresi seized upon a statement by the Supreme Court that "[c]ertification today covers territory once dominated by a deferral device called '*Pullman* abstention,'" relying on *Arizonans for Official English v. Arizona*, 520 U.S. 43 (2000). Judge Calabresi noted, "The teaching of *Arizonans*, therefore, is that we should consider certifying in more instances than had previously been thought appropriate, and do so even when the federal courts might think that the meaning of a state law is 'plain.'"

5. Challenged election cases also implicate a second abstention doctrine first identified in *Burford v. Sun Oil Co.*, 319 U.S. 315 (1943). *Burford* abstention is based on considerations of federalism and comity that require federal courts to resist disrupting the customary procedures of state law. In *Burford*, for example, the issue presented was whether federal court could abstain from exercising jurisdiction when a challenge to the reasonableness of an order of the Texas Railroad Commission would immerse a federal court in the center of the State's complicated oil regulatory apparatus. As a general matter, the *Burford* abstention doctrine is "justified if and only if (1) a state has created a complex regulatory system on a matter of substantial importance to the state, (2) there exist no federal interests in the matter that override the state interests, and (3) the state legislature has made the state courts integral to the administrative scheme by delegating to them broad discretion so that they may participate in the development of regulatory policy." Lewis C. Yelin, Note, *Burford Abstention in Actions for Damages*, 99 Colum. L. Rev. 1871, 1881 (1999). *Pullman* abstention and *Burford* abstention are motivated by different concerns. The former is based in the idea that courts should not decide constitutional issues if they can in any way avoid doing so. Because *Burford* is based in principles of comity and federalism, there is therefore a conspicuous balancing element in *Burford* that is not necessarily present in *Pullman* abstention cases. After *Growe*, however, the lines between the two abstention doctrines has blurred. Thus, in *Quackenbush v. Allstate Insurance Co.*, 517 U.S. 706 (1996), the Court held that there should be "a narrow range of circumstances in which *Burford* can justify dismissal of a federal action." As one court has summarized the state of uncertainty, "In light of the Supreme Court's decision between those circumstances that require dismissal of a suit and those that require postponing consideration of its merits, it may be more appropriate to refer to *Burford* abstention in this case as *Burford* 'deferral.' [citing *Growe*] Nonetheless, after more than a half-century in which courts and commentators have spoken of *Burford* abstention, the court believes that use of the phrase '*Burford* deferral' would be more confusing than clarifying." *In the Matter of Rehabilitation of the Universe Life Insurance Company*, 35 F.Supp. 2d 1297 (D. Kansas 1999).

6. In *Touchston v. McDermott*, 234 F.3d 1161 (11th Cir. 2000), the first federal court appeal in the Florida presidential controversy, the Eleventh Circuit confronted precisely these kind of abstention claims. Although the Court ultimately decided the case on a timing questions (discussed below), it decisively rejected arguments that the abstention doctrines could prove an obstacle to federal oversight:

> Defendants argue that we should abstain from hearing this case under *Burford v. Sun Oil Co.*, 319 U.S. 315 (1943), or under *Railroad Comm'n of Tex. v. Pullman Co.*, 312 U.S. 496 (1941). We conclude that abstention is not appropriate in this case.
>
> The *Burford* abstention doctrine allows a federal court to dismiss a case only if it presents difficult questions of state law bearing on policy problems of substantial public import whose importance transcends the result in the case then at bar, or if its adjudication in a federal forum would disrupt state efforts to establish a coherent policy with respect to a matter of substantial public concern. A central purpose furthered by *Burford* abstention is to protect complex state administrative processes from undue federal interference. The case before us does not threaten to undermine all or a substantial part of Florida's process of conducting elections and resolving election disputes. Rather, Plaintiffs' claims in this case target certain discrete practices set forth in a particular state statute. Further, *Burford* is implicated when federal interference would disrupt a state's effort, through its administrative agencies, to achieve uniformity and consistency in addressing a problem. *See, e.g., Quackenbush v. Allstate Ins. Co.*, 517 U.S. 706, 727-28 (1996). This case does not threaten to undermine Florida's uniform approach to manual recounts; indeed, the crux of Plaintiffs' complaint is the absence of strict and uniform standards for initiating or conducting such recounts. Finally, we note that *Burford* abstention represents an "extraordinary and narrow exception to the duty of a District Court to adjudicate a controversy properly before it." *County of Allegheny v. Frank Mashuda Co.*, 360 U.S. 185, 188 (1959). We do not believe that the concerns raised by Defendants in this case justify our abstention under this narrow doctrine.
>
> Perhaps the most persuasive justification for abstention advanced by Defendants is based on *Pullman*; however, we conclude that abstention under this doctrine would not be appropriate. Under the *Pullman* abstention doctrine, a federal court will defer to "state court resolution of underlying issues of state law." *Harman v. Forssenius*, 380 U.S. 528, 534 (1965). Two elements must be met for *Pullman* abstention to apply: (1) the case must present an unsettled question of state law, and (2) the question of state law must be dispositive of the case or   would materially alter the constitutional question

presented.   The purpose of *Pullman* abstention is to "avoid unnecessary friction in federal-state functions, interference with important state functions, tentative decisions on questions of state law, and premature constitutional adjudication." Because abstention is discretionary, it is only appropriate when the question of state law can be fairly interpreted to avoid adjudication of the constitutional question.

Plaintiffs claim that Florida's manual recount provision is unconstitutional because the statute does not provide sufficient standards to guide the discretion of county canvassing boards in granting a request for a manual recount or in conducting such a recount.   There has been no suggestion by Defendants that the statute is appropriately subject to a more limited construction than the statute itself indicates.

Our conclusion that abstention is inappropriate is strengthened by the fact that Plaintiffs allege a constitutional violation of their voting rights.   In considering abstention, we must take into account the nature of the controversy and the importance of the right allegedly impaired.   Our cases have held that voting rights cases are particularly inappropriate for abstention. In light of this precedent, the importance of the rights asserted by Plaintiffs counsels against our abstention in this case; although, as discussed below, we are mindful of the limited role of the federal courts in assessing a state's electoral process.

We therefore conclude that abstention is not appropriate.

7.   After *Touchston,* what is left of the abstention doctrines? Is there any way to distinguish federal voting claims from all other claims in which a specific federal constitutional or statutory interest is asserted? *Touchston* may be a clear articulation of the transformation of the jurisdictional abstention doctrines into prudential deferral doctrines, spelled out in a context where the federal concern seems particularly palpable. If so, however, it would be an odd development for abstention law to fall in an area where the federal interest, even if substantial, is so heavily defined by the proper use of established state procedures.

8.   Should federal court intervention depend on the availability of other institutional actors capable of redressing the claimed harms? Consider the processes for challenging disputed delegations to the Electoral College in light of the process failure arguments raised in *United States v. Carolene Products,* 304 U.S. 144, 152 n.4 (1944) and in Justice Clark's opinion in *Baker v. Carr,* 369 U.S. 186 (1962). Both *Carolene Products* and Justice Clark placed great emphasis on the need for federal court intervention when no other actors were capable of redressing a claimed harm through the normal operations of the political process. But consider the elaborate statutory scheme set forth in 3 U.S.C. §§ 2, 5 and 15. For example, § 2 provides that when a state "has failed to make a choice [of electors to the electoral college] on the day prescribed by law, the electors may be appointed on a subsequent day in such a manner as the legislature of such State may direct." In addition, § 5 requires that states make a "final determination of any controversy or contest concerning the appointment" of electors by six days prior to the meeting of the electoral college and deems such state determination to be "conclusive." Finally, §15 expressly anticipates that there might be unresolved controversies over which electors legitimately represent the state and that there could even be rival sets of electors each claiming to represent their states — as occurred with the Florida, Louisiana and South Carolina delegations in 1876. Resolution of such disputes is entrusted to independent determination by each branch of Congress — with a preference in case of a split between the House and Senate going to the delegation whose certificate of appointment bears the signature of the governor of their state of origin.   Given the availability of political organs resolving electoral college disputes, should federal courts refuse to hear contests involving the selection of electors to the electoral college?

9.   Although much of the caselaw on federal intervention into state election practices involves redistricting, there is nonetheless a discrete issue concerning federal oversight of state administration of *federal* elections. The clearest example is, of course, the scramble for judicial relief in the Florida presidential election. Unlike redistricting, presidential elections are subject to direct constitutional and federal statutory commands. The one-person, one-vote command for redistricting is a matter of constitutional construction that is not directly anticipated in the text of the Constitution. By contrast, Article II of the Constitution and the Presidential Elections Act directly regulate state conduct of presidential elections. Should that alter the principles of federal oversight?

Siegel v. LePore

120 F.Supp. 2d 1041 (S.D. Fla., Nov. 13, 2000)

■ DONALD M. MIDDLEBROOKS, U.S.D.J.

ORDER ON PLAINTIFFS' EMERGENCY MOTION FOR TEMPORARY RESTRAINING ORDER AND PRELIMINARY INJUNCTION

THIS CAUSE comes before the Court upon Plaintiffs' Emergency Motion for Temporary Restraining Order and Preliminary Injunction, filed November 11, 2000.

I. Introduction

Plaintiffs, consisting of individual registered Florida voters as well as the Republican candidates for President and Vice-President Governor George W. Bush and Richard Cheney, move for entry of a temporary restraining order and preliminary injunction against Defendants, individual members of the electoral canvassing boards of Palm Beach, Broward, Miami-Dade, and Volusia Counties. They request that the canvassing boards of Broward, Miami-Dade, Palm Beach, and Volusia Counties be enjoined from proceeding with manual recounts of the November 7th election.

The gravamen of their complaint is that a manual recount may diminish the accuracy of a vote count because of ballot degradation and the exercise of discretion on the part of the county canvassing boards in determining a voter's intent. Implicit in their argument is a concern that selected manual recounts in some counties but not others may skew the election results even if the hand count is accurate. This is so because the machine counting process may reject ballots which upon visual inspection can be determined to be valid, and the machine error rate is likely to be spread equally across all precincts. If only selected precincts or counties are manually counted, the hand count, assuming it is more accurate, may help the candidate favored in those areas.

These are serious arguments. The question becomes who should consider them. Under the Constitution of the United States, the responsibility for selection of electors for the office of President rests primarily with the people of Florida, its election officials and, if necessary, its courts. The procedures employed by Florida appear to be neutral and, while not yet complete, the process seems to be unfolding as it has on other occasions. For the reasons that follow, I believe that intervention by a federal district court, particularly on a preliminary basis, is inappropriate.

II. Factual Background

On November 7, 2000, the United States held a general election wherein Florida voters cast ballots for several offices, including votes for the twenty-five electors for President and Vice President of the United States. On November 8, 2000, the Division of Elections for the State of Florida reported that the Republican Party presidential ticket received 2,909,135 votes and the Democratic Party presidential ticket received 2,907,351 votes. Other candidates on the presidential ballot received a total of 139,616 votes. The margin of difference between the votes received by the Republic and Democratic presidential tickets was 1,784, or 0.0299% of the total Florida vote.

In Florida, the administration of elections includes statewide and local features. While the Secretary of State is the chief election officer of the state, see Fla. Stat. § 97.102(1), the actual conduct of elections occurs in Florida counties. Except for the appointed supervisor in Miami-Dade County, the county supervisor of elections is an elective office, chosen every four years. *See* Fla. Stat. § 98.015(1). The supervisor employs deputy supervisors. *See* Fla. Stat. § 98.015(8). The county canvassing board is an essential part of Florida's election scheme. Ordinarily, the board is made up of the supervisor of elections, a county court judge, and the chair of the board of county commissioners. *See* Fla. Stat. § 102.131(1). The canvassing boards are responsible for counting the votes given each candidate. *See* Fla. Stat. § 102.141(2). It is their responsibility to judge the accuracy of vote counts. In addition, a county canvassing board, on its own initiative, may order mechanical recounts "if there is a discrepancy which could affect the outcome of an election." Fla. Stat. § 102.166(3)(c). After the vote counts are certified, the results are forwarded to the Department of State for any election involving a federal or state officer. *See* Fla. Stat. § 102.111(1); Fla. Stat. § 102.112. Based on the sum total of the results generated locally, the Elections Canvassing Commission, consisting of the Governor, the Secretary of State, and the Director of the Division of Elections, is granted authority to "certify the returns of the election and determine and declare who has been elected for each office." Fla. Stat. § 102.111(1). The Commission also issues certificates of the result of the election for federal and state officers, including presidential electors. See Fla. Stat. § 102.121. County canvassing boards are obligated to file a report with the Division of Elections at the same time the results of an election are certified. See Fla. Stat. § 102.141(6). Using these reports, the Secretary of State may issue advisory opinions. See id.; see also Fla. Admin. Code 1S-2.010.

Candidates or voters can promptly protest "erroneous" returns. See Fla. Stat. § 102.166(1)-(2). Candidates and political parties also can request manual recounts. See Fla. Stat. § 102.166(4). The procedures for such manual recounts are described in the pertinent statutory provisions. See Fla. Stat. § 102.166(4)-(10). Following certification by the county canvassing board, a candidate or voter also may contest election results by filing a complaint in circuit court. See Fla. Stat. § 102.168 et seq. The circuit courts are authorized to provide any relief that is appropriate. See Fla. Stat. § 102.168(8). District courts of appeal and the Florida Supreme Court are available to review circuit court orders.

In this case, the initial phase of election verification began automatically because Florida Statutes, § 102.141(4), compels machine recount for electoral differentials of 0.5% or less. The law further provides that candidates, as well as political parties, can submit written requests for hand counts. If granted, the threshold hand count encompasses a minimum of three precincts or 1% of the count's vote, whichever is greater. If the results of the initial manual recount indicate a disparity with the machine count which could affect the outcome of the election, the canvassing board "shall" undertake a manual recount of all precincts. See Fla. Stat. § 102.166(5).

In this case, the Florida Democratic Party filed requests for manual recounts in Broward, Miami-Dade, Palm Beach, and Volusia Counties within seventy-two hours as required by Florida Statutes, § 102.166(4)(b). As required by the statute, those requests set forth reasons, which included the extraordinary closeness of the statewide margin, as well as concern as to whether the vote totals reliably reflected the true will of the Florida voters.

Broward County

On November 8, 2000, pursuant to Fla. Stat. § 102.141(4), the Broward Canvassing Board conducted a statutorily mandated machine recount which is now complete. As a result of that recount, Vice President Gore received an additional 43 votes and Governor Bush received an additional 44 votes. On November 9, 2000, within 72 hours after midnight on the date the election was held, the Broward County Democratic Party filed a request for a manual recount pursuant to Florida Statutes, § 102.166(4). Pursuant thereto, a meeting of the Broward Canvassing Board was scheduled for Friday, November 10, 2000, at 10:00 a.m. The Broward County Republican Party, through its chair, Ed Pozzuoli, was notified by telephone of the date and time of the meeting. The Broward County Republican Party appeared and participated at the hearing.

The Broward Canvassing Board authorized a manual recount in three of Broward County's precincts, comprising at least one percent of the total votes cast for Vice President Gore. Pursuant to Florida Statutes, § 102.166(4)(d), the Broward County Democratic Party chose the three precincts subject to the manual recount. The one percent recount has not been completed and will continue Monday, November 13, 2000.

Miami-Dade

The Canvassing Board received a request from the Miami-Dade Democratic Party on November 9, 2000 pursuant to Florida Statutes, § 102.166(4), to conduct a recount. That request was revoked and amended later the same day. The Republican Party of Dade County submitted a response opposing the request for a manual recount. The Canvassing Board has not yet decided whether to grant or deny the request for a recount and has scheduled a hearing for Tuesday, November 14, 2000, at 9:30 a.m. to consider the matter.

Palm Beach

On November 11, 2000, when the manual recount of one percent of Palm Beach voters established a net gain of nineteen votes for Vice President Gore, the Palm Beach Canvassing Board, by a 2-1 vote, directed a manual recount of all precincts in the county. That decision adhered to Florida Statutes, § 102.166(5)(c), requiring a full recount when the one percent result shows that the election outcome could be changed by a full manual recount.

Plaintiffs allege that the manual recount in Palm Beach County has been characterized by ad hoc and arbitrary decisions. They claim that Leon St. John, attorney for the Palm Beach Canvassing Board, and Bob Nichols, spokesperson for the Board, gave a confusing press briefing on November 11, 2000 in which, at different times, they stated varying standards the Board was using to determine if a ballot would be tallied or not. Plaintiffs also allege that during the first hour of the manual recount no procedural guidance was given to recount observers or party representatives, and that no written criteria or rules were ever promulgated by the Board. Finally, Plaintiffs allege that because there were not enough Republican employees in the Supervisor of Elections' office, certain teams of reviewers did not include any Republican members.

Volusia

The Canvassing Board was advised during the evening of November 7, 2000 that a malfunction of the diskette in the electronic ballot tabulating machine in precinct 216 caused an obviously erroneous report of the results in the presidential vote from that precinct. The supervisor supplied another diskette which was inserted in another electronic ballot tabulating machine and all paper ballots from that precinct were tabulated.

On November 8, 2000, Deanie Lowe, Supervisor of Elections for Volusia County, provided to the Canvassing Board the directive of the Florida Secretary of State to conduct a mandatory recount of the presidential election pursuant to Florida Statutes, §102.141(4). On November 8, 2000, the Canvassing Board conducted the mandatory recount by reconciling the printouts of all votes case from each electronic ballot tabulating machine with the compilation of results from the host computer. The mandatory recount revealed no variance from the original count. The ballots were not removed from their sealed containers or recounted electronically or manually, except for ballots from precinct 216. Representatives of the Florida Republican Party suggested and expressly agreed to a manual recount of precinct 216. The Canvassing Board conducted a manual recount of the ballots from precinct 216 and the result was identical to the result from the electronic tabulation received after the substitution of the diskette.

After the mandatory recount, on November 9, 2000, the Florida Democratic Party requested a manual recount of all ballots. The Canvassing Board granted the request. On November 12, 2000, the Canvassing Board began the manual visual recount of all ballots. Numerous teams of two county employees, who are registered electors, are reading and counting the ballots. Republic and Democratic parties have been afforded the opportunity to have one observer for each counting team. Security of ballot storage and the counting room is provided under the direction of the Canvassing Board with Florida Department of Law Enforcement and Volusia County Sheriffs Office personnel.

The Volusia Canvassing Board has adopted a motion stating that it will comply with the requirements of Florida Statutes, § 102.111, to certify the results of the election to the Department of State no later than 5:00 p.m. on Tuesday, November 14, 2000, unless the time is extended by lawful authority. The Canvassing Board also has authorized the County Attorney and such other attorneys as he may appoint to seek state or federal judicial relief from the time limit for certification provided in Florida Statutes, § 102.111.

* * * *

III. Analysis

Our review of Plaintiffs' claims necessarily begins with the United States Constitution. The Constitution does not provide for the popular election of a President or Vice President of the United States on either a national or a state-by-state basis. Instead, the Constitution delineates that "each State shall appoint, in such Manner as the Legislature thereof may direct, a Number of Electors . . . to choose a President and Vice President." U.S. Const., Art. II, § 1. This constitutional provision grants "extensive power to the States to pass laws regulating the selection of electors." *Williams v. Rhodes*, 393 U.S. 23 (1968); *see also McPherson v. Blacker*, 146 U.S. 1, 27 (1892) (noting that the Constitution "recognizes that the people act through their representatives in the legislature, and leaves it to the legislature exclusively to define the method of effecting the object [of selecting electors])"; *Fitzgerald v. Green*, 134 U.S. 377, 380 (1889) (observing that rather than "interfere with the manner of appointing electors, or, where [according to the now general usage] the mode of appointment prescribed by the law of the state is election by the people, to regulate the conduct of such election. . . ," Congress "has left these matters to the control of the states"). However, while this power is broad, "these granted powers are always subject to the limitation that they may not be exercised in a way that violates other specific provisions of the Constitution." *Id.*

Here, Plaintiffs assert that Florida Statutes, § 102.166(4) violates the First and Fourteenth Amendments. In adjudicating similar challenges to state electoral laws, the Supreme Court has adopted a balancing test which weighs "the character and magnitude of the asserted injury to the rights protected by the First and Fourteenth Amendments" versus the legitimacy, strength, and necessity of the state interests underlying the electoral scheme. *Anderson v. Celebrezze*, 460 U.S. 780, 789 (1983) (citing *Williams*, 393 U.S. at 30-31). More recently, the Court has observed:

> Under this standard, the rigorousness of our inquiry into the propriety of a state election law depends upon the extent to which a challenged regulation burdens First and Fourteenth Amendment rights. Thus, as we have recognized when those rights are subjected to 'severe' restrictions, the regulation must be 'narrowly drawn to advance a state interest of compelling importance.' *Norman v. Reed*, 502 U.S. 279, 289 (1992). But when a state election law provision imposes only 'reasonable, nondiscriminatory restrictions' upon the First and Fourteenth Amendment rights of voters, 'the State's important regulatory interests are generally sufficient to justify' the restrictions. *Anderson*, 460 U.S. at 788; *see also id.*, at 788-789, n.9.

Burdick v. Takushi, 504 U.S. 428, 433 (1992). A central precept of this approach is the recognition that while "election laws will invariably impose some burden upon individual voters. . . common sense, as well as constitutional law, compels the conclusion that government must play an active role in structuring elections . . . if they are to be fair and honest and if some sort of order, rather than chaos, is to accompany the democratic processes." *Id.* (citations omitted). It is within this framework that we address the specifics of Plaintiffs' claims.

Florida law outlines a structural process by which a candidate or political party "may file a written request with the county canvassing board for a manual recount." Fla. Stat. § 102.166(4)(a). Such a request "must be filed with the canvassing board prior to the time the canvassing board certifies the results for the office being protested or within 72 hours after midnight of the date the election was held, whichever occurs later." Fla. Stat. § 102.166(4)(b). Once a request is made, "the county canvassing board may authorize a manual recount. If a manual recount is authorized, the county canvassing board shall make reasonable effort to notify each candidate whose race is being recounted of the time and place of such recount." Fla. Stat. § 102.166(4)(c). If the board decides to conduct a manual recount, "the manual recount must include at least three precincts and at least 1 percent of the total votes cast for such candidate or issue. In the event there are less than three precincts involved in the election, all precincts shall be counted. The person who requested the recount shall choose three precincts to be recounted, and, if other precincts are recounted, the county canvassing board shall select the additional precincts." Fla. Stat. § 102.166(4)(d). "If the manual recount indicates an error in the vote tabulation which could affect the outcome of the election," the statute authorizes the canvassing board to undertake a variety of remedial measures, including the manual recount of all ballots. Fla. Stat. § 102.166(5).[6] The state law also provides that "any manual recount shall be open to the public," and outlines the procedures by which a manual recount must take place. Fla. Stat. § 102.166(6)-(10).[7]

This state election scheme is reasonable and non-discriminatory on its face. Unlike a ballot access restriction that burdens only certain candidates or parties, *see Anderson*, 460 U.S. at 787-89 (invalidating an early filing deadline for independent presidential candidates); *Williams*, 393 U.S. at 30-31 (striking down state election laws that imposed substantial ballot access restrictions on minority parties), Florida's manual recount provision is a "generally-applicable and evenhanded" electoral scheme designed to "protect the integrity and reliability of the electoral process itself" — the type of state electoral law often upheld in federal legal challenges. *Anderson*, 460 U.S. at 788 n.9. On its face, the manual recount provision does not limit candidates' access to the ballot or interfere with voters' right to associate or vote. Instead, the manual recount provision is intended to safeguard the integrity and reliability of the electoral process by providing a structural means of detecting and correcting clerical or electronic tabulating errors in the counting of election ballots. While discretionary in its application, the provision is not wholly standardless. Rather, the central purpose of the scheme, as evidenced by its plain language, is to remedy "an error in the vote tabulation which could affect the outcome of

---

6. This provision states, the county canvassing board shall:

(a) Correct the error and recount the remaining precincts with the vote tabulation system;
(b) Request the Department of State to verify the tabulation software; or
(c) Manually recount all ballots.

7. These procedures are as follows:

(a) The county canvassing board shall appoint as many counting teams of at least two electors as is necessary to manually recount the ballots. A counting team must have, when possible, members of at least two political parties. A candidate involved in the race shall not be a member of the counting team.

(b) If a counting team is unable to determine a voter's intent in casting a ballot, the ballot shall be presented to the county canvassing board for it to determine the voter's intent.
(8) If the county canvassing board determines the need to verify the tabulation software, the county canvassing board shall request in writing that the Department of State verify the software.
(9) When the Department of State verifies such software, the department shall:
(a) Compare the software used to tabulate the votes with the software filed with the Department of State pursuant to s. 101.5607; and
(b) Check the election parameters.
(10) The Department of State shall respond to the county canvassing board within 3 working days.

the election." Fla. Stat. § 102.166(5). In this pursuit, the provision strives to strengthen rather than dilute the right to vote by securing, as near as humanly possible, an accurate and true reflection of the will of the electorate. Notably, the four county canvassing boards challenged in this suit have reported various anomalies in the initial automated count and recount.[9] The state manual recount provision therefore serves important governmental interests.

In addition, the manual recount provision is the type of state electoral law that safely resides within the broad ambit of state control over presidential election procedures. As the Eleventh Circuit has explained, "'the functional structure embodied in the Constitution, the nature of the federal court system and the limitations inherent in the concepts both of limited federal jurisdiction and of the remedy afforded by § 1983 operate to restrict federal relief in the state election context." *Curry v. Baker*, 802 F.2d 1302, 1314 (11th Cir. 1986) (quoting *Gamza v. Aguirre*, 619 F.2d 449, 452 (5th Cir. 1980)); *see also Duncan v. Poythress*, 657 F.2d 691 (5th Cir. 1981). In Curry, the Eleventh Circuit rejected a substantive due process claim based on an Alabama subcommittee's use of polling data to determine the number of illegal votes cast in a Democratic gubernatorial runoff primary. The Court noted "although federal courts closely scrutinize state laws whose very design infringes on the rights of voters, federal courts will not intervene to examine the validity of individual ballots or supervise the administrative details of a local election. Only in extraordinary circumstances will a challenge to a state election rise to the level of a constitutional deprivation." *Id.* Moreover, the Supreme Court, in the analogous context of a state manual recount of a Senate election, stated:

> Unless Congress acts, Art. 1, § 4, empowers the States to regulate the conduct of senatorial elections. This Court has recognized the breadth of those powers: 'It cannot be doubted that these comprehensive words embrace authority to provide a complete code for congressional elections, not only as to times and places, but in relation to notices, registration, supervision of voting, protection of voters, prevention of fraud and corrupt practices, counting of votes, duties of inspectors and canvassers, and making and publication of election returns; in short, to enact the numerous requirements as to procedure and safeguards which experience shows are necessary in order to enforce the fundamental right involved.' Indiana has found, along with many other States, that one procedure necessary to guard against irregularity and error in the tabulation of votes is the availability of a recount. Despite the fact that a certificate of election may be issued

---

9. One of the main rationales behind a manual recount system is observe whether an imprecise perforation, called a "hanging chad," exists on the physical ballot. If the blunt-tipped voting stylus strikes the ballot imperfectly, the chad, the rectangular perforation designed to be removed from a punch card when punched, can remain appended to the ballot (although it is pushed out), and an automated tabulation will record a blank vote. This problem is particularly associated with counties that still rely on punch card technology. Palm Beach, Broward, and Miami-Dade all use punch card voting systems. The final county, Volusia County, found a series of irregularities with its automated tabulation results including reports of computer failure and statistical aberrations.

to the leading candidate within 30 days after the election, the results are not final if a candidate's option to compel a recount is exercised. A recount is an integral part of the Indiana electoral process and is within the ambit of the broad powers delegated to the States by Art. I. § 4.

Roudebush v. Hartke, 405 U.S. 15, 24 (1972).

The central thrust of these decisions is that federal courts should tread cautiously in the traditional state province of electoral procedures and tabulations. Simply put, "federal courts are not the bosses in state election disputes unless extraordinary circumstances affecting the integrity of the state's election process are clearly present in a high degree. This well-settled principle — that federal courts interfere in state elections as a last resort — is basic to federalism, and we should take it to heart." *Roe v. Evans*, 43 F.3d 574, 585 (11th Cir. 1995) (Edmondson, J., dissenting). These principles of comity and federalism equally apply to state electoral procedures for the selection of presidential electors given the broad ambit of state authority in this area as outlined in Article II, Section 1 of the United States Constitution. Otherwise, federal courts run the risk of being "thrust into the details of virtually every election, tinkering with the state's election machinery, reviewing petitions, registration cards, vote tallies, and certificates of election for all manner of error and insufficiency under state and federal law." *Duncan v. Poythress*, 657 F.2d 691, 701 (5th Cir. 1981).

The thrust of Plaintiffs' position is that Florida's decentralized county-by-county electoral system can yield disparate tabulating results from county to county. For instance, similarly-punched ballots in different counties may be tabulated differently in a manual recount due to the introduction of human subjectivity and error. Further, if manual recounts are held in certain counties but not others, ballots previously discarded by electronic tabulation in manual recount counties would be counted, while similarly-situated ballots in non-manual recount counties would not- thereby diluting the vote in non-manual recount counties." These concerns are real, and, in our view, unavoidable given the inherent decentralization involved in state electoral and state recount procedures. For instance, at least 48 states employ recount procedures — many of which differ in their methods of tabulation.[11] In Florida, 65 of 67 counties use one of many different electronic voting systems certified by the Division of Elections.[12] One county uses a mechanical lever machine and another county uses manually-tabulated paper ballots. Undoubtably, the use of these disparate tabulating systems will generate tabulation differences from county to county. Unless and until each electoral county in the United States uses the exact same automatic tabulation (and even then there may be system malfunctions and alike), there will be tabulating discrepancies depending on the method of tabulation. Rather than a sign of weakness or constitutional injury, some solace can be taken in the fact that no one centralized body or person can control the tabulation of an entire statewide or national election. For the more county boards and individuals involved in the electoral regulation process, the less likely it becomes that corruption, bias, or error can influence the ultimate result of an election.

Moreover, Plaintiffs have failed to demonstrate that manual recounts are so unreliable that their use rises to the level of a constitutional injury. The burden of proof rests squarely with Plaintiffs on this point. Manual recounts are available in numerous states, and have been used since the time of the Founding. While some level of error is inherent to manual tabulation, no method of tabulation is free from error. It has been submitted to this Court that electronic tabulation runs a five per cent error rate. In fact, the very premise of a manual recount after an electronic tabulation, as is the case here, is to provide an additional check on the accuracy of the ballot count. While manual recounts may produce verifiable errors in certain cases, we do not find sufficient evidence to declare a law authorizing the use of a manual recount to be unconstitutional on its face. As the Supreme Court has elucidated, "facial invalidation 'is, manifestly, strong medicine' that 'has been employed by the Court sparingly and only as a last resort.'" *National Endowment for the Arts v. Finley* 524 U.S. 569, 580 (1998); *see also New York State Club Ass'n, Inc. v. City of New York*, 487 U.S. 1, 11 (1988) (stating that "to prevail on a facial attack the plaintiff must demonstrate that the challenged law either 'could never be applied in a valid manner'"). Clearly, the manual recount process, unless rife with error (which has not been proven by Plaintiffs), has many conceivable constitutional applications that would help ensure an accurate vote tally. It is unconvincing to argue that a process structured to render a vote tally more accurate somehow structurally dilutes the voting rights of the electorate. Simply because the recount tally postdates the initial vote or, as in this case, prolongs the certification of an election result does not result in a dilution of voting rights — anymore than the tallying of lawfully-cast absentee

---

11. It has been represented to this Court by Plaintiffs that at least fifteen states employ some type of statutory manual recount scheme in presidential elections.

12. Of these, 26 use punch-card and 39 use optical scanning systems.

ballots dilutes the value of votes cast at polling precincts on election day.

* * * *

In short, I simply do not find Plaintiffs' claims to have demonstrated a clear deprivation of a constitutional injury or a fundamental unfairness in Florida's manual recount provision. While this dispute has assumed clear national prominence and importance due to the close and undecided outcome of the presidential election, the types of specific issues raised by Plaintiffs' motion— for example, that manual ballot recounts are unreliable — are similar to the "'garden-variety' election dispute[s]" over counting ballots which have not been found to "rise to the level of a constitutional deprivation" under our caselaw. *Curry*, 802 F.2d at 1315; *see also Welch v. McKenzie*, 765 F.2d 1311, 1317, vacated on other grounds and remanded, 777 F.2d 191 (5th Cir. 1985) (stating that "even though votes inadvertently counted incorrectly threw an election to the wrong candidate, this court refused to intervene" because our Constitution envisions such disputes to be regulated by state and not federal law); *Pettengill v. Putnam Cty. Sch. Dist., Unionsville, Missouri*, 472 F.2d 121 (8th Cir. 1973) (refusing to intervene in election controversy where plaintiffs claimed that the right to vote had been diluted by defendant's improper counting of ballots). I agree with the Curry Court that "a federal court should not be 'the arbiter of disputes' which arise in elections" because it is not "the federal court's role to 'oversee the administrative details of a local election.'" *Curry*, 802 F.2d at 1315. I also stress that this not a case alleging clear and direct infringements of the right of citizens to vote through either racial intimidation or fraudulent interference with a free election such as stuffing the ballot box or deliberately undercounting votes.

Finally, I conclude that the public interest is best served by denying preliminary injunctive relief in this instance. The mere possibility that the eventual result of the challenged manual recounts will be to envelop the president-elect in a cloud of illegitimacy does not justify enjoining the current manual recount processes underway. Central to our democratic process as well as our Constitution is the belief that open and transparent government, whenever possible, best serves the public interest. Nowhere can the public dissemination of truth be more vital than in the election procedures for determining the next presidency.

IV. Conclusion

While I share a desire for finality, I do not believe it can be accomplished through this request for an injunction. One of the strengths of our Constitution's method for selection of the President is its decentralization. Florida, one of the 50 states, has 67 counties, each with a supervisor of election, a canvassing board, and different voting and tabulation equipment. In a close statewide election, it is difficult to come to a final determination.

A federal court has a very limited role and should not interfere except where there is an immediate need to correct a constitutional violation. At this stage, there is no likelihood that such a showing can be made. The request for preliminary injunction is DENIED.

DONE AND ORDERED in Chambers, at Miami, Florida, this 13th day of November 2000.

NOTES AND QUESTIONS

1. Is the district court correct that no federal interest is implicated because of the decentralization of authority among the multiple states and multiple counties that control election processes? Note that there may be a very significant difference between when the federal courts should intervene as a prudential matter, and whether federal courts may intervene in light of the decentralized control over election processes.

2. Does the fact that the election at issue is a federal election, and a presidential one to boot, distinguish this case from state elections? The court here relies on *Roe v. Evans*, 43 F.3d 574 (11th Cir. 1995), for the proposition that federal courts should be reluctant to intervene in state electoral processes. Recall that in *Roe*, the final order certified the question to the Alabama Supreme Court for determination of the proper application of state electoral procedures. Is this case distinguishable from *Roe* on the grounds that greater deference should be paid to state processes in state elections? Or is the federal interest limited to insuring that state processes have been followed faithfully? In this regard, consider the approach taken by the 11th Circuit in *Touchston v. McDermott*, 234 F.3d 1161 (11th Cir., Nov. 17, 2000):

> After expeditious but thorough and careful review, we conclude that the Emergency Motion for Injunction Pending Appeal should be denied without prejudice. Several factors lead us to this conclusion. Both the Constitution of the United States and 3 U.S.C. §5 indicate that states have the primary authority to determine the manner of appointing Presidential Electors and to resolve most controversies concerning the appointment of Electors. The case law is to the same effect, although, of course, federal courts may act to preserve and decide claims of violations of the Constitution of the United States in certain circumstances, especially where a state remedy is inadequate. In this case, the State of Florida has enacted detailed election dispute procedures. These procedures have been invoked, and are in the process of being implemented, both in the form of administrative actions by state officials and in the form of actions in state courts, including the Supreme Court of Florida. It has been represented to us that the state courts will address and resolve any necessary federal constitutional issues presented to them, including the issues raised by Plaintiffs in this case. . . . If so, then state procedures are not in any way inadequate to preserve for ultimate review in the United States Supreme Court any federal questions arising out of such orders.
>
> Based on a thorough review of events as they now stand, we cannot conclude that Plaintiffs have demonstrated a substantial threat of an irreparable injury that would warrant granting at this time the

extraordinary remedy of an injunction pending appeal, and thus at this time we need not address the likelihood of success on the merits; nor do we address now the merits of the underlying appeal. Accordingly, the Emergency Motion for Injunction Pending Appeal is

DENIED WITHOUT PREJUDICE.

3. For those wishing to review additional materials, including briefs and pleadings, from the Florida litigation, these may be found at http://election2000.stanford.edu/.

CHAPTER 6

REMEDIAL POSSIBILITIES FOR DEFECTIVE ELECTIONS

As the preceding chapters show, constitutional and statutory violations can take many forms. In *Harper v. State Board of Elections*, one of the equal protection cases on which *Bush v. Gore* relied, the commonwealth of Virginia required citizens to pay a poll tax in order to vote. In *Reynolds v. Sims* and *Gray v. Sanders*, the other two principal equal protection cases cited by the Court, states froze into place apportionments that weighted citizens' votes in dramatically different ways depending on where they lived. And in *Bush v. Gore* itself, the 2000 presidential election in Florida was plagued with a series of problems ranging from ballot design to the refusal to allow some citizens to vote to the rules for manual recounts.

Finding that there has been some constitutional or statutory violation does not, of itself, necessarily determine what should be done. In particular, in cases where plaintiffs seek some kind of injunctive relief, many complex questions regarding the equity of various alternatives will arise. The following materials consider the range of potential remedies. They begin with various forms of injunctive relief, but they also consider the quite different possibilities offered by damages actions and criminal prosecutions.

A. ORDERING A NEW ELECTION

Bell v. Southwell
376 F.2d 659 (5th Cir. 1967)

■ JOHN R. BROWN, Circuit Judge.

A Georgia election was conducted under procedures involving racial discrimination which was gross, state-imposed, and forcibly state-compelled. Nevertheless the District Court by summary judgment held it could not set aside such election or order a new one even though in parallel cases the unconstitutional discriminatory practices were enjoined . . . . We reverse.

The underlying facts out of which the controversy grew may be quickly stated. The Justice of the Peace for the 789th Militia District in Americus, Sumter County, Georgia, died on June 23, 1965. . . . [A] special election to fill the vacancy . . . was held on July 20, 1965. Mrs. Mary F. Bell, one of the plaintiffs, a Negro, was a candidate as was the winner, J. W. Southwell, a defendant, and four other white men. Following Georgia procedure, the results of the election were canvassed and the defendant J. W. Southwell declared the winner. Of the 2,781 votes cast, Negroes actually voting numbered 403 out of a total of 1,223 registered and qualified Negro voters in the District. On July 29, 1965, and after the expiration of the time for election contest under Georgia laws, this suit was filed. The District Judge by opinion denied relief for [two] reasons . . . . First, even assuming the admitted racial discrimination intimidated Negroes from voting, if all of the qualified Negroes not voting were added to the . . . vote of Southwell's opponents, the result could not have been changed. Second . . . Federal Courts simply do not have power to void a state election.

This suit, brought on their own behalf and on behalf of other Negroes and other voters in the District by Mrs. Bell, a qualified elector and candidate, and two other named Negro qualified voters, against the defendants Southwell and Horne, the Ordinary [that is, the local official responsible for running the election], invoked the Civil Rights Acts, 42 U.S.C.A. §§ 1971, 1981, 1983, 1985, 28 U.S.C.A. § 1343(3), (4). The main charge was that the election officials including the Ordinary had conducted the election in violation of the rights established under the Constitution and laws of the United States. The specific allegations fell in two categories, one relating to the election system and the second to specific acts of intimidation. In the first it was alleged that voting lists for the election were segregated on the basis of race. Likewise, voting booths were segregated according to race, with one booth for "white males", another for "white women", and a third for Negroes. During the course of the election, a number of qualified Negro women voters were denied the right to cast their ballots in the "white women's" booth. In the second group were charges that the officials barred representatives of candidate Bell from viewing the voting, another was physically struck by an election official and police allowed a large crowd of white males to gather near the polls thus intimidating Negroes from voting. In addition, the plaintiffs were commanded by a deputy sheriff, acting under directions of the Ordinary, to leave the white women's polling booth and after their respectful refusal to do so on the ground that they had the constitutional right to vote without being subjected to racial discrimination, they were arrested. With precision, through simultaneous motions for temporary restraining order, preliminary injunction, show cause orders, and the immediate release from arrest, the plaintiffs requested that the Court declare the defendant Southwell was not the legally elected Justice of the Peace, that he be enjoined from taking office, and that the Ordinary be ordered to call a new election. . . .

It rounds out the picture to state that . . . two parallel companion cases were before the District Court, one by the United States against various officials of Sumter County, the other an identical suit by these appellants-plaintiffs against the same Georgia officials. Hearing them simultaneously with the application for preliminary relief in the instant case, the District

Judge in those two cases entered an injunction enjoining the defendants from maintaining racial segregation at the polls, from maintaining segregated voting lists, from arresting or interfering with Negro voters, and from prosecuting the plaintiffs for their conduct leading to their arrest on July 20, 1965 . . . .

By the decrees in the companion cases . . . , the trial Court in unmistakable terms and action characterized the practices as flagrant violations of the Constitution. These steps were taken, so the Judge said, "to insure that in the future, elections in Sumter County will be free from discrimination." Despite his determination that for the future these glaring racial discriminations could not go on, the trial Judge concluded that a Federal Court was either powerless -- or at least ought not to exercise power -- to set aside a State election. The Judge was apparently influenced by two factors. The first is one going to the existence of power or the propriety of its exercise. On the basis of *Reynolds v. Sims*,, and other reapportionment cases, the trial Court recognizing that a prohibitory decree could look to the future, nevertheless held that it could not rectify the past since, as the Judge put it, "only a few minutes' reflection is needed to realize that the implications of such a decision would be staggering." The second [factor that influenced the district judge was that,] granting the existence of this crude discrimination, there is no way to tell whether the result would have been different in its absence. Hence, no harm or injury is shown by these complainants. Neither of these factors warrant, in our view, the complete denial of relief.

Drastic, if not staggering, as is the Federal voiding of a State election, and therefore a form of relief to be guardedly exercised, this Court [has] . . . . expressly recognized the existence of this power. Of course . . . not every unconstitutional racial discrimination necessarily permits or requires a retrospective voiding of the election. But the power is present . . . .

As to the second [factor identified by the district court,] we do not think the Court could justify denial of effective, present relief because of any assumed inability to demonstrate that the outcome would have been different. The appellants seem to suggest that the existence of such flagrant racial discrimination would raise a presumption that the vote of every actual and potential voter was affected. On that approach, it is not Negroes alone who suffer, it is the body politic as a whole, both Negro and white. And this is certainly true at least to the extent that the trial Court legally could not assume -- as it evidently did -- that all white voters would vote for white candidates, all Negroes for Negroes, or that no whites would vote for Negroes in a free, untainted election.

[W]e think it is a mistake to cast this in terms of presumption. The fact is that there are certain discriminatory practices which, apart from demonstrated injury or the inability to do so, so infect the processes of the law as to be stricken down as invalid. Thus in jury-race exclusion cases, once the evidence, either direct or by inference from statistical percentages, establishes the existence of racial discrimination, the law requires that the indictment (or the petit jury verdict of guilty) be set side even though the accused is unable to demonstrate injury in fact. And at times demonstrated actual discrimination is not even required if the racially conscious system affords a ready opportunity for it in practice. Of course the Court discharging an accused from such indictment or conviction as a legalism finds that the accused was "prejudiced", but it is not in terms of the personal harm suffered or a factual demonstration that things would have turned out better. Rather, it is the law's recognition that in areas of such vital importance, state-imposed racial discrimination cannot be tolerated and to eliminate the practice or the temptation toward it, the law must extinguish the judgment wrought by such a procedure.

Even more directly, in connection with the elective process, the Supreme Court gave full play to this approach in striking down the Louisiana law requiring the designation of the race of each candidate on the ballot. *Anderson v. Martin*, 1964, 375 U.S. 399. It takes little transposition to substitute for the ballot's written racial candidate label the state-supplied racial marker for places and manner of voting. In each situation it is ". . . placing a racial label . . . at the most crucial stage in the electoral process -- the instant before the vote is cast . . . ." By each mechanism "the State furnishes a vehicle by which racial prejudice may be so aroused as to operate against one group because of race and for another." And in both situations this "is true because by directing the citizen's attention to the single consideration of race or color, the State indicates that . . . race or color is an important -- perhaps paramount -- consideration in the citizen's choice, which may decisively influence the citizen to cast his ballot along racial lines." And as much for one as for the other, the " vice lies not in the resulting injury but in the placing of the power of the State behind a racial classification that induces racial prejudice at the polls." 375 U.S. 399, 402. . . .

[With respect to the question whether the election should be set aside,] the Georgia authorities . . . insist here that the relief sought was properly denied since the injunction was requested after the election was over.

But we certainly inten[d] no such mechanical rule. In *Hamer [v. Campbell*, where we refused to order such relief,] the vice sought to be corrected was the denial of the right to vote to Negroes through operation of the registration procedure. That was known to exist before the election was held. It was also known that the effects could not be eradicated except through equitable court relief. Here, of course, the vice occurred on election day upon the opening of the polls. It might be suggested that the Negro voters should have anticipated that the traditional practice of racially segregated lists and polling places would be maintained. But it was equally permissible for them to think that at this late date and in the atmosphere of that moment and the passage of successive Civil Rights statutes increasing protection against racial discrimination, that these Georgia authorities would measure up to the demands of the Constitution.

There was really no effective relief available before the election. The moment the election process began, there was a protest by these Negro voters and others seeking an eradication of the discrimination and an opportunity for all members of that race, indeed for all voters, to vote without regard to race or color. That this self-help was not successful, indeed resulted in the unwarranted arrest and detention of those who protested, does not fault them for want of diligence. And within but a few days after the result of the election was published, this suit was filed as a part of an attack on many fronts.

Considering the gross, spectacular, completely indefensible nature of this state-imposed, state-enforced racial discrimination and the absence of an effective judicial remedy prior to the holding of the election, this is far removed from a belated effort to set aside retrospectively an election held long before on the ground that re-examination of the circumstances indicates a denial of constitutional rights on the part of candidates or voters, or both. The parties here moved with unusual diligence and . . . relief ". . . if it is to be had, must perforce come from the Court or the voters must simply be told to wait four more years."

In the face of gross, unsophisticated, significant, and obvious racial discriminations in the conduct of the election and the now established power of a Federal Court to extinguish its effects even to the point of setting aside the election, the [state law] reasons relied on by the District Judge warrant but a brief comment. The Court's fundamental mistake was in assuming that this was an election contest as such in which the winner is challenged because of ineligibility, fraud or irregularities in the conduct of the election, the receipt or counting of illegal ballots which would change the result and the like, and which, as a separate special statutory proceeding, must be timely filed by specified persons following statutory procedures and in particular tribunals. Mrs. Bell and her co-plaintiffs alone or as members of the class did not challenge the eligibility of Mr. Southwell or the fact that he received an overwhelming majority. Indeed, Mrs. Bell as a former candidate did not seek to be selected over Southwell or any other opponent. What, and all, she and others sought was an election conducted free of such indefensible, racial distinctions. That being so, it was not the usual simple case of counting votes and denying relief for want of affirmative proof of a different result. . . .

This leaves only a tag end. There is a suggestion that the District Court enjoining Southwell from taking office pursuant to the election would be powerless to grant affirmative relief requiring that the Ordinary call a special election. In this vital area of vindication of precious constitutional rights, we are unfettered by the negative or affirmative character of the words used or the negative or affirmative form in which the coercive order is cast. If affirmative relief is essential, the Court has the power and should employ it.

The cause must therefore be reversed and remanded for the entry of an appropriate order setting aside the election and requiring the calling of a special election.

NOTES AND QUESTIONS

1. For a general discussion of federal courts' power to set aside state elections, see Kenneth W. Starr, *Federal Judicial Invalidation as a Remedy for Irregularities in State Elections*, 49 N.Y.U.L. Rev. 1092 (1974). Starr noted that as of 1974, federal intervention in state elections was a relatively new phenomenon, in part as a product of the political question doctrine, which viewed elections generally, and state elections particularly, as not amenable

to judicial oversight.

Starr emphasized the equitable nature of the invalidation power, and discussed its relative advantages and disadvantages. On the one hand, purely prospective injunctive relief – e.g., an order forbidding the unconstitutional practice in the future – "necessarily leave[s] intact the results achieved under an unlawful scheme . . . until a new election is held in the natural course of events." *Id.* at 1103. Invalidation provides a more complete remedy since it returns the voters more nearly to the status quo ante in which a constitutional election can be conducted. At the same time, invalidation seemed to Starr a less intrusive federal remedy than structural reform – for example, the reapportionment decisions that precipitated major reorganization of states' election systems.

On the other hand, Starr noted that invalidation could involve costly new elections which might, among other things, depress voter participation, thereby not actually returning voters to the status quo ante. And the delays necessary to conduct new elections might leave incumbents in office who themselves might lack legitimacy.

Starr identified three theoretical bases for exercising the power to invalidate elections. The first was "invalidation as retribution" for outrageous, intentional, illegal conduct by government officials during the election process. *Id.* at 1115. Starr saw *Bell* as such a case. A second theory would authorize invalidations for the purpose of "ensuring electoral purity," *id.* at 1121, without regard to official intent, but such a per se rule seemed too automatic to him. Finally, a third approach, which Starr found the "most pragmatic," would contemplate invalidation when unconstitutional actions were "outcome-determinative," that is, when they might have affected the actual outcome of an election: "There is no logical correlation between the invalidation remedy and the violation if the violations which have occurred cannot reasonably be viewed as having affected the actual result of an election." *Id.* at 1125.

2.   The power exercised in *Bell* is quite rare. To get a sense of how reluctant courts are to order such a drastic remedy, consider the facts in *Hamer v. Ely*, 410 F.2d 152 (5th Cir. 1969). The case involved an election in Sunflower, Mississippi, for mayor and city council. The election was the first in which the majority-black town's black population was able to cast ballots. (Their ability to vote was the product of the Voting Rights Act of 1965 and a prior federal court order.) The election was a cause celebre, in part because of the presence of Fannie Lou Hamer, one of the key heroes of the Civil Rights Movement.

Every one of the black candidates lost. In a lawsuit asking the district court to set aside the election, the plaintiffs alleged that the local Election Commission refused to appoint any black election workers to help illiterate black voters cast their ballots. Instead, the Commission appointed, among other people, election officials who were employers or creditors of black voters. The plaintiffs argued that many illiterate black voters therefore cast their ballots without aid, rather than disclose how they voted. They pointed to the fact that a majority of the ballots rejected for irregularities contained votes only for black candidates and very few contained votes only for white candidates. Nonetheless, the district judge found it "significant that not one witness was offered, not one witness testified that he or she was illiterate and needed assistance in casting his ballot, but refused to ask for assistance because he did not want a white person to know how his vote was cast." The court of appeals agreed that the election was fundamentally fair:

> Of course, it would be naive to doubt that there must have been some Negroes who were unwilling to ask for aid because of a reluctance to disclose or fear of disclosing how they intended to vote. But this election was held in a fishbowl. The report of the federal observers is in the record. Commenting on the report the district judge said:

> "It speaks clearly and demonstrates that this election was fairly and properly held in every respect, and it is not questioned but that every person who was given assistance was assisted fairly and impartially with the ballot in each instance being marked in exact accord with the voter's wishes."

As for the way in which the local election commission provided assistance, the court of appeals stated:

> The [Voting Rights] Act requires that voters be apprised of their right to assistance, not that they be induced to accept it. In the Sunflower election, voters were apprised of their right and each was informed that he could request a federal observer to be with him in the voting booth to check the quality of assistance rendered by the election official.

> On the cold record before us, the attitude of Sunflower's Election Commissioners may have been shoddy, but it does not justify the "drastic, if not staggering" procedure, *Bell v. Southwell*, of a federal court's voiding a state election. Such "drastic" measures are properly reserved for cases involving serious violations of voting rights.

3. Most of the cases setting aside elections involve claims of racial discrimination. To what extent is the willingness of courts to intervene under these circumstances a product of their sense that race discrimination, as opposed to other explanations for why a particular election went wrong, is an ongoing problem that can be stopped only through drastic measures? For an example of a case not involving claims of racial discrimination in which an election was set aside on purely state-law grounds, consider *Akizaki v. Fong*, 51 Haw. 354 (1969). The case involved an election to the Hawaii state legislature. In the final tabulation of the votes for the sixth and final seat from a multimember district, the Republican candidate, Fong, received two more votes than the Democratic candidate, Akizaki. Akizaki contested the election proved before the trial court that at least nineteen absentee ballots were invalid because of late postmarks. Due to a mistake by election officials, these ballots were nevertheless opened and counted. Worse, they were "commingled" with validly cast absentee ballots and it could not later be determined for whom the invalid ballots had been cast. The trial court's solution was to discard 174 absentee ballots, among which were the 19 invalid ones. Once these 174 votes were thrown out, Akizaki had more votes than Fong, and the trial court declared him the winner.

The Hawaii Supreme Court reversed:

The fundamental interest to be protected here is that of the people of the Fifteenth Representative District in choosing whomever they please to represent them in the House of Representatives. The right to vote is perhaps the most basic and fundamental of all the rights guaranteed by our democratic form of government. Implicit in that right is the right to have one's vote count and the right to have as nearly perfect an election proceeding as can be provided. The result we reach must be consistent with these principles.

* * * *

It remains to be decided whether the result reached by the court below was correct. We hold that it was not, and that a new election should have been ordered. Because of the commingling of the valid and invalid absentee ballots, there is simply no way to determine what the actual result of the election was, and who should therefore be declared the winner. In such a situation, HRS § 12-103 directs the court to invalidate the election.[4]

The trial court's approach was plausible; but to excise the entire absentee vote contained in the 174 ballots excluded by the court, in order to eliminate the nineteen ballots known to be invalid, inflicts too harsh a result on those absentee voters whose votes were validly cast.

Pursuant to HRS § 12-105, this court may, in election contest cases, enter any judgment the circuit court would have been authorized to enter. Our judgment is, as provided in HRS § 12-103, that the election was invalid for the reason that a correct result cannot be ascertained because of the mistake we have noted on the part of the election officials in opening the late-postmarked envelopes and commingling those ballots with ballots validly cast. Therefore, in accordance with HRS § 12-103, and in order to protect the right of the people of the Fifteenth Representative District to choose their representatives, we invalidate the election as between Fong and Akizaki. As set out in HRS § 12-103, a certified copy of our judgment shall be filed with the governor, so that he may call a new election as between Fong and Akizaki as provided by the statute.

---

4. HRS § 12-103 provides, in part: ... The judgment may invalidate the election on the grounds that a correct result cannot be ascertained because of a mistake or fraud on the part of the election inspectors; .... If the judgment should be that the election was invalid, a certified copy thereof shall be filed with the governor, and he shall duly call a new election to be held within sixty days after the judgment is filed. ...

Many states have similar statutes requiring new elections when the result of an initial election cannot be determined. *See, e.g.*, N.Y. Elect. Law § 16-102 (1999) ("The court may direct . . . the holding of a new primary election . . . where it finds there has been such fraud or irregularity as to render impossible a determination as to who rightfully was nominated or elected.").

B. ENJOINING AN UPCOMING ELECTION

As the previous section suggested, courts will often refuse to set aside an election if the injured parties could have prevented the violation of their rights by seeking relief before the election. Sometimes pre-election relief will involve simply a declaratory judgment about a particular election practice or an injunction forbidding or requiring a particular action. For example, voters might decide to challenge an unconstitutional apportionment and seek an injunction forbidding the state from conducting an election under the challenged scheme.

Since the plaintiffs in such a lawsuit are seeking equitable relief, doctrines such as laches come into play. Every use of an unconstitutional or illegal election practice involves a new violation of voters' or candidates' rights -- in other words, there isn't a statute of limitations that immunizes a practice from challenge. (There almost always is, however, a statute of limitations with regard to challenging the *outcome* of a particular election. For example, in Florida, a challenge to the results of an election must be filed within a relatively few days after the election results are certified. *See* Fla. Stat. § 102.168(2).) But although a plaintiff can challenge an election law or regulation at any time, a court might refuse to afford immediate relief to a plaintiff who waits until the very eve of an election before bringing suit over a practice that she either knew or should have known would be in effect.

Even when plaintiffs do file their lawsuit in a timely manner, however, equitable considerations may play a substantial role in a court's decision whether to stop an upcoming election.

Chisom v. Roemer

853 F.2d 1186 (5th Cir. 1988)

■ HENRY POLITZ, Circuit Judge.

On August 3, 1988, following an expedited appeal, we vacated the preliminary injunction issued by the district court which had enjoined the election of a justice of the Louisiana Supreme Court from the First Supreme Court District, and ordered that "said election shall be conducted in accordance with the laws of the State of Louisiana at the times and in the manner specified therein." Consistent with a reservation then made, we now assign our reasons for that decision.

Background

On September 19, 1986 complainants, black registered voters in Orleans Parish, Louisiana, and an organization active in voting-rights issues, filed the instant suit, alleging that the present system of electing two justices to the Louisiana Supreme Court from the First Supreme Court District violates section 2 of the Voting Rights Act of 1965 as amended. Their complaint was met with a motion to dismiss under Rule 12(b)(6) of the Federal Rules of Civil Procedure, which the court granted, essentially based on the conclusion that section 2 did not apply to judicial elections. On appeal we reversed and remanded.

After an application for panel rehearing and for a rehearing en banc was declined, the case was returned to the district court. Thereafter, complainants applied for a preliminary injunction to prevent the election scheduled for October 1, 1988 of a justice from the First Supreme Court District, a position held by Justice Pascal F. Calogero, Jr. since 1972. Based on the evidence presented the district judge concluded that the election should be enjoined. Defendants appealed . . . .

* * * *

The trial court concluded that complainants had satisfied the tetrad test for issuance of a preliminary injunction which was synthesized, although not originated, in the oft-cited case of *Canal Authority of State of Florida v. Callaway,* 489 F.2d 567, 572 (5th Cir.1974), by showing:

(1) a substantial likelihood that plaintiff will prevail on the merits;

(2) a substantial threat that plaintiff will suffer irreparable injury if the injunction is not granted;

(3) that the threatened injury to plaintiff outweighs the threatened harm the injunction may do to defendant; and

(4) that granting the preliminary injunction will not disserve the public interest.

Analysis

Inasmuch as our decision is powered by a consideration of the essence and ramifications of the third and fourth factors, we pretermit a discussion of the first two, except for these limited comments. It remains to be seen whether the complainants will prevail on the merits, indeed the Supreme Court has yet to speak on the critical issue whether section 2 of the Voting Rights Act applies to judicial elections. And we can only speculate as to the state of the record in this case after trial on the merits.

As to irreparable injury, complainants urge a black-letter, per se rule to the effect that if an electoral standard, practice, or procedure abridges section 2 of the Voting Rights Act it automatically does irreparable injury to all or a portion of the body politic. Some district courts would agree. See *Dillard v. Crenshaw County*, 640 F. Supp. 1347 (M.D.Ala.1986); *Harris v. Graddick*, 593 F. Supp. 128 (M.D.Ala.1984); *Cook v. Luckett*, 575 F. Supp. 479 (S.D. Miss.1983). We do not. We are not prepared to adopt a per se rule in such a vital area of state-federal relations. We recognize and are in full accord with the teachings of the Supreme Court in *Reynolds v. Sims*, that "the right to vote freely for the candidate of one's choice is of the essence of a democratic society and any restrictions on that right strike at the heart of representative government. And the right of suffrage can be denied by a debasement or dilution of the weight of a citizen's vote just as effectively as by wholly prohibiting the free exercise." We are cognizant, however, that "'the possibility that . . . other corrective relief will be available at a later date, in the ordinary course of litigation, weighs heavily against a claim of irreparable harm.'" In this we agree with the commentators who suggest that "only when the threatened harm would impair the court's ability to grant an effective remedy is there really a need for preliminary relief." Wright & Miller, Federal Practice and Procedure § 2948 at 431-34 (1973).

Should the election be enjoined?

Assuming per arguendo that there has been a prima facie showing of likelihood of success on the merits, and irreparable injury, our disposition of this appeal turns on a negative response to the question: Does the public interest require that this election be enjoined? Would such an injunction be in the best interests of: all of the citizens of the State of Louisiana; the citizens of the First Supreme Court District; the black citizenry of Louisiana; that of the First Supreme Court District; or the black electorate of Orleans Parish? We are persuaded beyond peradventure that the answer must be a resounding "no" on behalf of all of these groupings of Louisianians.

Our analysis begins with the staunch admonition that a federal court should jealously guard and sparingly use its awesome powers to ignore or brush aside long-standing state constitutional provisions, statutes, and practices. There can be no doubt that under the Supremacy Clause, federal courts do and indeed must have this authority in our unique form of government. It is the use of this power that must be maintained in the balance, a balance which is more delicate than usual when a state's judicial process is involved.

It cannot be gainsaid that federal courts have the power to enjoin state elections. *Watson v. Commissioners Court of Harrison County*, 616 F.2d 105 (5th Cir.1980); *Hamer v. Campbell*, 358 F.2d 215 (5th Cir.), cert. denied, 385 U.S. 851 (1966). But, "intervention by the federal courts in state elections has always been a serious business," *Oden v. Brittain*, 396 U.S. 1210, (1969) (Black, J., opinion in chambers), not to be lightly engaged in. Indeed, even after an adjudication on the merits that a legislative apportionment plan violated the Constitution, the Supreme Court invited the use of a velvet glove over the mailed fist:

> In awarding or withholding immediate relief, a court is entitled to and should consider the proximity of a forthcoming election and the mechanics and complexities of state election laws, and should act and rely upon general equitable principles. With respect to the timing of relief, a court can reasonably endeavor to avoid a disruption of the election process which might result from requiring precipitate changes that could make unreasonable or embarrassing demands on a State in adjusting to the requirements of the court's decree.

Reynolds v. Sims, 377 U.S. at 585. *Sims* has been the guidon to a number of courts that have refrained from enjoining impending elections. In another instance, the Supreme Court stayed a district court's hand after a three-judge court found Indiana's multi-member districting provisions unconstitutional. *Whitcomb v. Chavis*, 396 U.S. 1055 and 396 U.S. 1064 (1970) (granting a stay pending appeal, 305 F. Supp. 1359, 1364 (S.D.Ind.1969)). *See also Maryland Citizens v. Governor of Maryland*, 429 F.2d 606 (4th Cir.1970); *Dillard v. Crenshaw County; Banks v. Bd. of Ed., City of Peoria*, 659 F. Supp. 394 (C.D.Ill.1987); *Knox v. Milwaukee County*, 581 F. Supp. 399 (E.D.Wis.1984).

We consider significant the Supreme Court's action in *Chavis*. In staying the reapportionment plan ordered by a three-judge court, the Supreme Court permitted the conduct of an election under the old scheme which had been found constitutionally infirm. In dissenting from the refusal to vacate their stay order, Justice Douglas pointedly stated: "The State contends that without a stay it will be forced to conduct the forthcoming election under the reapportionment plan of the District Court. By granting the stay, however, this Court has equally forced the appellees to go through the election under the present scheme which was held unconstitutional by the District Court." Nonetheless the court permitted the election to proceed.

The case at bar

Against this backdrop we consider the realities of the case at bar. The district court concluded that the issuance of an injunction would either be neutral, in ultimate result, or preferable to not enjoining the election. We do not find the court's reasoning persuasive. To the extent this is a factual finding by the trial court, we view it as clearly erroneous; to the extent it is a conclusion of law, we view it as erroneous.

Preventing this judicial election at this late stage is not a passive or neutral act. It is the proverbial gossamer-thin veil which is fraught with difficulties. The consequences to Louisiana's judicial system are as significant as they are uncertain. Indeed, the very uncertainties introduced account in large measure for the significance of the impact.

The core value of the law and its implementing judicial system is stability— the ability reasonably to anticipate the results of actions and proceedings, by individuals and by legal institutions. Staying the election for a justice of the First Supreme Court District casts a cloud over the Louisiana Supreme Court, as staying any judicial election would cast a cloud over the affected court. The Louisiana Constitution provides that the terms of the justices of its supreme court are ten years. The term of Justice Calogero expires on December 31, 1988. If the regularly scheduled election did not go forward, would Louisiana have seven justices on its highest court on January 1, 1989? If the election is enjoined and Justice Calogero continues to serve, will there be any question about the validity of his actions as a justice?

The Louisiana Constitution prescribes that four justices must concur to render judgment. Decisions in both civil and criminal cases decided on a 4-3 basis are not a rarity. The sparse offerings by the state in defense of the application for the preliminary injunction include the affidavit of the Director of the Louisiana Supreme Court's Central Staff of attorneys. He advises that since 1976 the Louisiana Supreme Court has reviewed 82 death penalty appeals. In 30 of those appeals the conviction was reversed or the death sentence was vacated. Twenty percent of those reversals were decided on a 4-3 vote. The record does not contain statistics for 4-3 renditions in civil cases, or in the denial of writs of certiorari or review, which require the agreement of four justices, but the number undoubtedly is very substantial. One need only thumb through a selective sampling of the Southern Reporter Second series for a feel of just how substantial that number is. What is the consequence if Justice Calogero is one of the four? Is an uncertainty introduced?

Does the general statutory provision declaring that public officers hold their offices until their successors are "inducted into office" apply in this instance? Our research reflects no case in which the Louisiana Supreme Court has applied this statute to a justice or judge. Until Louisiana's highest court resolves this question it remains just that, an open question and, as such, it casts a shadow on the functioning of the Louisiana Supreme Court.

Appellees and the trial court refer to the provision of the Louisiana Constitution which addresses the temporary posting of judicial vacancies. Article 5, § 22, provides that until a vacancy in a judicial office is filled "the supreme court shall appoint a person meeting the qualifications for the office . . . to serve at its pleasure. The appointee shall be ineligible as a candidate at the election to fill the vacancy." *Id.* § 22(B). If the election is enjoined, after midnight on December 31, 1988 is the post now held by Justice Calogero to be deemed vacant and subject to an appointment by his former-fellow justices? Because of the involvement of the federal court, and its preventing of the election, would this be a vacancy subject to appointment? If it is deemed such and Justice Calogero accepts an appointment, would he be eligible to seek reelection to the judicial post he has held since 1972 when the federal court did permit an election to proceed? More shadows on the otherwise clear patina of the Louisiana judicial system. Are such warranted? Can they be justified or permitted?

Further, in Article 5, § 6, the Louisiana Constitution establishes that "the judge oldest in point of service on the supreme court shall be chief justice." Justice Calogero currently is second in point of service to the chief justice. If the election is enjoined and his office is deemed vacant, should he not be offered, or should he decline an appointment out of caution for the Article 5, § 22(B) proscription; if he is reelected, would his service have been interrupted so as to cause a forfeiture of his claim to be oldest in point of service?

Finally, what about the litigants during this period? What will be the racial demographics of that group? Will they be affected adversely? Will that effect be significant? Can it be justified?

Appellees suggest that the specter of problems with and for the Louisiana Supreme Court are manageable. The trial court states: "Regardless of the state constitutional provisions, this Court has in any event the power under the Supremacy Clause to fashion both preliminary and final equitable relief that will both provide plaintiffs with a full and adequate remedy and protect other important state interests." Is this a suggestion that the chancellor will appoint a successor to Calogero, perhaps Calogero, and, out of a sense of fair play, decree that all state constitutional questions as to his service are to be taken for naught, that the proscription against his running for the office is nullified, and, further, order that no one may suggest a break in his service for purposes of eligibility for the office of chief justice? Is such necessary? Should the federal court even contemplate that scenario? We are most reluctant to do so.

Were we to countenance such a scenario, other interests would be disserved. As the *Dillard* court recognized, the extension of the terms of incumbents or the court's appointment of replacements, effectively denies "the entire electorate the right to vote and thus seem to offend basic principles..."

How long would this disenfranchisement of all of the voters of the First Supreme Court District continue? As discussed *infra*, this case must run its full course, and, thereafter, assuming violations are found, the Louisiana Legislature must be afforded an opportunity to repair the defects the court discloses. Is the electorate to have no say whatever as to the person to serve during that period? Can that conceivably be considered in the best interests of the citizenry?

In addition to the foregoing caution to the use of injunctive powers before trial on the merits, and indeed even after trial on the merits, we are also keenly mindful of another well-established rubric which must be brought to bear in the resolution of the present conundrum. It is now established beyond challenge that upon finding a particular standard, practice, or procedure to be contrary to either a federal constitutional or statutory requirement, the federal court must grant the appropriate state or local authorities an opportunity to correct the deficiencies. In *Reynolds v. Sims* the Supreme Court commended the district court for refraining from enjoining an impending election until the Alabama Legislature had been given an opportunity to remedy the defects in their legislative apportionment scheme. Further, after trial on the merits, and a declaration that an existing election scheme is unlawful, it is "appropriate, whenever practicable, to afford a reasonable opportunity for the legislature to meet constitutional [or federal statutory] requirements by adopting a substitute measure rather than for the federal court to devise and order into effect its own plan." *Wise v. Lipscomb*, 437 U.S. 535, 540 (1978). The court goes on to cite authorities for the proposition that the legislatures should first be given a chance, and quoting *Reynolds v. Sims*, the *Sanchez* court noted that "judicial relief becomes appropriate only when a legislature fails to reapportion according to federal constitutional requisites in a timely fashion after having had an adequate opportunity to do so." 452 U.S. at 150 n. 30; *Connor v. Finch*, 431 U.S. 407 (1977).

As found by the district court, the Louisiana Legislature has signaled no reluctance to address this matter. When this court held that section 2 applied to judicial elections, remedial legislation was offered and seriously considered in the just-recessed legislative session. This legislature gives every indication of promptly responding to a need for action should it occur.

We understand these precedents to mandate that the responsible state or local authorities must be first given an opportunity to correct any constitutional or statutory defect before the court attempts to draft a remedial plan. In the case at bar, that means that should the court rule on the merits that a statutory or constitutional violation exists the Louisiana Legislature should be allowed a reasonable opportunity to address the problem. We have no reason whatsoever to doubt that the governor and legislature will respond promptly . . . .

In the interim, we are convinced that the system in place for the election of the subject judicial officer should be left undisturbed. There are a number of variables and several contingencies. But notwithstanding their final alignment, at the appropriate time, should it become necessary, the federal courts may fashion whatever remedy the law, equity, and justice require.

The preliminary injunction is VACATED and it is ordered that the presently scheduled election for justice of the First Supreme Court District of Louisiana proceed in accordance with the laws of Louisiana.

NOTES AND QUESTIONS

1. The Court of Appeals' decision rests in part on the availability of "other corrective relief . . . at a later date, in the ordinary course of litigation." What does this mean? That if the election system is later held invalid a court can order a special election?

2. A major source of injunctive relief barring elections is section 5 of the Voting Rights Act of 1965, 42 U.S.C. § 1973c. Section 5 prohibits certain states and political subdivisions that had a history of discrimination and depressed political participation from making any changes with respect to their election systems unless they receive "preclearance," that is, prior approval from the U.S. Department of Justice or a federal district court in Washington, D.C.

In *Clark v. Roemer*, 500 U.S. 646 (1991), another case involving judicial elections in Louisiana, the Supreme Court described the principles that govern injunctions in section 5 cases:

Section 5 requires States to obtain either judicial or administrative preclearance before implementing a voting change. A voting change in a covered jurisdiction "will not be effective as law until and unless cleared" pursuant to one of these two methods. Failure to obtain either judicial or administrative preclearance "renders the change unenforceable." If voting changes subject to § 5 have not been precleared, § 5 plaintiffs are entitled to an injunction prohibiting the State from implementing the changes.

The District Court ignored these principles altogether. It presented a number of reasons for not enjoining the election, none of which we find persuasive. The court cited the short time between election day and the most recent request for injunction, the fact that qualifying and absentee voting had begun, and the time and expense of the candidates. But the parties, the District Court, and the candidates had been on notice of the alleged § 5 violations since appellants filed their July 1987 amended complaint. When Louisiana asked the Attorney General for reconsideration of its original preclearance decision in June 1990, it became apparent that the State intended to hold elections for the unprecleared seats in the fall of the same year. Less than a month later, and more than two months before the scheduled October 6, 1990, election, appellants filed a motion to enjoin elections for the unprecleared seats. Appellants displayed no lack of diligence in challenging elections for the unprecleared seats, and every participant in the process knew for over three years that the challenged seats were unprecleared, in violation of § 5. . . .

Nor did the District Court's vague concerns about voter confusion and low voter turnout in a special election for the unprecleared seats justify its refusal to enjoin the illegal elections. Voters may be more confused and inclined to avoid the polls when an election is held in conceded violation of federal law. Finally, the District Court's stated purpose to avoid possible challenges to criminal and civil judgments does not justify allowing the invalid elections to take place. To the contrary, this concern counsels in favor of enjoining the illegal elections, thus averting a federal challenge to state judgments.

The three-judge District Court, maintained that its decision to give provisional effect to elections conducted in violation of § 5 "closely paralleled" a number of our decisions, including *Perkins v. Matthews*, 400 U.S. 379 (1971), *NAACP v. Hampton County Election Comm'n*, 470 U.S. 166 (1985), *Berry v. Doles*, 438 U.S. 190 (1978), and *Georgia v. United States*, 411 U.S. 526 (1973). The cases are inapposite. *Perkins* stated that "in certain circumstances . . . it might be appropriate to enter an order affording local officials an opportunity to seek federal approval and ordering a new election only if local officials fail to do so or if the required federal approval is not forthcoming." 400 U.S. at 396-397. But in Perkins, as in *Hampton County, Berry*, and *Georgia*, the elections in question had been held already; the only issue was whether to remove the elected individuals pending preclearance. Here the District Court did not face the ex

post question whether to set aside illegal elections; rather, it faced
the ex ante question whether to allow illegal elections to be held at
all. On these premises, §5's prohibition against implementation of
unprecleared changes required the District Court to enjoin the
election. This is especially true because, unlike the circumstance in
Perkins, Hampton County, Berry, or *Georgia*, the Attorney General
interposed objections before the election.

We need not decide today whether there are cases in which a district
court may deny a § 5 plaintiff's motion for injunction and allow an
election for an unprecleared seat to go forward. An extreme
circumstance might be present if a seat's unprecleared status is not
drawn to the attention of the State until the eve of the election and
there are equitable principles that justify allowing the election to
proceed. No such exigency exists here. The State of Louisiana failed
to preclear these judgeships as required by § 5. It received official
notice of the defect in July 1987, and yet three years later it had still
failed to file for judicial preclearance, the "basic mechanism" for
preclearance, It scheduled elections for the unprecleared seats in the
fall of 1990 even after the Attorney General had interposed objections
under § 5. 5. In short, by the fall 1990 election, Louisiana had with
consistency ignored the mandate of § 5. The District Court should
have enjoined the elections.

An injunction in a § 5 case may prevent elections from occurring for a very long
time: in *Beer v. United States*, a case involving the New Orleans City Council,
elections were enjoined for over five years; elections were enjoined in
Richmond, Virginia during the pendency of *City of Richmond v. United States*,
for a similar period of time.

3.   In the context of section 5, Florida raises some interesting questions. Five
counties within the state are covered jurisdictions, which cannot make any
change respecting elections without first establishing that the proposed change
will have neither a discriminatory purpose nor a discriminatory effect. On the
other hand, the state as a whole is *not* a covered jurisdiction. Suppose the
Florida Legislature had decided to appoint its own slate of electors in light of
the uncertainty raised by the pending litigation. Would the decision to abolish,
at least for the 2000 election, determination of the electors by popular vote
have required preclearance? Cf. *Lopez v. Monterey County*, 525 U.S. 255
(1999) (discussing how the preclearance regime applies to partially covered
states).

C. ADJUSTING THE VOTE TOTALS

One issue that frequently arises in challenges to the outcomes of a
particular election— as opposed to challenges to the larger structural rules
within which elections take place— involves the question whether particular

ballots that were counted ought to have been excluded or particular ballots that were not counted ought to have been included. Often, as in the Florida presidential election of 2000, litigation follows some kind of administrative proceeding in which disappointed voters or candidates seek recounts and adjustments of the original totals.

States differ quite dramatically in their standards for deciding what counts as a legal ballot. At one end, Florida's courts have taken a relatively liberal view: in *Palm Beach County Canvassing Board v. Harris*, 772 So.2d 1243 (Fla. 2000), the Court relied on Fla. Election Code § 101.5614(5), which provides that "no vote shall be declared invalid or void if there is a clear indication of the intent of the voter as determined by the canvassing board" to hold that as long as a canvassing board could determine a voter's intent in a manual recount, the vote should not be discarded even if it had not been picked up during the machine tabulation because, for example, the voter had not completely dislodged the chad the way he had been instructed to do. On the other, some states have quite specific standards for what counts as a legal vote, and may end up invalidating particular ballots for quite technical reasons. For example, in jurisdictions using paper ballots, the Illinois Election Code expressly required that voters mark their paper ballots by making a cross (x) in the space next to the candidate of their choice. Ill. Election Code, ch. 10, § 17-11. Applying this hard-and-fast rule, Illinois courts held that votes would not be counted "unless two lines intersect in a cross in the appropriate place on the ballot, even if the voter's intent is clear." *Pullen v. Mulligan*, 561 N.E.2d 585, 609 (Ill.Sup. Ct. 1990). Thus, in one case, the court refused to count ballots which the voter had marked with a check, rather than a cross, or ballots on which the voter had written the word "yes," rather than marking the box with an "x". *Scribner v. Sachs*, 164 N.E.2d 481 (Ill. Sup. Ct. 1960). In other cases, lines that did not actually cross within the box were held not to constitute a legal vote, *Green v. Bjorseth*, 350 N.E.. 469, 481 (Ill. Sup. Ct. 1932), as were circles made within the circle next to a candidate's name. *Iseburg v. Martin*, 127 N.E. 663 (Ill. Sup. Ct. 1920).

In general, cases involving judicial orders to count additional ballots do not raise particularly complex legal issues. The exceptions – like the recent controversy in Florida – revolve, not around whether a particular ballot should have been included, but rather around whether recounts should be conducted at all and, if they should, what the standard ought to be.

Delahunt v. Johnston, 423 Mass. 731 (1996), is a fairly typical example of an additive case. The case involved the 1996 Democratic primary in the Tenth Congressional District. After the initial tabulation of the votes, Johnston was declared the winner with 266 more votes than Delahunt. After recounts pursuant to petitions in several municipalities, Johnston was again declared the winner, this time with 175 more votes than Delahunt.

Delahunt then filed a judicial challenge. The trial court reviewed 956 contested ballots, and counted as votes for either Delahunt or Johnston many ballots that had previously been recorded as blank. These ballots were cast on punch cards designed to be counted by computer. As in Florida, many of the ballots involved incompletely removed chads. Reflecting the newly identified votes, the judge concluded that Delahunt was the winner.

The question presented on appeal was:

> [W]hether a discernible indentation made on or near a chad should
> be recorded as a vote for the person to whom the chad is assigned.
> The trial judge concluded that a vote should be recorded for a
> candidate if the chad was not removed but an impression was made
> on or near it. We agree with this conclusion.

> We apply the standard that has been expressed in our cases
> concerning the counting of punch card (and other) ballots. "The
> cardinal rule for guidance of election officers and courts in cases of
> this nature is that if the intent of the voter can be determined with
> reasonable certainty from an inspection of the ballot, in the light of
> the generally known conditions attendant upon the election, effect
> must be given to that intent and the vote counted in accordance
> therewith, provided the voter has substantially complied with the
> requisites of the election law; if that intent cannot thus be fairly and
> satisfactorily ascertained, the ballot cannot rightly be counted."

Interestingly, the Supreme Judicial Court took the position that review of a
voter's intent is a question of law to be decided de novo and thus it reviewed
each of the disputed ballots itself.

On the merits, the Supreme Judicial Court found Johnston's contention
that many voters started to express a preference in the congressional contest,
pressed the card, but pulled the stylus back because they really did not want
to express a choice on that contest to be unpersuasive:

> The large number of ballots with discernible impressions makes such
> an inference unwarranted, especially in a hotly contested election . .
> . .

> Once one accepts, as we have, the presence of a discernible
> impression made by a stylus as a clear indication of a voter's intent,
> our task is to assess each of the 956 ballots. We have done so and
> have agreed with the trial judge's conclusions on all but twenty-eight
> ballots. Our totals concerning the contested ballots show that
> Delahunt gained 659 votes, Johnston gained 283 votes, and fourteen
> ballots were blank. This resulted in a net gain of 376 votes for
> Delahunt which more than offset Johnston's 175 vote lead before the
> contested ballots were counted.

The Court added a footnote explaining the disparity in recount results: "On
balance, we are slightly more willing to find an intention expressed on ballots
where the trial judge ruled there was none. The net effect of our willingness on
twenty-three additional ballots to identify voters' intentions (and of our other
disagreements with the judge [five ballots]) was insignificant. In the final
calculations, Delahunt gained twelve new votes, and Johnston gained ten."

For an example of how searching appellate judicial review can be, consider *Escalante v. City of Hermosa Beach,* 195 Cal. App. 3d 1009 (Cal. Ct. App. 1987). The case involved a ballot proposition in Hermosa Beach. The initial canvass produced a result of 2,397 voters having voted "yes," and 2,398 having voted "no." After a recount, the tally was adjusted to 2,398 "yes" votes and 2,400 "no" votes.

At that point, a voter who supported the ballot measure filed an election contest in state court. He claimed that illegal votes had been cast and that the city clerk and the recount board, in conducting the recount, made errors sufficient to change the result of the election. Voters who opposed the ballot measure filed a cross-statement on the same grounds, claiming the inititative was in fact defeated by a larger majority than that found on recount.

At trial, the Superior Court made eight sets of determinations about contested ballots: (1) the city clerk erroneously failed to count two "yes" votes of absentee voters who marked their punch card ballots with a pen on the chad designated "yes," rather than punching out the chad as directed; (2) the clerk properly counted as a "no" vote a ballot punched "no" with transparent adhesive tape on the reverse side holding the "yes" chad in place; (3) five ballots punched "no" that also had other chads punched out were properly counted as "no" votes; (4) one ballot punched "yes" with an additional chad punched so that it remained attached to the ballot by only one of its four arms was also properly counted; (5) two ballots with neither the "yes" or "no" chads punched out, but with nearby chads punched, were properly not counted; (6) the clerk erred in counting one voter's absentee ballot; and (7) the clerk properly counted the ballot of Anthony C. De Bellis, Jr., who had moved shortly before election day but who voted in his former precinct; and (8) the clerk acted within her discretion in refusing to count the absentee ballot of Jane R. Woods. After making these determinations, the result was 2,400 votes in favor of the ballot measure, and 2,399 against the measure, which then carried.

On appeal, the District Court of Appeal reviewed each of the Superior Court's determinations and upheld all of them except one: it held that DeBellis— ironically a member of the Hermosa Beach City Council— was not entitled to vote in the election because he had not properly complied with the provisions governing reregistration by voters who moved within a city. Since DeBellis had apparently testified at trial that he had voted in favor of the ballot measure, the Court of Appeal's rejection of the De Bellis "Yes" vote produced a tie: 2,399 votes for, and 2,399 votes against, the ballot measure. Since the contestant had failed to establish precinct board errors, or illegal votes, "sufficient to change the election result," Cal. Elect. Code §§ 20021(e), 20024, the election results were confirmed.

Notice, then, that there are two potential mechanisms for ensuring the kind of equal treatment of ballots that the Supreme Court's decision in *Bush v. Gore* suggested is required by the Fourteenth Amendment. Uniformity can be achieved through detailed substantive rules about what counts or does not count as a valid vote. But it can also be pursued "procedurally," rather than substantively, through protest, contest, and appeals processes, which ultimately place disputed ballots before a single arbiter:

The procedural solution creates uniformity not through the application of rigid rules but by channeling disputes into an arena where those disputes could be resolved consistently. That, in effect, is how the systems of *most* states' systems operate today: they do not have rigid rules, but rather employ procedural solutions for dealing with disagreements over what counts as a valid vote. That was one of the key premises of the dissenting opinions that Justices Souter and Breyer delivered: they thought that the Florida *courts* were the appropriate mechanism for making sure ballots were treated uniformly. And that solution generally works, unless time is too short to permit orderly procedures — a source of sharp disagreement within both the Florida and U.S. Supreme Courts — or unless one is so skeptical of judicial integrity that one thinks state judges will count a checkmark if it is next to Candidate X's name but not if it is next to Candidate Y's.

Pamela S. Karlan, *Equal Protection: Bush v. Gore and the Making of a Precedent* in The Unfinished Election of 2000 (Jack N. Rakove ed. 2001).

More often, election contests involve not the attempt to have votes counted that were initially omitted, but rather a request to have ballots thrown out that were originally included.

In re the Matter of the Protest of Election Returns
707 So.2d 1170 (Fla. Ct. App. 1998)

■ PER CURIAM:

This appeal involves an election contest which occurred during the November 4, 1997, Miami Mayoral election. After considering the evidence, the lower tribunal issued a Final Judgment which found that the evidence demonstrated an extensive "pattern of fraudulent, intentional and criminal conduct that resulted in such an extensive abuse of the absentee ballot laws that it can fairly be said that the intent of these laws was totally frustrated." The lower court ordered that the appropriate remedy was to declare the entire Mayoral election void and order that a new election be held within sixty (60) days. While we find that substantial competent evidence existed to support the trial court's findings of massive fraud in the absentee ballots, we disagree as to the appropriateness of the trial court's remedy in ordering a new election.

In July, 1996, Joe Carollo became the Mayor of the City of Miami. On November 4, 1997, a general election was held for the position of Executive Mayor, with Joe Carollo and Xavier Suarez as two of the contenders. Carollo received a majority of the precinct votes (51.41%) and Suarez received a majority of the absentee votes (61.48%), resulting in Carollo receiving 49.65% of the votes and Suarez receiving 46.80% of the votes when the absentee ballot votes were combined with the machine precinct votes.

Since neither of the parties received a majority of the overall votes, a run-off election was held on November 13, 1997. In that election, Suarez defeated

Carollo in both precinct votes and the absentee votes. On November 14, 1997, the results of the November 13, 1997, election were certified and Suarez assumed the position of Mayor of the City of Miami. On the same day, Carollo filed a protest to the run-off election pursuant to Section 102.166, Florida Statutes (1997), as well as the November 4th and November 13th election results, under Section 102.168, Florida Statutes (1997). The filings were consolidated. The principal relief sought by Carollo was to be declared the victor of the Mayoral election, having received a majority of the "untainted" precinct votes or, in the alternative, for a new election.

A bench trial was held and, on March 3, 1998, the trial court declared the Mayoral election void. This judgment was based on the trial court's finding of massive absentee voter fraud which affected the electoral process.

The uncontradicted statistical evidence presented by Kevin Hill, Ph.D., a political scientist and expert in research methodology and statistical analysis, indicated that the amount of fraud involved in the absentee ballots was of such consequence so as to have affected the outcome of the election. Dr. Hill analyzed the absentee ballot voting, finding that the absentee ballots cast in Commission District 3 could not be explained by any normal statistical measurement. District 3 is the area which the trial court found "was the center of a massive, well conceived and well orchestrated absentee ballot voter fraud scheme." Dr. Hill referred to the results of the absentee ballots as an "outlier" and an "aberrant case" so unlikely that it was "literally off the charts" of probability tables. The odds of this occurring by chance were 5,000 to 1.

Dr. Hill finally concluded it was "reasonable" that the absentee ballot deviation in favor of Suarez resulted only from voting fraud, ruling "out almost every other conceivable possibility to a high degree of probability."[2]

An expert documents examiner, Linda Hart, concluded that 225 illegal absentee ballots were cast, in contravention of statutory requirements. An FBI agent with 26 years of experience, Hugh Cochran, identified 113 confirmed false voter addresses. There was evidence of 14 stolen ballots, and of 140 ballots that were falsely witnessed. In addition, evidence was presented that more than 480 ballots were procured or witnessed by the 29 so-called "ballot brokers" who invoked their privilege against self-incrimination instead of testifying at trial.

The trial court specifically found that the above described absentee ballot voter fraud scheme, "literally and figuratively, stole the ballot from the hands of every honest voter in the City of Miami". The trial court further found that, as a result thereof, "the integrity of the election was adversely affected." Based on our review of the record, there was certainly ample evidence of fraud to support the findings of the trial court's Final Judgment.

---

2. Dr. Hill estimated that the "aberrant" absentee ballots in Commission District 3 cost Mr. Carollo more than the 160 votes that he needed in order to secure outright victory in the November 4, 1997, election.

We are confronted with the question of whether the trial court erred in finding that the remedy for the instant absentee voting fraud was to order a new election. We hold that it did.

An important decision concerning the issue of the appropriate remedy to be provided upon a finding that absentee ballot fraud has affected the electoral process is *Bolden v. Potter*, 452 So. 2d 564 (Fla. 1984). In that case, the Supreme Court of Florida held that: "Although the will of the electorate must be protected, so must the sanctity of the ballot and the integrity of the election. Courts cannot ignore fraudulent conduct which is purposefully done to foul the election or corrupt the ballot." The Supreme Court of Florida went on to expressly approve the trial court's remedy, which was to invalidate all of the absentee ballots and, thereafter, to solely rely on the machine vote to determine the outcome of the election. Similarly, in *Boardman v. Esteva*, 323 So. 2d 259 (Fla. 1975), *app. dism.*, 425 U.S. 967 (1976), the Supreme Court of Florida held that "The general rule is that where the number of invalid absentee ballots is more than enough to change the result of an election, then the election shall be determined solely upon the basis of machine vote."

We are mindful of the fact that the trial court found there was no evidence that Mr. Suarez knew of, or in any way participated in, the absentee voter fraud. However, as the Supreme Court stated in *Bolden v. Potter*:

> We also reject the district court's implication that the burden of proof, with regard to fraud or corruption, is dependent upon the status of the offender. It makes no difference whether the fraud is committed by candidates, election officials, or third parties. The evil to be avoided is the same, irrespective of the source. As long as the fraud, from whatever source, is such that the true result of the election cannot be ascertained with reasonable certainty, the ballots affected should be invalidated.

. . . . Mr. Suarez contends that to eliminate all of the absentee ballots would effectively disenfranchise those absentee voters who legally voted. We first note that unlike the right to vote, which is assured every citizen by the United States Constitution, the ability to vote by absentee ballot is a privilege. In fact, the Florida Legislature created this privilege by enacting statutory provisions separate from those applicable to voting at the polls....

Consistent with the fact that there is no legal precedent in Florida to support the action of the trial court in ordering a new election as the proper remedy upon a finding of massive absentee voter fraud is the public policy of the State of Florida to not encourage such fraud. Rather, it must be remembered that the sanctity of free and honest elections is the cornerstone of a true democracy. As the Supervisor of Elections, David Leahy, noted during his trial testimony, were we to approve a new election as the proper remedy following extensive absentee voting fraud, we would be sending out the message that the worst that would happen in the face of voter fraud would be another election . . . .

Further, we refuse to disenfranchise the more than 40,000 voters who, on

November 4, 1997, exercised their constitutionally guaranteed right to vote in the polling places of Miami. In the absence of any findings of impropriety relating to the machine vote in this election, public policy dictates that we not void those constitutionally protected votes, the majority of which were cast for Mr. Carollo. In addition, a candidate who wins an election by virtue of obtaining a majority of the votes cast is entitled to take office as a result thereof, and not be forced into a second election, whether it is a statutorily mandated run-off election or a court ordered special election, when the said second election only comes about due to absentee ballot fraud, in the first election, that favored one of his or her opponents . . . .

To the extent that the trial court's remedy, to correct the massive absentee ballot fraud that occurred in the November 4, 1997, election involved the holding of a completely new election which, in effect, invalidated all of the machine votes that were cast by the voters in person at the polls, we find that such a remedy is not warranted by Florida legal precedent. As a result, the voiding of the entire election and the ordering of a new election is hereby reversed, and this cause is remanded to the trial court with directions to enter a Final Judgment, forthwith, that voids and vacates the absentee ballots only and, furthermore, provides that the outcome of the November 4, 1997, City of Miami Mayoral election shall be determined solely upon the machine ballots cast at the polls, resulting in the election of Joe Carollo as Mayor of the City of Miami. Consequently, the trial court's Final Judgment shall delete the requirement of the holding of a new election since, by virtue of the foregoing, there is no need for such an election . . . .

NOTES AND QUESTIONS

1. Following the District Court of Appeals' decision, a group of voters who had cast legal absentee votes in the Miami mayoral election brought suit in federal court, claiming that their right to vote had been unconstitutionally denied. In *Scheer v. City of Miami*, 15 F. Supp. 2d 1338 (S.D. Fla. 1998), the district court rejected their challenge. As a preliminary matter, the district court held that the plaintiffs had standing. The defendants had argued that the plaintiffs lacked standing because even if their votes for Suarez had been counted, Carollo would still have won the election. But Chief Judge Davis found that the state courts had not identified "exactly" how many absentee ballots had been cast illegally:

> If they could, the remedy would have been obvious - invalidate the fraudulent votes and count the lawful ones. However, isolating the number of fraudulent votes is and was impossible. Therefore, it is also impossible to know for sure if Carollo would have won the election even counting the class in this case. Accordingly, Plaintiffs have standing because they have an identifiable harm— their votes were invalidated even though they were lawfully cast.

Leaving aside the remedial question, however, is the question of electoral outcome irrelevant to the issue of standing? That is, suppose a state electoral process threw out even a single legally cast ballot. Given the nature of the right to vote, wouldn't that voter have suffered an injury in fact sufficient to confer standing? Suppose, as we discuss later in this section, a voter sued for damages. It seems unlikely he would be required to prove as an element in his case that his vote would have changed the outcome.

On another preliminary question, Chief Judge Davis rejected the Florida court's right/privilege distinction. Regardless of whether Florida's conferral of the ability to vote by absentee ballot was a pure act of legislative grace, once the state had conferred that ability in a particular election, it could not change the rules after a ballot was cast.

On the merits, Chief Judge Davis refused to find that the state courts had violated a federal constitutional right in their decision to disregard all absentee ballots rather than requiring a special election:

> Our predecessor court in *Gamza v. Aguirre*, 619 F.2d 449, 453 (5th Cir. 1980), recognized a distinction between state laws and patterns of state action that systematically deny equality in voting, and episodic events that, despite non-discriminatory laws, may result in the dilution of an individual's vote. Unlike systematically discriminatory laws, isolated events that adversely affect individuals are not presumed to be a [constitutional violation]. . . .

The Ninth Circuit, in refusing to meddle with a state election, summarized the law in all of these election cases:

> A general pattern emerges from all of these cases taken together. Mere fraud or mistake will not render an election invalid. However, a court will strike down an election . . . if two elements are present: (1) likely reliance by voters on an established election procedure and/or official pronouncements about what the procedure will be in the coming election; and (2) significant disenfranchisement that results from a change in the election procedures.

> This case is about mere fraud - nothing more. It has nothing to do with reliance on an established procedure or a change in the election procedures. If anything, the voters must be presumed to have known of Florida's procedure of voiding all absentee votes if there was evidence of fraud. . . .

> Florida courts have established and followed this policy for good reason. The absentee voting scheme as it now exists in Florida lends itself to fraud, manipulation, and deceit. The state legislature continues to attempt improvements, but to date criminals have found ways to abuse the system. Accordingly, Florida courts for the past sixty years have constructed a means of dealing with absentee voter fraud. It is not this Court's province to upset this remedy as it has been well thought out by the state courts. For example, as the state appellate court in this case noted, "were we to approve a new election as the proper remedy following extensive absentee voting fraud, we would be sending out the message that the worst that would happen

in the face of voter fraud would be another election."

Even if Plaintiffs were able to set forth a constitutional violation, the Court must take into account equitable considerations in fashioning the appropriate remedy in each case. . . . A federal court reaching into the state political process to invalidate an election necessarily implicates important concerns of federalism and state sovereignty. It should not resort to this intrusive remedy until it has carefully weighed all equitable considerations." *Gjersten v. Board of Election Comm'rs,* 791 F.2d 472, 478 (7th Cir. 1986). . . .

The almost circus atmosphere surrounding this case makes the remedy Plaintiffs seek even more drastic and staggering. . . . The City of Miami has been scarred by the events that took place during and after the 1997 Mayoral election. The City and its citizens are finally starting to heal. Equity necessitates that the Court not re-open these wounds. . . .

Note the way in which Chief Judge Davis's treatment of the plaintiffs' claims mirrors the United States Supreme Court's treatment of claims of the denial of procedural due process in *Parratt v. Taylor*, 451 U.S. 527 (1981) and its progeny. (For a more detailed treatment of these cases, *see, e.g.*, John C. Jeffries, Jr., Pamela S. Karlan, Peter W. Low, & George A. Rutherglen, Civil Rights Actions: Enforcing the Constitution 240-70 (2000).) In these cases, the Court has held that a state's deprivation of a property or liberty interest – and state actors may perpetrate such deprivations quite often – rises to the level of a Fourteenth Amendment violation only when the state fails to provide adequate procedural protections. In cases where the deprivation is unauthorized or unforeseeable, such protection may be provided by a post-deprivation hearing.

2. The role of statistical evidence in election challenges is an interesting, and perhaps underanalyzed question. If a reviewing court or administrative body knows that some number of votes have been cast illegally, but does not know for whom those votes were cast, it turns out that courts' intuitions are often misguided.

In *Mathematical Probability In Election Challenges*, 73 Colum. L. Rev. 241 (1973), Michael O. Finkelstein and Herbert E. Robbins set out a formula: $Z = d* \sqrt{(s-k)}/sk$, where d is the winner's plurality, s is the number of votes cast for the winner or his challenger, and k is the number of invalid votes cast for the winner or his challenger. The value of z — which is a standard normal variate — can be found in virtually any statistics text. *See, e.g.*, Alan Agresti and Barbara Finley, Statistical Methods for the Social Sciences tbl. A (3d ed. 1997) determines the probability that the outcome would be reversed and as z increases, the probability that there would be a reversal declines very quickly. For example, if z is 0.5, the probability of reversal is .81, while if $z=1$, the probability is .16, and if $z=1.5$, the probability is .07. Thus, there is less than a one percent chance of reversal if z is greater than 2.4.

Consider a case like *Ippolito v. Power*, 22 N.Y.2d 594 (1968), which involved a primary election for positions in the state Democratic Party. There were 2,827 votes cast, and the winner's plurality was 17 votes. In order to vote, each voter was required to sign in on an individual voter registration card. The courts found 101 votes that were suspect "for some kind of irregularity without any evidence of fraud or intentional misconduct." Six voter sign-in cards had been submitted by registered Conservatives (who could not have voted in the election); seven cards had not been signed; one card was "irregular" in some undescribed way; nineteen cards were submitted without any indication of party enrollment; and there were 68 more votes than there were sign-in cards to begin with. The New York Court of Appeals affirmed a lower court's decision to order a new election because "it does not strain the probabilities to assume a likelihood that the questioned votes produced or could produce a change in the results." Finkelstein and Robbins point out that the probability of there being a different outcome in a case like *Ippolito* is roughly 5 percent. That is, if we imagine all of the votes as pebbles being placed in an urn, with the winner's pebbles being white and the loser's being red, and we were to draw 101 pebbles out of the urn, there is a five percent chance that the number of red pebbles remaining in the urn would exceed the number of white pebbles.

Had the New York Court of Appeals understood this, would they have found a significantly substantial probability to overturn the election? What does this say about margins of error generally?

Note that Finkelstein and Robbins's model presupposes that the illegally cast votes are not systematically biased towards one candidate. In cases where either eyewitness or statistical evidence suggests that a particular candidate was the disproportionate beneficiary of illegal votes, the likelihood of a changed outcome may be much higher. Obviously, if *all* of the voters who cast illegal ballots in *Ippolito* had supported the winning candidate, the probability that the outcome would have been different in the absence of improper votes would have been 100 percent.

3. Setting aside all absentee ballots as the remedy in a case where only some absentee ballots were cast illegally may seem a draconian remedy. Of course if it were possible to identify precisely which ballots were invalid, the remedy would be clear: disregard those ballots and only those ballots. Despite the general sanctity of the secret ballot, it may sometimes be possible to do so. Consider, for example, N.J. Stat. § 19:29-7 (2000), and N.J.R. Evid.513, which govern state election contests in New Jersey. Section 19:29-7 provides that in an election contest, "[t]he judge may require any person called as a witness who voted at such election to answer touching his qualification as a voter, and if the court, from his examination, or otherwise, is satisfied that he was not a qualified voter in the election district where he voted, he may compel him to disclose for whom he voted." And Rule 513 provides that "[e]very person has a privilege to refuse to disclose the tenor of his vote at a political election unless the judge finds that the vote was cast illegally." The predecessor versions of these provisions were implicitly approved against federal constitutional attack in *Hoch v. Phelan*, 796 F. Supp. 130 (D.N.J. 1992).

Even in the case where it is impossible to identify and disregard individual illegal ballots, there is a potential compromise position between excluding all potentially tainted ballots or conducting a new election. It may be possible to reduce each candidate's total according to some formula that allocates improperly cast votes among them. For a discussion of this issue, see the wonderfully captioned *In re the Purported Election of Bill Durkin*, 299 Ill. App.3d 192 (Ill. App. Ct. 1998). Durkin, Finn, and Tenpas were candidates for mayor of Waukegan, Illinois. Durkin, the Democratic candidate, received 4,296 total votes, Finn, an independent, received 4,260 total votes, and Tenpas, whose party affiliation was not noted by the court, received of 1,069.

Finn challenged the results and showed that 71 absentee ballots were invalid, because the voter had failed to provide a reason on his or her application, as required by state law. The absentee ballots in each precinct were commingled with the votes cast in person, so that it was not possible to ascertain the specific candidate for whom the illegal absentee ballots were cast (although it was possible to determine how many absentee votes there were in each precinct).

Finn argued that since 51 of the 71 absentee voters whose votes were determined to be illegal had declared their political party membership as Democrats in a primary election held on February 25, 1997, the "party affiliation method" should be used to allocate those votes. Those 51 votes should be subtracted from Durkin's vote total because Durkin was the Democratic candidate in the general election. The other 20 votes should be deducted from Durkin, Finn, and Tenpas according to the percentages of votes each candidate received in the precincts in which these votes were cast. The net effect of Finn's proposed allocation was a lowering of Durkin's vote total to 4,232 votes and a lowering of Finn's vote total to 4,254 votes. Thus, according to Finn's proposed allocation of the 71 illegal votes, he was the winner of the election.

Not surprisingly, Durkin (and the county canvassing board of which he was a member) proposed using the "proportion method" alone. Durkin's proposal apportioned the 71 illegal votes between Finn and Durkin on the basis of the percentage of votes each candidate received in the precincts where the illegal votes had been cast. According to this proposed allocation, Durkin would lose 49.8675 votes and Finn would lose 17.7329 votes. This would lower Durkin's total votes received to 4,246.1325 votes and petitioner's total votes received to 4,242.2671 votes, leaving Durkin still as the winner, albeit now by only four votes.

The courts agreed with Durkin, rejecting the party affiliation method because this contest involved an independent candidate:

> It is well established that a court may use party affiliation to determine the candidate for whom illegal votes were cast and, when such votes have been identified, to allocate such illegal votes against that candidate by deducting them from that candidate's vote total. *See, e.g., Talbott v. Thompson*, 350 Ill. 86, 97-98, 182 N.E. 784 (1932) (party affiliation raises presumption voter cast ballot for nominee of her or his political party, and presumption determines for whom

ballot was cast in absence of countervailing evidence); *Leach v. Johnson*, 20 Ill. App. 3d 713, 718-19, 313 N.E.2d 636 (1974) (absent better evidence, party affiliation is best evidence for determining candidate for whom illegal vote was cast). This is the party affiliation method of allocating illegal votes.

It is also well established that, when the evidence does not disclose the recipient of illegal votes, such votes should be eliminated by allocating them to the candidates in the same proportion that each candidate received votes in the precincts where the illegal votes were cast. This is the proportion method of allocating illegal votes. . . .

Using the party affiliation method in this case would be unfair because, as the trial court noted, only candidates affiliated with a political party can lose votes when this method is applied, while an independent candidate cannot lose votes. Of course, if the party affiliation method reliably determined the candidate for whom the illegal votes were cast, its use would be appropriate. However, we believe that the circumstances of this case cast doubt on the reliability of the party affiliation method in determining the candidate for whom the illegal votes were cast. We believe that determining party affiliation, and therefore how votes were cast, in a general election that includes a strong independent candidate based on the voting records from a previous primary election in which the independent candidate did not participate, as in this case, is not a reliable method of determining how votes were cast. Because the independent candidate did not participate in the primary election, voters in that election did not have a chance to vote for the independent candidate at that time. Based on the strong showing of petitioner, the independent candidate for mayor in the general election, it is reasonable to conclude that many of the voters who participated in the primary election split their tickets and voted for the independent candidate in the general election. Without evidence of the numbers of such voters, the party affiliation established by the primary election records is unreliable.

4. If there are only two candidates in an election, throwing out illegally cast votes — if they can be identified — may be an entirely adequate remedy. Subtracting votes to which a candidate is not entitled poses no theoretical problem. But what happens if the problem isn't that the votes are illegal, and thus shouldn't be counted at all, but rather than the votes should be reassigned to a different candidate? Is it possible, or desirable, to *add* votes to a candidate's total? The controversy in Florida during the 2000 election over the so-called "butterfly ballot" in Palm Beach County poses this question in a particularly dramatic form.

Palm Beach County, like roughly 20 percent of the counties in the United States, uses a punchcard voting system. Voters insert blank cards into machines that list the candidates for office and using a stylus punch out pre-scored holes. In the 2000 presidential election, Palm Beach County used a ballot design in which the holes were placed between two columns of candidates. George W. Bush was the first candidate listed in the left-hand column (because, as a matter of state law, the candidate whose party received the highest number of votes in the previous gubernatorial election receives the first spot on the ballot), and Al Gore was the second candidate listed in the left-hand column (because the Democrats had received the second highest number of votes in the last gubernatorial election). Pat Buchanan, a conservative candidate of the Reform Party, was the first candidate listed in the right-hand column.

Given the two columns of candidates, the first hole was that for Bush. But the second hole did not correspond to the second candidate on the ballot, Gore. Rather, it corresponded to the first candidate in the *right-hand column*, namely, Buchanan. The hole for Gore was thus the third hole.

On Election Day itself, voters in Palm Beach County began to complain about the form of the ballot and to claim that they had mistakenly voted for Buchanan when they meant to vote for Gore. A group of voters filed suit in Florida state court, claiming that the ballot had violated various state-law requirements regarding the order of candidates' names on the ballot and the placement of the holes. Ultimately, their claims were rejected by the trial court and the Florida Supreme Court, which held that the ballot did not violate state law. *Fladell v. Palm Beach County Canvassing Board*, 772 So.2d 1240 (Fla. 2000).

Leaving aside the question of the ballot's legality under state law, the possibility that the ballot might have affected the outcome of the election in Florida, and thus across the nation, seems fairly well established. A group of political scientists used a variety of techniques to study the Palm Beach results. In an analysis of returns from 4300 counties across the United States (in every state but Michigan [where Buchanan was not on the ballot], Alaska, Hawaii, and Delaware), they concluded that Palm Beach County produced the second most anamolous result "in terms of having exceptionally high support for Buchanan that deviates from expected patterns." Jonathan N. Wand, Kenneth W. Shotts, Jasjeet S. Sekhon, Walter R. Mebane, Jr. and Michael C. Herron, *Voting Irregularities in Palm Beach County* (2000) (available from http://elections.fas.harvard.edu/wssmh/). The authors analyzed county-by-county data from Florida and concluded, first, that "compared to other Florida counties as measured in a number of ways, the Palm Beach County vote share for Buchanan is extremely large. In fact, what we know about other counties in Florida implies that this vote share is so large as to be practically unbelievable. It is virtually certain that there is something unique about Palm Beach County, and the only obvious factor that is unique to Palm Beach County is its ballot format," and, second, using census data, that "Palm Beach County actually contains relatively few Buchanan supporters."

Other social scientists estimated that roughly 2000 of the 3400 votes Buchanan received in Palm Beach County had been cast by voters who thought they were voting for Gore. *See, e.g.,* Henry E. Brady, *Report on Voting and Ballot Form in Palm Beach County* (Nov. 16, 2000) (available from http://elections.fas.harvard.edu/statement/hbrady/).

What sorts of remedies might be available to a court that found the Palm Beach ballot to be illegal? In the special context of the presidential election, a new election was never a realistic possibility. Among other things, the requirement for a uniform national election day seemed to preclude it. But suppose this had been an election for statewide office. Could a court reallocate votes on the basis of statistical evidence regarding the "expected" outcome?

In this context, consider how courts and the public have thought about an analogous issue – how to conduct the decennial census. Most social scientists agree that it is more accurate to use "adjusted" figures than to rely on the initial count, since statistical techniques can correct predictable under- and over-counts of identifiable groups. Nonetheless, Congress has mandated using the unadjusted figures to apportion congressional seats among the states, and many states also require use of the uncorrected figures. To some extent, this choice may reflect predictions about the partisan political consequences of choosing one set of numbers over the other. But there may also be a visceral preference for using the actual numbers because a sample just doesn't "feel" like an actual enumeration. Consider in this light the pressure for a manual recount in Florida. In an essay in the New York Times, Lawrence M. Krauss, the head of the physics department at Case Western Reserve University wrote that the so-called "law of large numbers suggests that roughly 68 percent of the time, if one performed precisely the same experiment on precisely the same system over and over again," that is, if one counted and recounted Florida's six million ballots repeatedly, "the total number of events [i.e., votes] counted would be expected to vary by at least 2,000 events." *Analyze This: A Physicist on Applied Politics*, N.Y. Times, Nov. 21, 2000, at F4. Thus, there may be no scientific reason to expect one counting method rather than another to produce the most reliable result, especially if the standard for a legally cast ballot is not clear in the first place.

Is there in fact anything different about reallocating votes among candidates on the basis of statistical estimates as opposed to simply invalidating votes?

D. PERMANENTLY ENJOINING A PARTICULAR ELECTION PRACTICE

The remedies discussed in the preceding sections all focus, to one degree or another, on discrete elections. In those kinds of litigation, plaintiffs seek to change election outcomes. But there are other remedies that focus not on the results of a particular election, but rather on more systemic change. The usual context in which such questions arise is litigation by plaintiffs who seek declaratory judgments or permanent injunctive relief against the use of practices that deny, dilute, or abridge their rights.

The general equitable principles that govern such cases can be stated relatively simply, although in practice they can raise difficult questions. Having found a statutory or constitutional violation, the courts are to order relief that remedies the violation as completely as possible. *See, e.g.,* S. Rep. No. 97-417, p. 31 (1982) (stating, with respect to violations of § 2 of the Voting Rights Act that "[t]he court should exercise its traditional equitable powers to fashion the relief so that it completely remedies the prior dilution of minority voting strength and fully provides equal opportunity for minority citizens to participate and to elect candidates of their choice."). At the same time, precisely because regulation of the political process trenches so intimately on core state decisionmaking, the courts are required to give states a fair opportunity to propose a remedy before imposing one of their own devising. *See, e.g., Reynolds v. Sims,* 376 U.S. 533, 586 (1964) (finding that, even once the district court had found a violation of one-person, one-vote, it "acted wisely in declining to stay the impending primary election," "properly refrained from acting further until the Alabama Legislature had been given an opportunity to remedy the admitted discrepancies in the State's legislative apportionment scheme," and "correctly recognized that legislative reapportionment is primarily a matter for legislative consideration and determination, and that judicial relief becomes appropriate only when a legislature fails to reapportion according to federal constitutional requisites in a timely fashion after having had an adequate opportunity to do so.")

Oddly enough, relatively little of the extensive federal case law on equitable remedies and the political process focuses on the nitty-gritty of balloting itself. But in the wake of *Bush v. Gore,* this may well change. There, the Court noted that "[t]his case has shown that punch card balloting machines can produce an unfortunate number of ballots which are not punched in a clean, complete way by the voter. After the current counting, it is likely legislative bodies nationwide will examine ways to improve the mechanisms and machinery for voting." The Court's decision prompted several lawsuits, in Florida and elsewhere, challenging the use of punch card systems. For copies of the pleadings in these cases, see http://election2000.stanford.edu. Is there also a role for courts in policing voting technologies?

One source of litigation might be section 2 of the Voting Rights Act of 1965 as amended, 42 U.S.C. § 1973. Essentially, section 2 forbids the use of any voting "qualification or prerequisite to voting or standard, practice, or procedure" that makes it more difficult for minority voters than for other voters to participate in the political process or to elect the candidate of their choice. A different section of the Voting Rights Act, § 14(c)(3), defines "voting" to include "all action necessary to make a vote effective in any primary, special, or general election, including, but not limited to, registration, listing pursuant to this Act, or other action required by law prerequisite to voting, casting a ballot, *and having such ballot counted properly and included in the appropriate totals of votes cast* with respect to candidates for public or party office and propositions for which votes are received in an election." 42 U.S.C. § 1973*l*(c)(3) (emphasis added). Interestingly enough, most litigation under the Act has concentrated on rules for aggregating votes – such as the use of at-large elections or the choice among district boundaries in reapportionment plans – rather than on the nuts and bolts of the actual voting process. In part, this may be a function of a general lack of awareness about problems with electoral technology: since most elections do not appear to be very close, the public generally may not be concerned with how votes are counted. In part, it may also be a function of the major impetus behind voting rights litigation: the desire of politically active minority individuals and organizations to obtain election rules that enable them to elect candidates. At-large elections and districting plans that dilute minority voting strength are more obvious targets for such lawsuits.

There are, however, cases in which the Voting Rights Act has been applied to election technologies. The leading section 5 coverage case, *Allen v. State Board of Elections*, 393 U.S. 44 (1969), held that Virginia was required to seek preclearance of changes in the way illiterate voters could cast write-in votes. And in the wake of empirical studies following the 2000 election that suggest that ballot spoilage rates may be higher among minority voters, there may be an increase in section 2 challenges to voting technologies.

For one example of such a lawsuit, consider *Roberts v. Wamser*, 679 F. Supp. 1513 (E.D. Mo, 1987), *rev'd*, 883 F.2d 617 (8th Cir. 1989), also discussed *supra* on pages 93-94. The plaintiff, a minority candidate for office who lost in a close election, challenged the punch card system used in St. Louis, Missouri, a city with a large black community.

The district court found that the system, at least as it was operated in St. Louis, violated section 2. It observed that there were a variety of reasons why a voter's ballot might contain an "undervote" or "overvote," that is, votes not counted by the automatic tabulating equipment: apathy; interest; protest voting; trying to correct a mistaken vote; voter fatigue due to placement on a large ballot; and education of the voter. Minority voters were on average less well educated than white voters, and this might account for a differential spoilage rate.

The district court relied on testimony by the plaintiff's experts that showed that 7.22 % of the ballots cast by black voters in the election being challenged were not counted, whereas only 1.77 % of ballots cast by white voters were not counted and that in the last four primary elections, votes cast in "black" wards were about three times more likely not to be counted as votes cast in "white" wards.

The court found no persuasive reason for the city's election practices:

[T]he record does not clearly establish the reason for not manually reviewing ballots not counted by the automatic tabulating equipment. The record discloses that the Board's change from the lever voting machines to the present punch card voting system may have been for administrative convenience and efficiency in terms of storage between elections and transportation of the equipment to and from the polling places. Moreover, without dispute the record shows the use of the new system is not "tenuous." That use in and of itself is, however, not at issue here. Rather, the resulting failure of the new system to prevent overvotes, the significant numbers of uncounted ballots in the black community since use of the new system, and the Board's apparent failure explicitly to address that problem are part and parcel of plaintiff's present claim. Without an explanation for the Board's failure manually to review ballots rejected by the equipment, and to see whether such ballots should in fact be counted rather than rejected, the Court is unable to say any such Board practice or policy is anything but tenuous. . . .

In light of the present record, the Court sustains plaintiff's challenge to the Board's failure manually to review cast ballots rejected by the tabulating equipment and finds, under the circumstances, that that failure constitutes a violation of the Voting Rights Act. The record shows the Board's failure to review and, if appropriate, count such ballots has resulted in the City's black voters having less opportunity than other members of the City's electorate to participate in the political process and to elect representatives of their choice. It is not the use of the punch card voting system and automated tabulating equipment alone, but the Board's blanket failure to review rejected ballots, that resulted in the disenfranchisement of City voters.

The district court therefore issued an injunction requiring the board of elections

(a) to take appropriate steps manually to count all ballots validly cast by voters of the City of St. Louis but rejected by the tabulating equipment;

(b) to target for voter education on the proper use of the punch card voting system those wards from which the Board receives over a reasonable period of time a relatively high number of uncounted ballots (five percent of the total ballots cast in such wards); and

(c) to offer to voters at the polling places explanations and demonstrations of the proper use of the punch card voting system
. . . .

On appeal, a divided panel of the Eighth Circuit reversed the district court. *Roberts v. Wamser*, 883 F.2d 617 (8th Cir. 1989). The majority held that Roberts lacked standing, as a candidate, to challenge the use of punchcard ballots under the Voting Rights Act. The court noted that the Act expressly conferred standing only upon the Attorney General. It recognized that the Supreme Court had held that a private citizen attempting to protect his right to vote was a proper party to effectuate the goals of the Act, and therefore enjoyed an implied right of action, and that Congress had ratified this holding when it amended the Act in 1975.

Here, Roberts is not an aggrieved voter suing to protect his right to vote. Nowhere in his complaint (or anywhere else) does Roberts claim that his right to vote has been infringed because of his race. Nor does Roberts allege that he is suing on behalf of persons who are unable to protect their own rights. The asserted personal injury for which Roberts seeks a remedy is not the denial of his right to vote, but rather the loss of the votes that he claims he would have received if not for the allegedly disproportionate difficulties of black voters in coping with punch-card voting. Because Roberts is not seeking to enforce his right to vote, but rather to improve the odds of his being elected, the question becomes whether he is an "aggrieved person" within the meaning of the Voting Rights Act.

We conclude that an unsuccessful candidate attempting to challenge election results does not have standing under the Voting Rights Act. . . . The purpose of the Voting Rights Act is to protect minority voters, not to give unsuccessful candidates for state or local office a federal forum in which to challenge elections. In addition, we see good reasons why Congress would not have wished to confer standing on defeated candidates. First, because of the potential divergence between the interests of a candidate seeking office and citizens attempting to enforce their right to vote, it is difficult to see an aggrieved candidate as being a proper party to bring a Voting Rights Act action. And second, because state and local election contests are quintessential state and local matters, to extend standing to an unsuccessful candidate to challenge his electoral defeat under the Voting Rights Act would violate principles of federalism in a highly radical way— an intention that we should not attribute to Congress except upon its unmistakably clear manifestation in the statutory language. . . .

We also observe that Roberts's claim to standing in this case is not dependent upon his being a member of a minority group protected by the Voting Rights Act, but rather on his simply being a candidate for public office. Under Roberts's (and the District Court's) theory of standing, any candidate, without regard to his or her race, could challenge an election result by alleging that something about the manner in which the election was conducted infringed upon the voting rights of blacks or other protected groups. If such a theory of standing were accepted, the potential Voting Rights Act challenges to state elections by losing candidates would be endless. We cannot believe that Congress intended such a result. More importantly, we cannot find anything in the language of the Voting Rights Act that makes manifest a congressional intent to bring about such a counter-intuitive result.

If Roberts did not having standing to challenge St. Louis's use of punchcard ballots as a violation of § 2 because he was a candidate, not a voter, how is it that George W. Bush had standing to challenge – as an equal protection clause violation – to challenge Florida's recount procedure? As Professor Karlan notes:

[T]he injuries the Supreme Court [saw] are the exclusion of valid undervotes by stringent counties and exclusionary counting teams and the exclusion of valid overvotes by an incomplete recount process . . . .

[George W. Bush] is not an excluded voter himself. So unless he has third-party standing, he is not a proper champion of the excluded voters' claims. Moreover, unless and until the Supreme Court is prepared to say that his supporters are disproportionately likely not to have their votes recovered under the prescribed process, he is an especially unlikely candidate for third party standing. It is hard to see George W. Bush as the champion of a claim by undervoters in overwhelmingly Democratic Palm Beach County that they are being denied equal protection because their votes would have been included under the more liberal Broward County standard. Indeed, Bush's third-party complaint in *Gore v. Harris* -- the source of his intervention in the case which the Supreme Court decided as *Bush v. Gore* -- alleged, among other things, that the standard used in Broward County was partisan, inconsistent, and unfair. The relief he sought was a declaration that "the illegal votes counted in Broward County under the news rules established after the election should be excluded under the Due Process Clause and 3 U.S.C. § 5." Nothing in that proposed remedy vindicates the rights of excluded voters in Palm Beach County or elsewhere except in the brute realist sense that they might be content to have their votes excluded if that means that a disproportionate number of votes by the other guy's supporters get excluded as well.

Pamela S. Karlan, *Nothing Personal: The Evolution of the Newest Equal Protection from Shaw v. Reno to Bush v. Gore*, 79 N.C.L. Rev. ___ (2001); see also Pamela S. Karlan, *The Newest Equal Protection: Regressive Doctrine on a Changeable Court* in The Vote: Bush, Gore and the Supreme Court (Cass R. Sunstein and Richard A. Epstein eds. 2001) (further discussing the issue of standing).

E. DAMAGES

In *Memphis Community School District v. Stachura*, 477 U.S. 299, 312 n.14 (1986), the Supreme Court noted a long series of cases in which plaintiffs who were illegally prevented from voting in state elections suffered compensable injury. These cases extend back at least to *Ashby v. White*, 2 Ld. Raym. 938, 92 Eng. Rep. 126 (1703).

A number of nineteenth century cases involved damages. For example, purely as a matter of state law, the Maine Supreme Judicial Court in *Sanders v. Getchell*, 76 Me. 158 (1884), ordered the award of $25 in damages to a plaintiff whom the Waterville selectmen refused to place on the town's voting rolls because he had moved to the town to attend an educational institution. (The ability of students to register where they attend school remains a live issue today.) The Supreme Judicial Court held that under the circumstances of this case — the plaintiff was 32 years old at the time he sought to register and had lived in Waterville for many years – "[t]o deprive him of his right to vote . . . was not reasonable." At the same time, the court disagreed with the plaintiff that "the damages should be either exemplary or severe. We think the wisest and most just conclusion, in view of all the circumstances, will be to accord to the plaintiff no greater damages than sufficient to carry the costs."

In the early twentieth century, many of the White Primary cases that challenged the exclusion of black voters in the South from Democratic Party primaries. were brought as damages actions. In *Nixon v. Herndon*, 273 U.S. 536 (1927), for example, the plaintiff— a black registered voter from El Paso — sued the Judges of Elections for refusing to permit him to vote in a primary election. He claimed damages of $5,000. Texas had enacted a statute that provided that "in no event shall a negro be eligible to participate in a Democratic party primary election held in the State of Texas . . . ."

The defendants moved to dismiss the complaint on the ground that case raised a nonjusticiable political question. The Supreme Court, in an opinion by Justice Holmes, unanimously disagreed:

> The objection that the subject matter of the suit is political is little more than a play upon words. Of course the petition concerns political action but it alleges and seeks to recover for private damage. That private damage may be caused by such political action and may be recovered for in a suit at law hardly has been doubted for over two hundred years, since *Ashby v. White*, 2 Ld. Raym. 938, 3 id. 320, and has been recognized by this Court. *Wiley v. Sinkler*, 179 U.S. 58, 64, 65. *Giles v. Harris*, 189 U.S. 475, 485. *See also* Judicial Code, § 24 (11), (12), (14). Act of March 3, 1911, c. 231; 36 Stat. 1087, 1092. If the defendants' conduct was a wrong to the plaintiff the same reasons that allow a recovery for denying the plaintiff a vote at a final election allow it for denying a vote at the primary election that may determine the final result.

The Court's citation of *Wiley v. Sinkler*, 179 U.S. 58 (1900), illustrates a practical problem with using damages actions. The plaintiff, a resident of Charleston, South Carolina, sued the city's board of election managers to recover damages in the sum of $2500 for wrongfully and wilfully rejecting his vote in the 1894 congressional elections. The Supreme Court unanimously recognized a qualified voter's right to sue for damages:

> The right to vote for members of the Congress of the United States is not derived merely from the constitution and laws of the State in which they are chosen, but has its foundation in the Constitution of the United States. . . .

> This action is brought against election officers to recover damages for their rejection of the plaintiff's vote for a member of the House of Representatives of the United States. The complaint, by alleging that the plaintiff was at the time, under the constitution and laws of the State of South Carolina and the Constitution and laws of the United States, a duly qualified elector of the State, shows that the action is brought under the Constitution and laws of the United States.

> The damages are laid at the sum of $2500. What amount of damages the plaintiff shall recover in such an action is peculiarly appropriate for the determination of a jury, and no opinion of the court upon that subject can justify it in holding that the amount in controversy was insufficient to support the jurisdiction of the Circuit Court.

Nonetheless, the Court unanimously affirmed the dismissal of the plaintiff's complaint because he could not show that he had been properly registered to vote under South Carolina's draconian registration scheme (which had been designed essentially to disenfranchise black voters.) That conclusion, jarring as it might seem to contemporary eyes, is not surprising: in *Giles v. Harris*, 189 U.S. 475 (1903), decided a few years later, the Supreme Court showed itself essentially unwilling at the turn of the century to order injunctive relief against discriminatory registration systems.

By contrast, consider the one reported federal case in which damages were awarded.

Wayne v. Venable
260 F. 64 (8th Cir. 1919)

■JOHN SANBORN, Circuit Judge.

[The plaintiffs in this case, J.A. Venable and J.V. Boyd sued the defendants] for $5,000 damages and $10,000 punitive damages, because, as each of the plaintiffs alleged, [the defendants] conspired and combined with each other and others to prevent them . . . from casting their votes . . . for presidential electors, United States Senator, and a member of Congress at the general election in the [Eagle] township on November 7, 1916 . . . . [T]he two actions were consolidated and tried together, and they resulted in a verdict in favor of each of the plaintiffs against Wayne and Alexander for $2,000. Judgments accordingly were rendered. . . .

The right of qualified electors to vote for a member of Congress at a general state election, which is also an election at which a Congressman is to be lawfully voted for and elected, is a right "fundamentally based upon the Constitution [of the United States], which created the office of member of Congress, and declared it should be elective, and pointed to the means of ascertaining who should be electors." *Ex parte Yarbrough*, 110 U.S. 655, 664, 665.

An action for damages in the proper federal court lies by a qualified elector for his wrongful deprivation of this right by a defendant or by an effective conspiracy of several defendants who deprive him thereof. . . .

In the eyes of the law this right is so valuable that damages are presumed from the wrongful deprivation of it without evidence of actual loss of money, property, or any other valuable thing, and the amount of the damages is a question peculiarly appropriate for the determination of the jury, because each member of the jury has personal knowledge of the value of the right. . . .

The record in this case convinces that while there was a conflict in the evidence regarding nearly all the material issues of fact, there was at the close of the evidence substantial evidence of these facts. The plaintiffs were qualified electors of Eagle township at the election therein on November 7, 1916, at which election a United States Senator and a member of Congress were lawfully to be voted for and elected. At this election in Eagle township, Harry A. Wayne, Walter Alexander, and T. L. Hughes were the judges of the election. After they met at the polling place on election day they appointed James T. Ritchie a special deputy sheriff to assist in conducting the election, and instructed him how he should admit into a schoolroom, where the voting was conducted, those desiring to vote, and that he should admit them one at a time . . . . Mr. Leach, a qualified voter in Eagle township, had a store 50 or 75 feet from the voting place. He testified that he tried to vote half a dozen times, but Mr. Ritchie was in charge of the door and would not let him in, although automobiles were coming in and the people from them voted in preference to those theretofore at the polling place waiting for an opportunity to vote . . . .

The Statutes of Arkansas (Kirby's Dig. § 2812) provided: "The polls shall be opened at eight o'clock a.m. and shall remain continuously opened until half-past six o'clock p.m." The polls were not opened for voting until about 9:30 a.m., and a recess was taken for lunch. There were about 220 votes usually cast at an election in Eagle township generally, but at this election only about 105 were received. When the polls were opened, and for an hour or more before that time, there were about 100 men waiting for the polls to open so that they could vote. The electors were not admitted in the order of their arrival or their proximity to the polling place, but Mr. Ritchie, by calling or beckoning, selected those who should vote and admitted them, while at the same time he repeatedly refused to admit those nearer the entrance who had been waiting longer. Automobile loads of voters came to the polls from Mr. Swartz's place and Mr. Wilder's place, while many voters who had been waiting to vote and had repeatedly been refused admission to the polling room by Mr. Ritchie were still waiting to vote. Mr. Swartz came out of the polling room to these men as they came up in the automobiles, led them up to the door, and they were admitted by Ritchie and permitted to vote one after the other until they had all voted, before any other voter who had been refused admission was permitted to enter the polling place. The voting was very slow— from 5 to 20 minutes were used to get in a single vote, only one voter was admitted to the polling place at a time, and no other one was admitted until he came out, save in exceptional instances until about 15 minutes before the polls closed, when announcement was made that the polls would close in 15 minutes, the door of the polling room was opened, and during that 15 minutes voters were admitted more rapidly, but it was too late for all those present to vote, and 40 or 50 of them were still there trying to get in and vote when the polls closed, while many others who had repeatedly tried to vote and had been turned back during the day, had become satisfied that they would not be permitted to vote, and had gone away and were in that way deprived of their rights to vote. Each of the plaintiffs waited long, repeatedly advanced towards the door and tried to vote, and was repeatedly prevented by Ritchie from so doing, and in this way each of the plaintiffs was deprived of his vote and of his right to vote for any of the candidates at this election. . . .

The suggestion of counsel for the defendants that the federal court has no jurisdiction over these actions because the plaintiffs produced no direct testimony that they wanted or intended to vote at this election for a candidate for United States Senator, or for a candidate for Congressman, while they proved that they were deeply interested in the election of a candidate for a justice of the peace, is insignificant and negligible. They pleaded in their complaint that they were deprived of their right to vote for a candidate for United States Senator and for a candidate for Congressman by the conspiracy of these defendants which they alleged and the attainment of its object. They proved to the satisfaction of the jury that they were deprived of their right to vote for any one at this election by the conspiracy and the attainment of its object, and as the whole is greater than any of its parts and includes all of them, they proved that they were deprived of their rights to vote for a candidate for United States Senator and for a candidate for Congressman, and that constitutes proof of a cause of action over which the federal court has jurisdiction. . . .

NOTES AND QUESTIONS

1. In *Memphis Community School District v. Stachura*, 477 U.S. 299, 312 n.14 (1986), the Supreme Court, after noting the long series of cases in which plaintiffs who were illegally prevented from voting were held to have suffered compensable injury, explained that "the 'value of the right' [to vote] in the context of these decisions is the money value of the particular loss that the plaintiff suffered— a loss of which 'each member of the jury has personal knowledge.' It is not the value of the right to vote as a general, abstract matter, based on its role in our history or system of government." How, then, ought a jury to determine the appropriate measure of damages? Is the way in which a plaintiff's rights have been denied relevant? For example, some denials may inflict greater dignitary interests than others. If the election is close and the vote of the plaintiff (or, more plausibly, a group of similarly situated plaintiffs) might have affected the outcome, are the damages greater? In *Santana v. Registrars of Voters of Worcester*, 398 Mass. 862 (1986), plaintiffs sought $25,000 in compensatory damages and $25,000 in punitive damages, introducing evidence that "the defendants' actions had caused them to become upset, angry, humiliated, distraught, frustrated and embarrassed. One plaintiff complained of a pounding headache while another said she now feels nervous, anxious and fearful when going to vote." Nonetheless, the trial judge found that none of the plaintiffs suffered financial loss or physical or emotional injury. As a result, he awarded only nominal damages and denied the plaintiffs' request for compensatory or punitive damages. The Massachusetts Supreme Judicial Court affirmed, and noted that after *Stachura*, "presumed" damages were no longer appropriate, and a plaintiff could recover for emotional distress only if it was accompanied by physical injury or was the product of willful, rather than negligent government acts.

Note also that damages are decided by juries, or at least either party to a damages lawsuit is entitled to ask for a jury. What effect will this have on a plaintiff's ability to obtain substantial damages, particularly if the plaintiff is a member of an unpopular group?

Finally, there are very few contemporary reported cases involving the award of damages to voters whose rights have been denied. There is dicta in *Palmer v. Board of Education*, 46 F.3d 682, 686 (7th Cir. 1995), suggesting that damages remain available, although voters today normally seek injunctive relief. Compare the Supreme Court's reference in *Stachura* to "whatever the wisdom of th[e] decisions [authorizing damages] in the context of the changing scope of compensatory damages over the course of this century. . . ." Why *don't* plaintiffs seek compensatory (or punitive) damages? Is it because they want to avoid trial before juries? Are there other strategic or tactical reasons?

2. As a matter of federal statutory law, the vehicle for seeking damages is most likely 42 U.S.C. § 1983, which provides for damages whenever a person acting under color of state law "subjects . . . any citizen of the United States . . . to the deprivation of any rights, privileges, or immunities secured by the Constitution and laws." But there is two significant limitations on a plaintiff's ability to obtain damages (as opposed to prospective, injunctive relief). First, with respect to lawsuits against local governments (section 1983 does not permit lawsuits against states themselves), the plaintiff must show that the deprivation was pursuant to an official custom or policy, and this can be difficult to do if there is no statute involved. Second, with respect to lawsuits against individual government officials, the question of qualified immunity arises. Plaintiffs can obtain damages only for violations of clearly established law: if the scope of the plaintiff's right is unclear, the official is immune from damages liability. For extensive treatment of the general questions of qualified immunity and governmental liability, see John C. Jeffries, Jr., et al. Civil Rights Actions: Enforcing the Constitution (2000); Martin A. Schwartz & John E. Kirklin, Section 1983 Litigation: Claims and Defenses (3d ed.1997).

3. Although damages actions are apparently available, this does not mean that damages offer a sufficiently complete form of relief so as to obviate the need for injunctive relief. *See, e.g., Dillard v. Crenshaw County*, 640 F. Supp. 1347, 1363 (M.D. Ala. 1986) ("Given the fundamental nature of the right to vote, monetary remedies would obviously be inadequate in this case; it is simply not possible to pay someone for having been denied a right of this importance.").

4. Do disappointed *candidates* have the ability to seek compensatory or punitive damages?

Hutchinson v. Miller
797 F.2d 1279 (4th Cir. 1986)

■ J. HARVIE WILKINSON, Circuit Judge:

Plaintiffs are three unsuccessful candidates for public office who seek to recover approximately $9 million in damages under 42 U.S.C. § 1983, 18 U.S.C.

§ 1964 (Racketeer Influenced and Corrupt Organizations Act— RICO), and the common law of West Virginia, for alleged irregularities in the 1980 general election. . . .

We conclude that federal courts are not available for awards of damages to defeated candidates. . . .

I

Plaintiffs were Democratic candidates in the 1980 general election in West Virginia. John Hutchinson sought re-election to the United States House of Representatives in the Third Congressional District of West Virginia. This district included Kanawha and Boone Counties — where the disputed elections occurred — as well as twelve other counties. Plaintiff Leonard Underwood was the incumbent delegate to the state house from Kanawha County, and plaintiff William Reese sought election as a County Commissioner for Kanawha County. Hutchinson and Reese were defeated by wide margins, while Underwood's loss was a narrow one.

Underwood requested a recount of all computer punchcard ballots cast in the election. When the Kanawha County Commission denied this request, Underwood sought a writ of mandamus in the Circuit Court of Kanawha County to compel a hand count of ballots. That action was dismissed, and a similar attempt before the state Supreme Court was found to be time barred. Hutchinson filed a formal election complaint with the United States Attorney in January, 1981. The resolution of that complaint is not revealed in the record, but apparently was not satisfactory to Hutchinson. Plaintiffs filed their original complaint in this suit in February, 1983.

As amended, the complaint in essence charges that the election night totals were pre-determined by defendants, who then conspired to cover up their activities. Named as defendants in the suit were both local officials and private citizens alleged to have acted in concert with those officials. The officials included Margaret Miller, Clerk of the County Commission of Kanawha County; Carolyn Critchfield, Ann Carroll, Darlene Dotson and Clayton Spangler, employees in the clerk's office; James Roark, the Prosecuting Attorney of Kanawha County in 1980; and Bernard Meadows, employed by the Clerk of the County Commission of Boone County. Private citizens named as defendants included Steven Miller, husband of Margaret Miller; David Staton, the successful Congressional candidate in the 1980 election; and John Cavacini, who in 1980 was associated with the campaign of Governor John D. Rockefeller, IV. Finally, plaintiffs sued Computer Election Systems, Inc. (CES), which provided computer vote tabulating systems in Kanawha County, and four employees of CES — Keith Long, Carl Clough, Cherrie Lloyd, and William Biebel.

Plaintiffs allege that a conspiracy among the defendants began as early as January, 1979, when Kanawha County Commissioners considered the use of electronic voting equipment. They suggest that the Millers' support for the

CES system and their role in the bidding process reveals the genesis of a scheme to fix the 1980 election. This purported scheme continued as CES employees helped county officials prepare for the use of CES equipment in the November election. Defendants, by contrast, describe the selection and preparation of CES equipment as legitimate and lawful activity designed to assist them in the efficient conduct of the election.

The CES system provided the county with electronic punch card vote tabulation, in which voters indicated their choices on computer punch cards. After polls were closed, these cards were transported to countywide tabulation centers in locked and sealed ballot boxes. The ballots were removed by teams of workers, who arranged them for feeding into the computer and noted in log books the time when ballot boxes were opened. Plaintiffs cite as evidence of election fraud the fact that the log shows one box was opened after the computer tabulation was printed out.

Plaintiffs' main allegations focus on events at the central tabulation center for Kanawha County. They rely largely on the testimony of Walter Price, incumbent candidate for the House of Delegates who was at the center on election night. Price testified that he observed Margaret Miller manipulating computer toggle switches during the election count, purportedly in an attempt to alter vote counts. He saw an "unknown gentleman" — whom plaintiffs identify as Carl Clough — placing a phone receiver into his briefcase. Plaintiffs suggest that this activity is consistent with the use of a portable modem, perhaps in an effort to change vote totals. Price also testified that Stephen Miller took computer cards from his coat pocket and gave them to his wife, who allegedly fed the cards into the computer.

Finally, plaintiffs assert that numerous irregularities occurred after the election, including improper handling of the ballots and release of exact returns prior to the canvass, and destruction of ballots that violated the terms of W. Va. Code § 3-6-9. Plaintiffs make similar, though less detailed, allegations with respect to the election process in Boone County . . . .

The court considered motions for directed verdicts at the close of plaintiffs' case. It found that plaintiffs' claims failed for several reasons. The court held that plaintiffs had failed to prove a conspiracy, noting that the only evidence the election was rigged was "purely speculative . . . mere suspicion." It also found that plaintiffs Reese and Hutchinson had not shown that they were harmed by the alleged actions; there was no evidence that their large losses would have been victories in the absence of the alleged conspiracy. Further, finding only "mere election irregularities" and no evidence to suggest that the election was fundamentally unfair, the court held that plaintiffs had failed to prove a deprivation of a constitutional right essential to a § 1983 action. Finally, the court dismissed plaintiffs' claims under RICO, finding "absolutely no proof" that would allow it to consider the claim.

II

Though our disposition of this dispute rests on the view that damages are unavailable to defeated candidates as a method of post-election relief, we are guided by an awareness of the broader context in which this suit arises. The plaintiffs ask us to arbitrate what is essentially a political dispute over the results of an election. We find it useful, for proper understanding of this case, to discuss the structural characteristics and mechanisms for review of disputed elections. This examination reveals both the proper sphere and the limits of judicial oversight of controversies in the electoral process.

As in any suit under § 1983 the first inquiry is "whether the plaintiff has been deprived of a right 'secured by the Constitution and laws.'" *Baker v. McCollan,* 443 U.S. 137, 140 (1979). In their complaint, plaintiffs alleged that defendants deprived them of "their constitutionally protected right to participate fully and fairly in the electoral process," and "their constitutional right to vote or receive votes," and their Fifth Amendment right to hold property, in this case public office. The district court found that plaintiffs proceeded at trial as "defeated or disenfranchised candidates rather than as . . . disenfranchised voters." Thus, plaintiffs essentially assert that they have been deprived of their "right to candidacy."

Courts have recognized that some restrictions on political candidates violate the Constitution because of their derivative effect on the right to vote. We assume, without deciding, that plaintiffs have sufficiently alleged a deprivation of constitutional rights to meet the basic requirements of a § 1983 cause of action. That assumption, however, cannot end the matter. . . .

We first acknowledge and affirm the significant duty of federal courts to preserve constitutional rights in the electoral process. Our role, however, primarily addresses the general application of laws and procedures, not the particulars of election disputes. Federal courts have, for example, invalidated class-based restrictions of the right to vote. The dilution of votes through malapportionment has also been a major concern of the federal judiciary. Courts have also acted to further the congressional mandate, as expressed in the Voting Rights, that race shall not affect the right to vote. Intervention for reasons other than racial discrimination "has tended, for the most part, to be limited to striking down state laws or rules of general application which improperly restrict or constrict the franchise" or otherwise burden the exercise of political rights. By these means, federal courts have assumed an active role in protecting against dilution of the fundamental right to vote and the denial of this right through class disenfranchisement.

By contrast, "circuit courts have uniformly declined to endorse action under § 1983 with respect to garden variety election irregularities." *See, e.g., Welch v. McKenzie,* 765 F.2d 1311 (5th Cir. 1985); *Gamza v. Aguirre,* 619 F.2d 449 (5th Cir. 1980); *Hennings v. Grafton,* 523 F.2d 861 (7th Cir. 1975); *Pettengill v. Putnam County R-1 School District,* 472 F.2d 121 (8th Cir. 1973); *Powell v. Power,* 436 F.2d 84 (2d Cir. 1970). These courts, mainly considering disputes involving state elections, have declined to interfere because of the constitutional recognition that "states are primarily responsible for their own elections," *Welch,* 765 F.2d at 1317, and that alternative remedies are adequate to guarantee the integrity of the democratic process. The discussion of those alternative means of resolving electoral disputes is the focus of the following section.

III

We note initially that the Constitution anticipates that the electoral process is to be largely controlled by the states and reviewed by the legislature. This control reaches elections for federal and state office. Article I, sec. 4, cl. 1, grants to the states the power to prescribe, subject to Congressional preemption, the "Times, Places and Manner of holding Elections for Senators and Representatives." In addition, states undoubtedly retain primary authority "to regulate the elections of their own officials."

Where state procedures produce contested results, the Constitution dictates that, for congressional elections, "Each House shall be the Judge of the Elections, Returns and Qualifications of its own Members." Art. I, Sec. 5, cl. 1. The House accordingly has the authority "to determine the facts and apply the appropriate rules of law, and, finally, to render a judgment which is beyond the authority of any other tribunal to review." This plenary power is paralleled at the state level by the power of the West Virginia legislature to review the elections of its own members. Contests for county offices, such as that of plaintiff Reese, are resolved by county courts.

We thus proceed with awareness that the resolution of particular electoral disputes has been primarily committed to others in our system. The express delegation to Congress and the states of shared responsibility for the legitimation of electoral outcomes and the omission of any constitutional mandate for federal judicial intervention suggests the inadvisability of permitting a § 1983 or civil RICO action to confer upon federal judges and juries "a piece of the political action," no matter what relief is sought. Consideration of the various ways in which these other bodies have regulated and monitored the integrity of elections only confirms our hesitation to consider the disputed details of political contests.

Those with primary responsibility have not abandoned their duty to ensure the reliability and fairness of democratic elections. The House of Representatives, for example, has developed a body of guiding precedent regarding election contests, *see* 2 Deschler's Precedents of the United States House of Representatives, 323-888 (1977), and has enacted detailed procedures designed to ensure due process and just consideration of disputes. *See* Federal Contested Elections Act, 2 U.S.C. §§ 381-396. The operation of these procedures was illustrated recently in the review of a close election contest for the House of Representatives in Indiana. *See generally* H. R. Rep. No. 58, 99th Cong., 1st Sess. (1985). The partisan and acrimonious nature of that debate only reaffirms the wisdom of avoiding judicial embroilment and of leaving disputed political outcomes to the legislative branch. Had the framers wished the federal judiciary to umpire election contests, they could have so provided. Instead, they reposed primary trust in popular representatives and in political correctives.

Dissatisfied candidates for office in West Virginia are also presented with numerous avenues by which to challenge election results, some of which parallel the federal model. The legislature is directed by Art. 4, § 11 of the West Virginia Constitution "to prescribe the manner of conducting and making returns of elections, and of determining contested elections . . . ," and has accordingly enacted procedures for ballot control and recounts, W. Va. Code §§ 3-6-6 to 3-6-9 and election contests, W. Va. Code §§ 3-7-1 to 3-7-9. Initially, of course, the election returns are counted and certified by a board of canvassers. W. Va. Code § 3-6-9. West Virginia courts have long exercised "election mandamus" powers by which they may "compel any [election] officer . . . to do and perform legally any duty herein required of him." W. Va. Code § 3-1-45. Appellant Underwood, in fact, attempted to employ this very procedure to compel a recount, but his writ was denied as untimely.

State and federal legislatures, moreover, are not concerned solely with election results, but have subjected the entire electoral process to increasing regulation . . . . Thus it seems fair to conclude that the demonstration of judicial restraint under 42 U.S.C. § 1983 will not leave American elections unsupervised or unregulated.

Finally, both state and federal authorities have employed criminal penalties to halt direct intrusions on the election itself. Federal conspiracy laws such as 18 U.S.C. § 241 have been applied to those engaged in corruption of election procedures. *See also* 18 U.S.C. § 594 (prohibiting intimidation of voters); 18 U.S.C. § 600 (prohibiting promise of employment or other benefit for political activity). Criminal sanctions are also available under West Virginia law for those found to have filed false returns, tampered with ballots, bought or sold votes, and the like. *See* W. Va. Code §§ 3-9-1 to 3-9-24. A state grand jury investigated the very allegations at issue here, and issued one indictment, which did not result in a conviction.

IV

Though the presence of even exhaustive alternative remedies does not usually bar an action literally within § 1983 or other statutes, *Patsy v. Board of Regents*, 457 U.S. 496 (1982); *Monroe v. Pape*, 365 U.S. 167 (1961), we are persuaded in this context that we must refrain from considering the particulars of a disputed election, especially in a suit for damages. To do otherwise would be to intrude on the role of the states and the Congress, to raise the possibility of inconsistent judgments concerning elections, to erode the finality of results, to give candidates incentives to bypass the procedures already established, to involve federal courts in the details of state-run elections, and to constitute the jury as well as the electorate as an arbiter of political outcomes. These costs, we believe, would come with very little benefit to the rights fundamentally at issue here — the rights of voters to fair exercise of their franchise. Instead, plaintiffs, who voluntarily entered the political fray, would stand to reap a post-election recovery that might salve feelings of rejection at the polls or help retire debts from the campaign but would bear very little relationship to the larger public interest in partisan debate and competition undeterred by prospects of a post-election suit for damages.

Plaintiffs' theories in this case illustrate the ways in which a lawsuit such as this could intrude on the role of states and Congress to conduct elections and adjudge results. In their complaint, plaintiffs allege damages including, inter alia, loss of income (salary from holding public office), earning capacity, time expended for election purposes and various election expenses, as well as injury to reputation. These losses, of course, would have resulted from election defeat absent any conspiracy by defendants. Injury to reputation, for example, may inhere in any political loss where exposure of opposition blemishes has from the earliest days of the Republic been a part of the quest for public office. Loss of the public official's salary is, ipso facto, an element of each and every political defeat.

Thus, plaintiffs in order to recover damages must perforce rely on the theory that defendants' alleged conspiracy cost them an election they otherwise would have won. In presenting their case plaintiffs would essentially ask a jury to review the outcome of the election. As explained above, however, the task is reserved for states and legislatures, and though the jury's review would not directly impair their primary responsibility to adjudge elections, its re-examination of election results would be inconsistent with proper respect for the role of others whose job it is to canvass the returns and declare a prevailing party. This intrusion, moreover, would not be limited to that of a jury, for the judiciary itself would doubtless be asked to review the jury's judgment of the election in post-trial motions. Principles of separation of powers and federalism, therefore, dictate that both jury and court avoid this inquiry.

Just as the review of electoral results by judge or jury is inconsistent with proper respect for the role of states and Congress, so too the outcomes of these deliberations are potentially inconsistent with the results of the electoral process. Were plaintiffs successful in convincing the jury that they should have won the election or should receive an award of damages, the courts would enter a judgment at odds with the judgment of Congress and of West Virginia, which have seated the apparent victors in these elections. The difficulties inherent in such continuing assaults on political legitimacy would be obvious and might impair the respect to which the enactments of those duly elected are entitled.

Closely related to the problem of inconsistent judgments is the need for finality in elections. Inconsistent judgments, of course, call into question the results of an election in a way that detracts from finality. Even without inconsistent judgments, suits asking federal courts to replay elections cast into limbo contests that should have been long since decided. This case is illustrative. The election at issue occurred in 1980. Plaintiffs did not even bring their suit until 1983, after plaintiff Hutchinson's term would have expired. Now, nearly six years after the election, the parties remain in court essentially to contest the integrity of the election. So long as such avenues are available to defeated candidates, the apparent finality of election outcomes will be illusory.

Maintenance of this action might also provide incentives to losing candidates to ignore the principal routes established to challenge an election and to proceed instead to have the election reviewed in federal courts in hopes of gaining monetary compensation. Plaintiffs in this case, for example, made incomplete use of state and federal procedures yet still seek to recover millions of dollars in this action. Underwood pursued his efforts to secure a recount in an untimely fashion; though Hutchinson filed a complaint with the United States Attorney, there is no evidence that he pursued other avenues available to contest the election; Reese apparently made no attempts to employ available procedures. To allow these plaintiffs access to the federal courts would undermine the processes that are intended to serve as the primary routes to election control: "federal courts would adjudicate every state election dispute, and the elaborate state election contest procedures, designed to assure speedy and orderly disposition of the multitudinous questions that may arise in the electoral process, would be superseded by a section 1983 gloss."

We further believe that federal courts are ill-equipped to monitor the details of elections and resolve factual disputes born of the political process. As one court has noted, "were we to embrace plaintiffs' theory, this court would henceforth be thrust into the details of virtually every election, tinkering with the state's election machinery, reviewing petitions, election cards, vote tallies, and certificates of election for all manner of error and insufficiency under state and federal law." *Powell v. Power*, 436 F.2d 84, 86 (2d Cir. 1970). Elections are, regrettably, not always free from error. Voting machines malfunction, registrars fail to follow instructions, absentee ballots are improperly administered, poll workers become over-zealous, and defeated candidates are, perhaps understandably, inclined to view these multifarious opportunities for human error in a less than charitable light. Quite apart from the serious problems of federalism and separation of powers problems raised by these tasks, we find sifting the minutiae of post-election accusations better suited to the factual review at the administrative and legislative level, where an awareness of the vagaries of politics informs the judgment of those called upon to review the irregularities that are inevitable in elections staffed largely by volunteers.

To ask a jury to undertake such tasks, moreover, is to risk the intrusion of political partisanship into the courtroom, where it has no place. From the exercise of jury strikes to the final rendering of verdict, the spectre of partisanship would intrude and color court proceedings. Such disputes belong, and have been placed, in the political arena, and we cannot accept the substitution of the civil jury for the larger, more diverse, and more representative political electorate that goes to the polls on the day of the election.

These concerns suggest that the federal judiciary should proceed with great caution when asked to consider disputed elections, and have caused many courts to decline the requests to intervene except in extraordinary circumstances. . . . [P]laintiffs' suit for damages strikes us as an inapt means of overseeing the political process. It would provide not so much a correction of electoral ills as a potential windfall to plaintiffs and political advantage through publicity. Those who enter the political fray know the potential risks of their enterprise. If they are defeated by trickery or fraud, they can and should expect the established mechanisms of review— both civil and criminal— to address their grievances, and to take action to insure legitimate electoral results. In this way, they advance the fundamental goal of the electoral process — to determine the will of the people — while also protecting their own interest in the electoral result. A suit for damages, by contrast, may result principally in financial gain for the candidate. We can imagine no scenario in which this gain is the appropriate result of the decision to pursue elected office, and we can find no other case in which a defeated candidate has won such compensation. Nor do we believe, in light of the multitude of alternative remedies, that such a remedy is necessary either to deter misconduct or to provide incentives for enforcement of election laws. . . .

NOTES AND QUESTIONS

1. The Fourth Circuit's opinion makes explicit a distinction that lurks within many of the cases you have looked at. Just whose rights are being vindicated in post-election contests? In this light, consider the United States Supreme Court's decision in *Bush v. Gore*, 531 U.S. 98 (2000). The Court decided the case on an equal protection theory. Precisely whose equal protection rights were being vindicated? As Professor Karlan has pointed out in a related context, "[t]he general assumption in contemporary equal protection law, which seems to play out most of the time, is that faced with a finding of unconstitutionality, the state will remedy the inequality by providing the benefit to the previously excluded group (that is, by "levelling up") rather than by depriving the previously included group ("leveling down"). The few examples in ordinary equal protection of leveling down—the closing of the schools in Prince Edward County, Virginia, or the swimming pools in Jackson, Mississippi – stand out precisely because of their rarity." Pamela S. Karlan, *Race, Rights and Remedies in Criminal Adjudication,* 96 Mich. L. Rev. 2001, 2027 (1998). *Bush II* is essentially a leveling down case: since Florida could not conduct a manual recount that comported with the Supreme Court's definition of equal protection within the constricted time period, the Court held essentially that *none* of the as-yet uncounted votes should be included. From the tactical perspective of candidate Bush, this was of course an acceptable solution. But which *voters* had cognizable interests that were vindicated by the Court's decision? Is there any voter who is better off than she was before in a sense that the legal system can or should recognize? See Pamela S. Karlan, *The Newest Equal Protection: Regressive Doctrine on a Changeable Court* in The Vote: Bush, Gore and the Supreme Court (Cass R. Sunstein and Richard A. Epstein eds. 2001) (discussing the standing issue in *Bush v. Gore* in greater detail.)

F. CRIMINAL PROSECUTION

In addition to the full panoply of civil remedies – preliminary and permanent injunctive relief and damages – violations of state and federal election laws, particularly violations committed by government officials, may often trigger criminal liability. During the 2000 election, for example, Republican election officials in two Florida counties permitted party officials to fill in parts of absentee ballot applications, arguably in violation of Florida law. Nonetheless, in light of the overall thrust of Florida's election code, which is that ballots should not be discarded for technical violations as long as they were cast by qualified voters, the circuit court and the Florida Supreme Court refused to exclude the challenged ballots. But the Florida Supreme Court's opinion states that:

> We find the Supervisor's conduct in this case troubling and we stress that our opinion in this case is not to be read as condoning anything less than strict adherence by election officials to the statutorily mandated election procedures. . . . "[T]his case [does not] concern[] potential sanctions for election officials who fail to faithfully perform their duties. It is for the legislature to specify what sanction should be available for enforcement against election officials who fail to faithfully perform their duties."

Jacobs v. Seminole County Canvassing Board, 773 So.2d 519, 524 (Fla. 2000) (quoting *Beckstrom v. Volusia County Canvassing Board*, 707 So. 2d 720, 725-26 (Fla. 1998)). And in a footnote the Florida Supreme Court observed that "chapter 104 of the Florida Election Code provides certain penalties for election officials and others who violate the Code. However, violations of the Code will not necessarily invalidate the votes of innocent electors."

Criminal prosecutions of government officials, or voters themselves, are infrequent, but by no means unheard of. And criminal prosecutions often produce important principles of law that affect future civil cases. For example, consider *Guinn v. Oklahoma*, 238 U.S. 347 (1915), discussed in Chapter 2. In *Guinn*, the United States Supreme Court struck down Oklahoma's "grandfather clause," which had effectively disenfranchised African Americans. The case involved a criminal prosecution of Oklahoma election officials under the predecessor to 18 U.S.C. § 241, which provides, in pertinent part that "[i]f two or more persons conspire to injure, oppress, threaten, or intimidate any person . . . in the free exercise or enjoyment of any right or privilege secured to him by the Constitution or laws of the United States, . . . [t]hey shall be fined . . . or imprisoned . . . or both . . . ." The Court held that the grandfather clause violated the Fifteenth Amendment because, although it was neutral on its face, it clearly had been adopted for the purpose of preventing blacks from registering and voting. Having recognized that principle in *Guinn*, the Court and lower courts then applied it to other facially neutral but purposefully discriminatory practices such as literacy tests, at-large elections, and dilutionary redistricting schemes.

Federal law has a number of criminal provisions that have been used to protect the right to vote. Some, like 18 U.S.C. § 241 and 18 U.S.C. § 242, which makes it a crime for a person acting "under color of [state] law" to "willfully subjec[t] any person . . . to the deprivation of any rights, privileges, or immunities secured or protected by the Constitution or laws of the United States," penalize the denial of constitutional rights generally. Other provisions, such as Chapter 29 of Title 18, or section 11 of the Voting Rights Act, are directed specifically at election-related offenses. In light of the discussions throughout the book about the delicate questions of federalism and the distinctive federal interests involved in elections, it is not surprising that federal statutes often use a jurisdictional handle that requires the presence of a candidate for federal office on the ballot. So, for example, 18 U.S.C. § 594 makes it a crime to "intimidat[e], threate[n], coerc[e], or attemp[t] to intimidate, threaten, or coerce, any other person for the purpose of interfering with the right of such other person to vote or to vote as he may choose, or of causing such other person to vote for, or not to vote for, any candidate for the office of President, Vice President, Presidential elector, Member of the Senate, Member of the House of Representatives, Delegate from the District of Columbia, or Resident Commissioner, at any election held solely or in part for the purpose of electing such candidate . . . ." And the provisions of section 11 of the Voting Rights Act that deal with what might be viewed as "retail" fraud also require that the election be held held "solely or in part for the purpose of selecting or electing" candidates to federal office.

States, too, have extensive criminal codes regulating elections. For example, Florida has provisions in Chapter 104 of its election code that parallel the federal criminal provisions regarding vote buying and selling, intimidation and use of force, vote fraud and the like. In addition, Florida law criminalizes various forms of official malfeasance. *See, e.g.*, Fla. Stat. § 104.051 (2000), which provides, in pertinent part:

> (2) Any official who willfully refuses or willfully neglects to perform his or her duties as prescribed by this election code is guilty of a misdemeanor of the first degree, punishable as provided in s. 775.082 or s. 775.083.

> (3) Any official who performs his or her duty as prescribed by this election code fraudulently or corruptly is guilty of a felony of the third degree, punishable as provided in s. 775.082, s. 775.083, or s. 775.084.

> (4) Any supervisor, deputy supervisor, or election employee who attempts to influence or interfere with any elector voting a ballot commits a felony of the third degree, punishable as provided in s. 775.082, s. 775.083, or s. 775.084.

In considering the relative efficacy of criminal prosecutions, think about the deterrence value these pack for individual voters who are inclined to commit what might be called "retail" fraud – that is, to cast a ballot they are not entitled to, or to accept a payment for voting or not voting in a particular way – as opposed to the impact of criminal sanctions on actors within the political system who are more prone to "wholesale" fraud.

There is a rich, and growing, literature on one aspect of the criminal law surrounding elections, namely, vote buying. For representative articles, see, e.g., Richard L. Hasen, *Vote Buying*, 88 Calif. L. Rev. 1323 (2000); Pamela S. Karlan, *Not By Money but by Virtue Won? Vote Trafficking and the Voting Rights System*, 80 Va. L. Rev. 1455 (1994); Pamela S. Karlan, *Politics By Other Means*, 85 Va. L. Rev. 1697 (1999); Saul Levmore, *Voting with Intensity*, 53 Stan. L. Rev. 111 (2000).

DOCUMENTARY APPENDIX

THE UNITED STATES CONSTITUTION
(SELECTED PROVISIONS)

We the People of the United States, in order to form a more perfect Union, establish Justice, insure domestic tranquility, provide for common defense, promote the general Welfare, and secure the Blessings of Liberty to ourselves and our Posterity, do ordain and establish this Constitution for the United States of America.

Article I

Section 1.
All legislative Powers herein granted shall be vested in a Congress of the United States, which shall consist of a Senate and House of Representatives.

Section 2.
The House of Representatives shall be composed of Members chosen every second Year by the People of the several States, and the Electors in each State shall have the Qualifications requisite for Electors of the most numerous Branch of the State Legislature.

No Person shall be a Representative who shall not have attained to the Age of twenty five Years, and been seven Years a Citizen of the United States, and who shall not, when elected, be an Inhabitant of that State in which he shall be chosen.

Representatives and direct Taxes shall be apportioned among the several States which may be included within this Union, according to their respective numbers, which shall be determined by adding to the whole Number of free Persons, including those bound to Service for a Term of Years, and excluding Indians not taxed, three fifths of all other Persons. The actual Enumeration shall be made within three Years after the first Meeting of the Congress of the United States, and within every subsequent Term of ten Years, in such Manner as they shall by Law direct. The Number of Representatives shall not exceed one for every thirty Thousand, but each State shall have at Least one Representative; and until such enumeration shall be made, the State of New Hampshire shall be entitled to choose three, Massachusetts eight, Rhode-Island and Providence Plantations one, Connecticut five, New-York six, New Jersey four, Pennsylvania eight, Delaware one, Maryland six, Virginia ten, North Carolina five, South Carolina five, and Georgia three.

The House of Representatives shall chuse their Speaker and other Officers; and shall have the sole Power of Impeachment.

* * * *

Section 4.
The Times, Places and Manner of holding Elections for Senators and Representatives, shall be prescribed in each State by the Legislature thereof; but the Congress may at any time by Law make or alter such Regulations, except as to the Places of choosing Senators.

The Congress shall assemble at least once in every Year, and such Meeting shall be on the first Monday in December, unless they shall by Law appoint a different Day.

Section 5.
Each House shall be the Judge of the Elections, Returns and Qualifications of its own Members, and a Majority of each shall constitute a Quorum to do Business; but a smaller Number may adjourn from day to day, and may be authorized to compel the Attendance of absent Members, in such Manner, and under such Penalties as each House may provide.

Each House may determine the Rules of its Proceedings, punish its Members for disorderly Behaviour, and, with the Concurrence of two thirds, expel a Member.

Each House shall keep a Journal of its Proceedings, and from time to time publish the same, excepting such Parts as may in their Judgment require Secrecy; and the Yeas and Nays of the Members of either House on any question shall, at the Desire of one fifth of those Present, be entered on the Journal.

Neither House, during the Session of Congress, shall, without the Consent of the other, adjourn for more than three days, nor to any other Place than that in which the two Houses shall be sitting.

* * * *

Section 8.
The Congress shall have Power To lay and collect Taxes, Duties, Imposts and Excises, to pay the Debts and provide for the common Defense and general Welfare of the United States; but all Duties, Imposts and Excises shall be uniform throughout the United States; . . . – And

To make all Laws which shall be necessary and proper for carrying into Execution the foregoing Powers, and all other Powers vested by this Constitution in the Government of the United States, or in any Department or Officer thereof.

* * * *

Article II

Section 1.

The executive Power shall be vested in a President of the United States of America. He shall hold his Office during the Term of four Years, and, together with the Vice President, chosen for the same Term, be elected, as follows

Each State shall appoint, in such Manner as the Legislature thereof may direct, a Number of Electors, equal to the whole Number of Senators and representatives to which the State may be entitled in the Congress: but no Senator or Representative, or Person holding an Office of Trust or Profit under the United States, shall be appointed an Elector.

The Electors shall meet in their respective States, and vote by Ballot for two Persons, of whom one at least shall not be an Inhabitant of the same State with themselves. And they shall make a List of all the Persons voted for, and of the Number of Votes for each; which List they shall sign and certify, and transmit sealed to the Seat of the Government of the United States, directed to the President of the Senate. The President of the Senate shall, in the Presence of the Senate and House of Representatives, open all the Certificates, and the Votes shall then be counted. The Person having the greatest Number of Votes shall be the President, if such Number be a Majority of the whole Number of Electors appointed; and if there be more than one who have such Majority, and have an equal Number of Votes, then the House of Representatives shall immediately chuse by Ballot one of them for President; and if no Person have a Majority, then from the five highest on the List the said House shall in like Manner chuse the President. But in chusing the President, the Votes shall be taken by States, the Representation from each State having one Vote; A quorum for this Purpose shall consist of a Member or Members from two thirds of the States, and a Majority of all the States shall be necessary to a Choice. In every Case, after the Choice of the President, the Person having the greatest Number of Votes of the Electors shall be the Vice President. But if there should remain two or more who have equal Votes, the Senate shall chuse from them by Ballot the Vice President.

The Congress may determine the Time of chusing the Electors, and the Day on which they shall give their Votes; which Day shall be the same throughout the United States.

No Person except a natural born Citizen, or a Citizen of the United States, at the time of the Adoption of this Constitution, shall be eligible to the Office of President; neither shall any Person be eligible to that Office who shall not have attained to the Age of thirty five Years, and been fourteen Years a Resident within the United States.

In Case of the Removal of the President from Office, or of his Death, Resignation, or Inability to discharge the Powers and Duties of the said Office, the Same shall devolve on the Vice President, and the Congress may by Law provide for the Case of Removal, Death, Resignation or Inability, both of the President and Vice President, declaring what Officer shall then act as

President, and such Officer shall act accordingly, until the Disability be removed, or a President shall be elected.

* * * *

Article III

Section 1.
The judicial Power of the United States, shall be vested in one supreme Court, and in such inferior Courts as the Congress may from time to time ordain and establish. The Judges, both of the supreme and inferior Courts, shall hold their Offices during good Behaviour, and shall, at stated Times, receive for their Services, a Compensation, which shall not be diminished during their Continuance in Office.

Section 2.
The judicial Power shall extend to all Cases, in Law and Equity, arising under this Constitution, the Laws of the United States, and Treaties made, or which shall be made, under their Authority;--to all Cases affecting Ambassadors, other public Ministers and Consuls;--to all Cases of admiralty and maritime Jurisdiction;--to Controversies to which the United States shall be a Party;--to Controversies between two or more States;--between a State and Citizens of another State; between Citizens of different States,—between Citizens of the same State claiming Lands under Grants of different States, and between a State, or the Citizens thereof, and foreign States, Citizens or Subjects.

In all Cases affecting Ambassadors, other public Ministers and Consuls, and those in which a State shall be Party, the supreme Court shall have original Jurisdiction. In all the other Cases before mentioned, the supreme Court shall have appellate Jurisdiction, both as to Law and Fact, with such Exceptions, and under such Regulations as the Congress shall make.

* * * *

Article IV

* * * *

Section 4.
The United States shall guarantee to every State in this Union a Republican Form of Government, and shall protect each of them against Invasion; and on Application of the Legislature, or of the Executive (when the Legislature cannot be convened) against domestic Violence.

Article V

The Congress, whenever two thirds of both Houses shall deem it necessary, shall propose Amendments to this Constitution, or, on the Application of the Legislatures of two thirds of the several States, shall call a Convention for proposing Amendments, which, in either Case, shall be valid to all Intents and Purposes, as Part of this Constitution, when ratified by the Legislatures of three fourths of the several States, or by Conventions in three fourths thereof, as the one or the other Mode of Ratification may be proposed by the Congress; Provided that no Amendment which may be made prior to the Year One thousand eight hundred and eight shall in any Manner affect the first and fourth Clauses in the Ninth Section of the first Article; and that no State, without its Consent, shall be deprived of its equal Suffrage in the Senate.

Article VI

* * * *

This Constitution, and the Laws of the United States which shall be made in Pursuance thereof; and all Treaties made, or which shall be made, under the Authority of the United States, shall be the supreme Law of the Land; and the Judges in every State shall be bound thereby, any Thing in the Constitution or Laws of any State to the Contrary notwithstanding.

* * * *

SELECTED AMENDMENTS

AMENDMENT IX
(Ratified in 1791.)
The enumeration in the Constitution, of certain rights, shall not be construed to deny or disparage others retained by the people.

AMENDMENT X
(Ratified in 1791.)
The powers not delegated to the United States by the Constitution, nor prohibited by it to the States, are reserved to the States respectively, or to the people.

AMENDMENT XII
(Ratified in 1804.)
The Electors shall meet in their respective states and vote by ballot for President and Vice-President, one of whom, at least, shall not be an inhabitant of the same state with themselves; they shall name in their ballots the person voted for as President, and in distinct ballots the person voted for as Vice-President, and they shall make distinct lists of all persons voted for as President, and of all persons voted for as Vice-President, and of the number of votes for each, which lists they shall sign and certify, and transmit sealed to the seat of the government of the United States, directed to the President of the Senate;— The President of the Senate shall, in the presence of the Senate and House of Representatives, open all the certificates and the votes shall then be counted;— The person having the greatest number of votes for President, shall be the President, if such number be a majority of the whole number of Electors appointed; and if no person have such majority, then from the persons having the highest numbers not exceeding three on the list of those voted for as President, the House of Representatives shall choose immediately, by ballot, the President. But in choosing the President, the votes shall be taken by states, the representation from each state having one vote; a quorum for this purpose

shall consist of a member or members from two-thirds of the states, and a majority of all the states shall be necessary to a choice. And if the House of Representatives shall not choose a President whenever the right of choice shall devolve upon then, before the fourth day of March next following, then the Vice-President shall act as President, as in the case of the death or other constitutional disability of the President.— The person having the greatest number of votes as Vice-President, shall be the Vice-President, if such number be a majority of the whole number of Electors appointed, and if no person have a majority, then from the two highest numbers on the list, the Senate shall choose the Vice-President; a quorum for the purpose shall consist of two-thirds of the whole number of Senators, and a majority of the whole number shall be necessary to a choice. But no person constitutionally ineligible to the office of President shall be eligible to that of Vice-President of the United States.

AMENDMENT XIV
(Ratified in 1868.)
Section 1.
All persons born or naturalized in the United States, and subject to the jurisdiction thereof, are citizens of the United States and of the
State wherein they reside. No State shall make or enforce any law which shall abridge the privileges or immunities of citizens of the United States; nor shall any State deprive any person of life, liberty, or property, without due process of law; nor deny to any person within its jurisdiction the equal protection of the laws.

Section 2.
Representatives shall be apportioned among the several States according to their respective numbers, counting the whole number of persons in each State, excluding Indians not taxed. But when the right to vote at any election for the choice of electors for President and Vice President of the United States, Representatives in Congress, the Executive and Judicial officers of a State, or the members of the Legislature thereof, is denied to any of the male inhabitants of such State, being twenty-one years of age, and citizens of the United States, or in any way abridged, except for participation in rebellion, or other crime, the basis of representation therein shall be reduced in the proportion which the number of such male citizens shall bear to the whole number of male citizens twenty-one years of age in such State.

Section 3.
No person shall be a Senator or Representative in Congress, or elector of President and Vice President, or hold any office, civil or military, under the United States, or under any State, who, having previously taken an oath, as a member of Congress, or as an officer of the United States, or as a member of any State legislature, or as an executive or judicial officer of any State, to support the Constitution of the United States, shall have engaged in insurrection or rebellion against the same, or given aid or comfort to the enemies thereof. But Congress may by a vote of two-thirds of each House, remove such disability.

* * * *

Section 5.
The Congress shall have power to enforce, by appropriate legislation, the provisions of this article.

AMENDMENT XV
(Ratified in 1870.)
Section 1.
The right of citizens of the United States to vote shall not be denied or abridged by the United States or by any State on account of race, color, or previous condition of servitude.

Section 2.
The Congress shall have power to enforce this article by appropriate legislation.

AMENDMENT XVII
(Ratified in 1913.)
The Senate of the United States shall be composed of two Senators from each State, elected by the people thereof for six years; and each Senator shall have one vote. The electors in each State shall have the qualifications requisite for electors of the most numerous branch of the State legislatures. When vacancies happen in the representation of any State in the Senate, the executive authority of such State shall issue writs of election to fill such vacancies: Provided, That the legislature of any State may empower the executive thereof to make temporary appointments until the people fill the vacancies by election as the legislature may direct. This amendment shall not be so construed as to affect the election or term of any Senator chosen before it becomes valid as part of the Constitution.

AMENDMENT XIX
(Ratified in 1920.)
The right of citizens of the United States to vote shall not be denied or abridged by the United States or by any State on account of sex. Congress shall have power to enforce this article by appropriate legislation.

AMENDMENT XX
(Ratified in 1933.)
Section 1.
The terms of the President and Vice President shall end at noon on the 20th day of January, and the terms of Senators and Representatives at noon on the 3d day of January, of the years in which such terms would have ended if this article had not been ratified; and the terms of their successors shall then begin.

Section 2.
The Congress shall assemble at least once in every year, and such meeting shall begin at noon on the 3d day of January, unless they shall by law appoint a different day.

Section 3.

If, at the time fixed for the beginning of the term of the President, the President elect shall have died, the Vice President elect shall become President. If a President shall not have been chosen before the time fixed for the beginning of his term, or if the President elect shall have failed to qualify, then the Vice President elect shall act as President until a President shall have qualified; and the Congress may by law provide for the case wherein neither a President elect nor a Vice President elect shall have qualified, declaring who shall then act as President, or the manner in which one who is to act shall be selected, and such person shall act accordingly until a President or Vice President shall have qualified.

Section 4.

The Congress may by law provide for the case of the death of any of the persons from whom the House of Representatives may choose a President whenever the right of choice shall have devolved upon them, and for the case of the death of any of the persons from whom the Senate may choose a Vice President whenever the right of choice shall have devolved upon them.

Section 5.

Sections 1 and 2 shall take effect on the 15th day of October following the ratification of this article.

Section 6.

This article shall be inoperative unless it shall have been ratified as an amendment to the Constitution by the legislatures of three-fourths of the several States within seven years from the date of its submission.

AMENDMENT XXIII
(Ratified in 1961.)
Section 1.

The District constituting the seat of Government of the United States shall appoint in such manner as the Congress may direct: A number of electors of President and Vice President equal to the whole number of Senators and Representatives in Congress to which the District would be entitled if it were a State, but in no event more than the least populous State; they shall be in addition to those appointed by the States, but they shall be considered, for the purposes of the election of President and Vice President, to be electors appointed by a State; and they shall meet in the District and perform such duties as provided by the twelfth article of amendment.

Section 2.

The Congress shall have power to enforce this article by appropriate legislation.

AMENDMENT XXIV
(Ratified in 1964.)
Section 1.

The right of citizens of the United States to vote in any primary or other election for President or Vice President, for electors for President or Vice President, or for Senator or Representative in Congress, shall not be denied or abridged by the United States or any State by reason of failure to pay any poll tax or other tax.

Section 2.
The Congress shall have power to enforce this article by appropriate legislation.

AMENDMENT XXVI
(Ratified in 1971.)
Section 1.
The right of citizens of the United States, who are eighteen years of age or older, to vote shall not be denied or abridged by the United States or by any State on account of age.

Section 2.
The Congress shall have power to enforce this article by appropriate legislation.

* * * *

THE ELECTORAL COUNT ACT
UNITED STATES CODE
TITLE 3. THE PRESIDENT
CHAPTER 1--PRESIDENTIAL ELECTIONS AND VACANCIES

§ 1. Time of appointing electors

The electors of President and Vice President shall be appointed, in each State, on the Tuesday next after the first Monday in November, in every fourth year succeeding every election of a President and Vice President.

§ 2. Failure to make choice on prescribed day

Whenever any State has held an election for the purpose of choosing electors, and has failed to make a choice on the day prescribed by law, the electors may be appointed on a subsequent day in such a manner as the legislature of such State may direct.

§ 3. Number of electors

The number of electors shall be equal to the number of Senators and Representatives to which the several States are by law entitled at the time when the President and Vice President to be chosen come into office; except, that where no apportionment of Representatives has been made after any enumeration, at the time of choosing electors, the number of electors shall be according to the then existing apportionment of Senators and Representatives.

§ 4. Vacancies in electoral college

Each State may, by law, provide for the filling of any vacancies which may occur in its college of electors when such college meets to give its electoral vote.

§ 5. Determination of controversy as to appointment of electors

If any State shall have provided, by laws enacted prior to the day fixed for the appointment of the electors, for its final determination of any controversy or contest concerning the appointment of all or any of the electors of such State, by judicial or other methods or procedures, and such determination shall have been made at least six days before the time fixed for the meeting of the electors, such determination made pursuant to such law so existing on said day, and made at least six days prior to said time of meeting of the electors, shall be conclusive, and shall govern in the counting of the electoral votes as provided in the Constitution, and as hereinafter regulated, so far as the ascertainment of the electors appointed by such State is concerned.

§ 6. Credentials of electors; transmission to Archivist of the United States and to Congress; public inspection

It shall be the duty of the executive of each State, as soon as practicable after the conclusion of the appointment of the electors in such State by the final ascertainment, under and in pursuance of the laws of such State providing for such ascertainment, to communicate by registered mail under the seal of the State to the Archivist of theUnited States a certificate of such ascertainment of the electors appointed, setting forth the names of such electors and the canvass or other ascertainment under the laws of such State of the number of votes given or cast for each person for whose appointment any and all votes have been given or cast; and it shall also thereupon be the duty of the executive of each State to deliver to the electors of such State, on or before the day on which they are required by section 7 of this title to meet, six duplicate-originals of the same certificate under the seal of the State; and if there shall have been any final determination in a State in the manner provided for by law of a controversy or contest concerning the appointment of all or any of the electors of such State, it shall be the duty of the executive of such State, as soon as practicable after such determination, to communicate under the seal of the State to the Archivist of the United States a certificate of such determination in form and manner as the same shall have been made; and the certificate or certificates so received by the Archivist of the United States shall be preserved by him for one year and shall be a part of the public records of his office and shall be open to public inspection; and the Archivist of the United States at the first meeting of Congress thereafter shall transmit to the two Houses of Congress copies in full of each and every such certificate so received at the National Archives and Records Administration.

§ 7. Meeting and vote of electors

The electors of President and Vice President of each State shall meet and give their votes on the first Monday after the second Wednesday in December next following their appointment at such place in each State as the legislature of such State shall direct.

§ 8. Manner of voting

The electors shall vote for President and Vice President, respectively, in the manner directed by the Constitution.

§ 9. Certificates of votes for President and Vice President

The electors shall make and sign six certificates of all the votes given by them, each of which certificates shall contain two distinct lists, one of the votes for President and the other of the votes for Vice President, and shall annex to each of the certificates one of the lists of the electors which shall have been furnished to them by direction of the executive of the State.

§ 10. Sealing and endorsing certificates

The electors shall seal up the certificates so made by them, and certify upon each that the lists of all the votes of such State given for President, and of all the votes given for Vice President, are contained therein.

§ 11. Disposition of certificates

The electors shall dispose of the certificates so made by them and the lists attached thereto in the following manner:

First. They shall forthwith forward by registered mail one of the same to the President of the Senate at the seat of government.

Second. Two of the same shall be delivered to the secretary of state of the State, one of which shall be held subject to the order of the President of the Senate, the other to be preserved by him for one year and shall be a part of the public records of his office and shall be open to public inspection.

Third. On the day thereafter they shall forward by registered mail two of such certificates and lists to the Archivist of the United States at the seat of government, one of which shall be held subject to the order of the President of the Senate. The other shall be preserved by the Archivist of the United States for one year and shall be a part of the public records of his office and shall be open to public inspection.

Fourth. They shall forthwith cause the other of the certificates and lists to be delivered to the judge of the district in which the electors shall have assembled.

§ 12. Failure of certificates of electors to reach President of the Senate or Archivist of the United States; demand on State for certificate

When no certificate of vote and list mentioned in sections 9 and 11 of this title from any State shall have been received by the President of the Senate or by the Archivist of the United States by the fourth Wednesday in December, after the meeting of the electors shall have been held, the President of the Senate or, if he be absent from the seat of government, the Archivist of the United States shall request, by the most expeditious method available, the secretary of state of the State to send up the certificate and list lodged with him by the electors of such State; and it shall be his duty upon receipt of such request immediately to transmit same by registered mail to the President of the Senate at the seat of government.

§ 13. Same; demand on district judge for certificate

When no certificates of votes from any State shall have been received at the seat of government on the fourth Wednesday in December, after the meeting of the electors shall have been held, the President of the Senate or, if he be absent from the seat of government, the Archivist of the United States shall send a special messenger to the district judge in whose custody one certificate of votes from that State has been lodged, and such judge shall forthwith transmit that list by the hand of such messenger to the seat of government.

§ 14. Forfeiture for messenger's neglect of duty

Every person who, having been appointed, pursuant to section 13 of this title, to deliver the certificates of the votes of the electors to the President of the Senate, and having accepted such appointment, shall neglect to perform the services required from him, shall forfeit the sum of $1,000.

§ 15. Counting electoral votes in Congress

Congress shall be in session on the sixth day of January succeeding every meeting of the electors. The Senate and House of Representatives shall meet in the Hall of the House of Representatives at the hour of 1 o'clock in the afternoon on that day, and the President of the Senate shall be their presiding officer. Two tellers shall be previously appointed on the part of the Senate and two on the part of the House of Representatives, to whom shall be handed, as they are opened by the President of the Senate, all the certificates and papers purporting to be certificates of the electoral votes, which certificates and papers shall be opened, presented, and acted upon in the alphabetical order of the States, beginning with the letter A; and said tellers, having then read the same in the presence and hearing of the two Houses, shall make a list of the votes as they shall appear from the said certificates; and the votes having been ascertained and counted according to the rules in this subchapter provided, the result of the same shall be delivered to the President of the Senate, who shall thereupon announce the state of the vote, which announcement shall be deemed a sufficient declaration of the persons, if any, elected President and Vice President of the United States, and, together with a list of the votes, be entered on the Journals of the two Houses. Upon such reading of any such certificate or paper, the President of the Senate shall call for objections, if any. Every objection shall be made in writing, and shall state clearly and concisely, and without argument, the ground thereof, and shall be signed by at least one Senator and one Member of the House of Representatives before the same shall be received. When all objections so made to any vote or paper from a State shall have been received and read, the Senate shall thereupon withdraw, and such objections shall be submitted to the Senate for its decision; and the Speaker of the House of Representatives shall, in like manner, submit such objections to the House of Representatives for its decision; and no electoral vote or votes from any State which shall have been regularly given by electors whose appointment has been lawfully certified to according to section 6 of this title from which but one return has been received shall be rejected, but the two Houses concurrently may reject the vote or votes when they agree that such vote or votes have not been so regularly given by electors whose appointment has been so certified. If more than one return or paper purporting to be a return from a State shall have been received by the President of the Senate, those votes, and those only, shall be counted which shall have been regularly given by the electors who are shown by the determination mentioned in section 5 of this title to have been appointed, if the determination in said section provided for shall have been made, or by such successors or substitutes, in case of a vacancy in the board of electors so ascertained, as have been appointed to fill such vacancy in the mode provided by the laws of the State; but in case there shall arise the question which of two or more of such State authorities determining what electors have been appointed, as mentioned in section 5 of this title, is the lawful tribunal of such state, the votes regularly given of those electors, and those only, of such State shall be counted whose title as electors the two Houses, acting separately, shall concurrently decide is supported by the decision of such State so authorized by its law; and in such case of more than one return or paper purporting to be a return from a State, if there shall have been no such determination of the question in the State aforesaid, then those votes, and those only, shall be counted which the two Houses shall concurrently decide were cast by lawful electors appointed in accordance with the laws of the State, unless the two Houses, acting separately, shall concurrently decide such votes not to be the lawful votes of the legally appointed electors of such State. But if the two Houses shall disagree in respect of the counting of such votes, then, and in that case, the votes of the electors whose appointment shall have been certified by the executive of the State, under the seal thereof, shall be counted. When the two Houses have voted, they shall immediately again meet, and the presiding officer shall then announce the decision of the questions submitted. No votes or papers from any other State shall be acted upon until the objections previously made to the votes or papers from any State shall have been finally disposed of.

§ 16. Same; seats for officers and Members of two Houses in joint meeting

At such joint meeting of the two Houses seats shall be provided as follows: For the President of the Senate, the Speaker's chair; for the Speaker, immediately upon his left; the Senators, in the body of the Hall upon the right of the presiding officer; for the Representatives, in the body of the Hall not provided for the Senators; for the tellers, Secretary of the Senate, and Clerk of the House of Representatives, at the Clerk's desk; for the other officers of the two Houses, in front of the Clerk's desk and upon each side of the Speaker's platform. Such joint meeting shall not be dissolved until the count of electoral votes shall be completed and the result declared; and no recess shall be taken unless a question shall have arisen in regard to counting any such votes, or otherwise under this subchapter, in which case it shall be competent for either House, acting separately, in the manner hereinbefore provided, to direct a recess of such House not beyond the next calendar day, Sunday excepted, at the hour of 10 o'clock in the forenoon. But if the counting of the electoral votes and the declaration of the result shall not have been completed before the fifth calendar day next after such first meeting of the two Houses, no further or other recess shall be taken by either House.

§ 17. Same; limit of debate in each House

When the two Houses separate to decide upon an objection that may have been made to the counting of any electoral vote or votes from any State, or other question arising in the matter, each Senator and Representative may speak to such objection or question five minutes, and not more than once; but after such debate shall have lasted two hours it shall be the duty of the presiding officer of each House to put the main question without further debate.

§ 18. Same; parliamentary procedure at joint meeting

While the two Houses shall be in meeting as provided in this chapter, the President of the Senate shall have power to preserve order; and no debate shall be allowed and no question shall be put by the presiding officer except to either House on a motion to withdraw.

THE VOTING RIGHTS ACT OF 1965
(SELECTED SECTIONS)
UNITED STATES CODE
TITLE 42
CHAPTER 20 – ELECTIVE FRANCHISE

§ 1973. Denial or abridgement of right to vote on account of race or color through voting qualifications or prerequisites; establishment of violation

(a) No voting qualification or prerequisite to voting or standard, practice, or procedure shall be imposed or applied by any State or political subdivision in a manner which results in a denial or abridgement of the right of any citizen of the United States to vote on account of race or color, or in contravention of the guarantees set forth in section 4(f)(2) [protecting language minorities], provided in subsection (b).

(b) A violation of subsection (a) is established if, based on the totality of circumstances, it is shown that the political processes leading to nomination or election in the State or political subdivision are not equally open to participation by members of a class of citizens protected by subsection (a) in that its members have less opportunity than other members of the electorate to participate in the political process and to elect representatives of their choice. The extent to which members of a protected class have been elected to office in the State or political subdivision is one circumstance which may be considered: Provided, That nothing in this section establishes a right to have members of a protected class elected in numbers equal to their proportion in the population.

§ 1973c. Alteration of voting qualifications and procedures; action by State or political subdivision for declaratory judgment of no denial or abridgement of voting rights; three-judge district court; appeal to Supreme Court

Whenever a [covered] State or political subdivision . . . shall enact or seek to administer any voting qualification or prerequisite to voting, or standard, practice, or procedure with respect to voting different from that in force or effect on [the date which prompted its being listed as a covered jurisdiction], . . . such State or subdivision may institute an action in the United States District Court for the District of Columbia for a declaratory judgment that such qualification prerequisite, standard, practice, or procedure does not have the purpose and will not have the effect of denying or abridging the right to vote on account of race or color, or in contravention of the guarantees set forth in section 4(f)(2), and unless and until the court enters such judgment no person shall be denied the right to vote for failure to comply with such qualification, prerequisite, standard, practice, or procedure: Provided, That such qualification, prerequisite, standard, practice, or procedure may be enforced without such proceeding if the qualification, prerequisite, standard, practice, or procedure has been submitted by the chief legal officer or other appropriate official of such State or subdivision to the Attorney General and the Attorney General has not interposed an objection within sixty days after such submission, or upon good cause shown, to facilitate an expedited approval within sixty days after such submission, the Attorney General has affirmatively indicated that such objection will not be made. Neither an affirmative indication by the Attorney General that no objection will be made, nor the Attorney General's failure to object, nor a declaratory judgment entered under this section shall bar a subsequent action to enjoin enforcement of such qualification, prerequisite, standard, practice, or procedure. In the event the Attorney General affirmatively indicates that no objection will be made within the sixty-day period following receipt of a submission, the Attorney General may reserve the right to reexamine the submission if additional information comes to his attention during the remainder of the sixty-day period which would otherwise require objection in accordance with this section. Any action under this section shall be heard and determined by a court of three judges in accordance with the provisions of section 2284 of title 28 of the United States Code and any appeal shall lie to the Supreme Court.

§ 1973l(c)(3) Definitions.

(1) The terms "vote" or "voting" shall include all action necessary to make a vote effective in any primary, special, or general election, including, but not limited to, registration, listing pursuant to this Act, or other action required by law prerequisite to voting, casting a ballot, and having such ballot counted properly and included in the appropriate totals of votes cast with respect to candidates for public or party office and propositions for which votes are received in an election.

* * * *

(3) The term "language minorities" or "language minority group" means persons who are American Indian, Asian American, Alaskan Natives or of Spanish heritage.

SELECTED PROVISIONS OF THE FLORIDA ELECTION CODE IN FORCE DURING THE 2000 ELECTION

101.015 Standards for voting systems.--

(1) The Department of State shall adopt rules which establish minimum standards for hardware and software for electronic and electromechanical voting systems. Such rules shall contain standards for:

(a) Functional requirements;

(b) Performance levels;

(c) Physical and design characteristics;

(d) Documentation requirements; and

(e) Evaluation criteria.

(2) Each odd-numbered year the Department of State shall review the rules governing standards and certification of voting systems to determine the adequacy and effectiveness of such rules in assuring that elections are fair and impartial.

(3) The Department of State shall adopt rules to achieve and maintain the maximum degree of correctness, impartiality, and efficiency of the procedures of voting, including write-in voting, and of counting, tabulating, and recording votes by voting systems used in this state.

(4)(a) The Department of State shall adopt rules establishing minimum security standards for voting systems.

(b) Each supervisor of elections shall establish written procedures to assure accuracy and security in his or her county, and such procedures shall be reviewed in each odd-numbered year by the Department of State.

(c) Each supervisor of elections shall submit any revisions to the security procedures to the Department of State at least 45 days before the first election in which they are to take effect.

(5)(a) The Department of State shall adopt rules which establish standards for provisional approval of hardware and software for innovative use of electronic and electromechanical voting systems. Such rules shall contain standards for:

1.   Functional requirements;

2.   Performance levels;

3.   Physical and design characteristics;

4.   Documentation requirements;

5.   Evaluation criteria;

6.   Audit capabilities; and

7.   Consideration of prior use of a system.

(b)   A voting system shall be provisionally approved for a total of no more than 2 years, and the Department of State has the authority to revoke such approval. Provisional approval of a system shall not be granted by the Department of State to supersede certification requirements of this section.

(c)   1.   No provisionally approved system may be used in any election, including any municipal election, without the authorization of the Department of State.

2.   An application for use of a provisionally approved system shall be submitted at least 120 days prior to the intended use by the supervisor of elections or municipal elections official. Such application shall request authorization for use of the system in a specific election. Each application shall state the election, the number of precincts, and the number of anticipated voters for which the system is requested for use.

3.   The Department of State shall authorize or deny authorization of the use of the provisionally approved system for the specific election and shall notify the supervisor of elections or municipal elections official in writing of the authorization or denial of authorization, along with the reasons therefor, within 45 days after receipt of the application.

(d)   A contract for the use of a provisionally approved system for a specific election may be entered into with the approval of the Department of State. No contract for title to a provisionally approved system may be entered into.

(e)   The use of any provisionally approved system shall be valid for all purposes.

(6)   All electronic and electromechanical voting systems purchased on or after January 1, 1990, must meet the minimum standards established under subsection (1). All electronic and electromechanical voting systems in use on or after July 1, 1993, must meet the minimum standards established under subsection (1) or subsection (5).

101.46 Instruction to electors before election.--

The authorities in charge of elections, where voting machines are used, shall designate suitable and adequate times and places for giving instructions to electors who apply, and the machines shall contain a sample ballot showing the title of offices to be filled, and, so far as practicable, the names of candidates to be voted on at the next election. No voting machine which is to be assigned for use in an election shall be used for instruction after having been prepared and sealed for the election. During the public exhibition of any voting machine for any instruction, the counting mechanism shall be concealed, but the doors may be temporarily opened when authorized by the supervisor of elections.

101.5601 Short title.--

Sections 101.5601 through 101.5615 shall be known as the "Electronic Voting Systems Act."

101.5602 Purpose.--

The purpose of this act is to authorize the use of electronic and electromechanical voting systems in which votes are registered electronically or are tabulated on automatic tabulating equipment or data processing equipment.

101.5603 Definitions relating to Electronic Voting Systems Act.--

As used in this act, the term:

(1) "Automatic tabulating equipment" includes apparatus necessary to automatically examine, count, and record votes.

(2) "Ballot" means the card, tape, or other vehicle upon which the elector's choices are recorded.

(3) "Ballot information" means the material containing the names of offices and candidates and the questions to be voted on.

(4) "Electronic or electromechanical voting system" means a system of casting votes by use of voting devices or marking devices and counting ballots by employing automatic tabulating equipment or data processing equipment.

(5) "Marking device" means either an approved apparatus used for the piercing of ballots by the voter or any approved device for marking a ballot with ink or other substance which will enable the ballot to be tabulated by means of automatic tabulating equipment.

(6) "Secrecy envelope" means an opaque device, used for enclosing a marked ballot, which conceals the voter's choices.

(7) "Software" means the programs and routines used to employ and control the capabilities of data processing hardware, including, without limitation,

operating systems, compilers, assemblers, utilities, library routines, maintenance routines, applications, and computer networking programs.

(8) "Voting device" means either an apparatus in which ballots are inserted and used in connection with a marking device for the piercing of ballots by the voter or an apparatus by which votes are registered electronically.

101.5605 Examination and approval of equipment.--

(1) The Department of State shall publicly examine all makes of electronic or electromechanical voting systems submitted to it and determine whether the systems comply with the requirements of s. 101.5606.

(2)(a)   Any person owning or interested in an electronic or electromechanical voting system may submit it to the Department of State for examination. The vote counting segment shall be certified after a satisfactory evaluation testing has been performed according to electronic industry standards. This testing shall include, but is not limited to, testing of all software required for the voting system's operation; the ballot reader; the rote processor, especially in its logic and memory components; the digital printer; the fail-safe operations; the counting center environmental requirements; and the equipment reliability estimate. For the purpose of assisting in examining the system, the department shall employ or contract for services of at least one individual who is expert in one or more fields of data processing, mechanical engineering, and public administration and shall require from the individual a written report of his or her examination. . . .

101.5606 Requirements for approval of systems.--

No electronic or electromechanical voting system shall be approved by the Department of State unless it is so constructed that:

(1) It permits and requires voting in secrecy.

(2) It permits each elector to vote at any election for all persons and offices for whom and for which the elector is lawfully entitled to vote, and no others; to vote for as many persons for an office as the elector is entitled to vote for; and to vote for or against any question upon which the elector is entitled to vote.

(3) The automatic tabulating equipment will be set to reject all votes for any office or measure when the number of votes therefor exceeds the number which the voter is entitled to cast or when the voter is not entitled to cast a vote for the office or measure.

(4) It is capable of correctly counting votes. . . .

(6) At presidential elections it permits each elector, by one operation, to vote for all presidential electors of a party or for all presidential electors of candidates for President and Vice President with no party affiliation.

(7) It provides a method for write-in voting.

(8) It is capable of accumulating a count of the specific number of ballots tallied for a precinct, accumulating total votes by candidate for each office, and accumulating total votes for and against each question and issue of the ballots tallied for a precinct. . . .

(10) It is capable of automatically producing precinct totals in printed, marked, or punched form, or a combination thereof.

(11) If it is of a type which registers votes electronically, it will permit each voter to change his or her vote for any candidate or upon any question appearing on the official ballot up to the time that the voter takes the final step to register his or her vote and to have the vote computed.

(12) It is capable of providing records from which the operation of the voting system may be audited.

. . . .

101.5609 Ballot requirements.--

. . . .

(2) The ballot information shall, as far as practicable, be in the order of arrangement provided for paper ballots. Ballots for all questions or propositions to be voted on shall be provided in the same manner and shall be arranged on or in the voting device, if necessary, in the places provided for such purposes.

. . . .

(6) Voting squares may be placed in front of or in back of the names of candidates and statements of questions and shall be of such size as is compatible with the type of system used. Ballots and ballot information shall be printed in a size and style of type as plain and clear as the ballot spaces reasonably permit. . . .

101.5611 Instructions to electors.--

(1) For the instruction of voters on election day, the supervisor of elections shall provide at each polling place one instruction model illustrating the manner of voting with the system. Each such instruction model shall show the arrangement of party rows, office columns, and questions to be voted on. Such model shall be located at a place which voters must pass to reach the official voting booth.

(2) Before entering the voting booth each voter shall be offered instruction in voting by use of the instruction model, and the voter shall be given ample opportunity to operate the model by himself or herself. In instructing voters, no precinct official may show partiality to any political party or candidate.

. . . .

101.5614 Canvass of returns.--

(1)(a)   In precincts in which an electronic or electromechanical voting system is used, as soon as the polls are closed, the election board shall secure the voting devices against further voting. The election board shall thereafter open the ballot box in the presence of members of the public desiring to witness the proceedings and count the number of voted ballots, unused ballots, and spoiled ballots to ascertain whether such number corresponds with the number of ballots issued by the supervisor. If there is a difference, this fact shall be reported in writing to the county canvassing board with the reasons therefor if known. The total number of voted ballots shall be entered on the forms provided. The proceedings of the election board at the precinct after the polls have closed shall be open to the public; however, no person except a member of the election board shall touch any ballot or ballot container or interfere with or obstruct the orderly count of the ballots.

(b)   In lieu of opening the ballot box at the precinct, the supervisor may direct the election board to keep the ballot box sealed and deliver it to a central or regional counting location. In this case, the election board shall count the stubs removed from the ballots to determine the number of voted ballots.

(2)(a)   If the ballots are to be tallied at a central location or at no more than three regional locations, the election board shall place all ballots that have been cast and the unused, void, and defective ballots in the container or containers provided for this purpose, which shall be sealed and delivered forthwith to the central or regional counting location or other designated location by two inspectors who shall not, whenever possible, be of the same political party. The election board shall certify that the ballots were placed in such container or containers and each container was sealed in its presence and under its supervision, and it shall further certify to the number of ballots of each type placed in the container or containers.

(b)   If ballots are to be counted at the precincts, such ballots shall be counted pursuant to rules adopted by the Department of State, which rules shall provide safeguards which conform as nearly as practicable to the safeguards provided in the procedures for the counting of votes at a central location.

(3)(a)   All proceedings at the central or regional counting location or other designated location shall be under the direction of the county canvassing board and shall be open to the public, but no person except a person employed and authorized for the purpose shall touch any ballot or ballot container, any item of automatic tabulating equipment, or any return prior to its release. If the ballots are tabulated at regional locations, one member of the canvassing board or a person designated by the board to represent it shall be present at each location during the testing of the counting equipment and the tabulation of the ballots.

(b)   If ballots are tabulated at regional locations, the results of such election may be transmitted via dedicated teleprocessing lines to the main computer system for the purpose of compilation of complete returns. The security guidelines for transmission of returns by dedicated teleprocessing lines shall conform to rules adopted by the Department of State pursuant to s. 101.015.

. . . .

(5)   If any ballot card of the type for which the offices and measures are not printed directly on the card is damaged or defective so that it cannot properly be counted by the automatic tabulating equipment, a true duplicate copy shall be made of the damaged ballot card in the presence of witnesses and substituted for the damaged ballot. Likewise, a duplicate ballot card shall be made of a defective ballot which shall not include the invalid votes. All duplicate ballot cards shall be clearly labeled "duplicate," bear a serial number which shall be recorded on the damaged or defective ballot card, and be counted in lieu of the damaged or defective ballot. If any ballot card of the type for which offices and measures are printed directly on the card is damaged or defective so that it cannot properly be counted by the automatic tabulating equipment, a true duplicate copy may be made of the damaged ballot card in the presence of witnesses and in the manner set forth above, or the valid votes on the damaged ballot card may be manually counted at the counting center by the canvassing board, whichever procedure is best suited to the system used. If any paper ballot is damaged or defective so that it cannot be counted properly by the automatic tabulating equipment, the ballot shall be counted manually at the counting center by the canvassing board. The totals for all such ballots or ballot cards counted manually shall be added to the totals for the several precincts or election districts. No vote shall be declared invalid or void if there is a clear indication of the intent of the voter as determined by the canvassing board. After duplicating a ballot, the defective ballot shall be placed in an envelope provided for that purpose, and the duplicate ballot shall be tallied with the other ballots for that precinct.

(6)   If an elector marks more names than there are persons to be elected to an office or if it is impossible to determine the elector's choice, the elector's ballot shall not be counted for that office, but the ballot shall not be invalidated as to those names which are properly marked.

. . . .

101.5615 Recounts and election contests.--

and election contests shall be conducted as provided for in this code. The automatic tabulating equipment shall be tested prior to the recount or election contest, as provided in s. 101.5612, if the official ballots or ballot cards are recounted on the automatic tabulating equipment. Each duplicate ballot shall be compared with the original ballot to ensure the correctness of the duplicate.

101.572 Public inspection of ballots.--

The official ballots and ballot cards received from election boards and removed from absentee ballot mailing envelopes shall be open for public inspection or examination while in the custody of the supervisor of elections or the county canvassing board at any reasonable time, under reasonable conditions . . . .

102.111 Elections Canvassing Commission.--

(1) Immediately after certification of any election by the county canvassing board, the results shall be forwarded to the Department of State concerning the election of any federal or state officer. The Governor, the Secretary of State, and the Director of the Division of Elections shall be the Elections Canvassing Commission. The Elections Canvassing Commission shall, as soon as the official results are compiled from all counties, certify the returns of the election and determine and declare who has been elected for each office. In the event that any member of the Elections Canvassing Commission is unavailable to certify the returns of any election, such member shall be replaced by a substitute member of the Cabinet as determined by the Director of the Division of Elections. If the county returns are not received by the Department of State by 5 p.m. of the seventh day following an election, all missing counties shall be ignored, and the results shown by the returns on file shall be certified.

(2) The Division of Elections shall provide the staff services required by the Elections Canvassing Commission.

102.112 Deadline for submission of county returns to the Department of State; penalties.--

(1) The county canvassing board or a majority thereof shall file the county returns for the election of a federal or state officer with the Department of State immediately after certification of the election results. Returns must be filed by 5 p.m. on the 7th day following the first primary and general election and by 3 p.m. on the 3rd day following the second primary. If the returns are not received by the department by the time specified, such returns may be ignored and the results on file at that time may be certified by the department.

(2) The department shall fine each board member $200 for each day such returns are late, the fine to be paid only from the board member's personal funds. Such fines shall be deposited into the Election Campaign Financing Trust Fund, created by s. 106.32.
(3) Members of the county canvassing board may appeal such fines to the Florida Elections Commission, which shall adopt rules for such appeals.

102.121 Elections Canvassing Commission to issue certificates.--

The Elections Canvassing Commission shall make and sign separate certificates of the result of the election for federal and state officers, which certificates shall be written and contain the total number of votes cast for each person for each office. The certificates, the one including the result of the election for presidential electors and representatives to Congress, and the other including the result of the election for state officers, shall be recorded in the Department of State in a book to be kept for that purpose.

102.131 Returns before canvassing commission.--

If any returns shall appear to be irregular or false so that the Elections Canvassing Commission is unable to determine the true vote for any office, nomination, constitutional amendment, or other measure presented to the electors, the commission shall so certify and shall not include the returns in its determination, canvass, and declaration. The Elections Canvassing Commission in determining the true vote shall not have authority to look beyond the county returns. The Department of State shall file in its office all the returns, together with other documents and papers received by it or the commission. The commission shall canvass the returns for presidential electors and representatives to Congress separately from their canvass of returns for state officers.

102.141 County canvassing board; duties.--

(1) The county canvassing board shall be composed of the supervisor of elections; a county court judge, who shall act as chair; and the chair of the board of county commissioners. In the event any member of the county canvassing board is unable to serve, is a candidate who has opposition in the election being canvassed, or is an active participant in the campaign or candidacy of any candidate who has opposition in the election being canvassed, such member shall be replaced as follows:

(a) If no county court judge is able to serve or if all are disqualified, the chief judge of the judicial circuit in which the county is located shall appoint as a substitute member a qualified elector of the county who is not a candidate with opposition in the election being canvassed and who is not an active participant in the campaign or candidacy of any candidate with opposition in the election being canvassed. In such event, the members of the county canvassing board shall meet and elect a chair.

(b) If the supervisor of elections is unable to serve or is disqualified, the chair of the board of county commissioners shall appoint as a substitute member a member of the board of county commissioners who is not a candidate with opposition in the election being canvassed and who is not an active participant in the campaign or candidacy of any candidate with opposition in the election being canvassed. The supervisor, however, shall act in an advisory capacity to the canvassing board.

(c) If the chair of the board of county commissioners is unable to serve or is disqualified, the board of county commissioners shall appoint as a substitute member one of its members who is not a candidate with opposition in the election being canvassed and who is not an active participant in the campaign or candidacy of any candidate with opposition in the election being canvassed.

(d) If a substitute member cannot be appointed as provided elsewhere in this subsection, the chief judge of the judicial circuit in which the county is located shall appoint as a substitute member a qualified elector of the county who is not a candidate with opposition in the election being canvassed and who is not an active participant in the campaign or candidacy of any candidate with opposition in the election being canvassed.

(2)   The county canvassing board shall meet in a building accessible to the public in the county where the election occurred at a time and place to be designated by the supervisor of elections to publicly canvass the absentee electors' ballots as provided for in s. 101.68. Public notice of the time and place at which the county canvassing board shall meet to canvass the absentee electors' ballots shall be given at least 48 hours prior thereto by publication once in one or more newspapers of general circulation in the county or, if there is no newspaper of general circulation in the county, by posting such notice in at least four conspicuous places in the county. As soon as the absentee electors' ballots are canvassed, the board shall proceed to publicly canvass the vote given each candidate, nominee, constitutional amendment, or other measure submitted to the electorate of the county, as shown by the returns then on file in the office of the supervisor of elections and the office of the county court judge.

(3)   The canvass, except the canvass of absentee electors' returns, shall be made from the returns and certificates of the inspectors as signed and filed by them with the county court judge and supervisor, respectively, and the county canvassing board shall not change the number of votes cast for a candidate, nominee, constitutional amendment, or other measure submitted to the electorate of the county, respectively, in any polling place, as shown by the returns. All returns shall be made to the board on or before noon of the day following any primary, general, special, or other election. If the returns from any precinct are missing, if there are any omissions on the returns from any precinct, or if there is an obvious error on any such returns, the canvassing board shall order a recount of the returns from such precinct. Before canvassing such returns, the canvassing board shall examine the counters on the machines or the tabulation of the ballots cast in such precinct and determine whether the returns correctly reflect the votes cast. If there is a discrepancy between the returns and the counters of the machines or the tabulation of the ballots cast, the counters of such machines or the tabulation of the ballots cast shall be presumed correct and such votes shall be canvassed accordingly.

(4)   If the returns for any office reflect that a candidate was defeated or eliminated by one-half of a percent or less of the votes cast for such office, that a candidate for retention to a judicial office was retained or not retained by one-half of a percent or less of the votes cast on the question of retention, or that a measure appearing on the ballot was approved or rejected by one-half of a percent or less of the votes cast on such measure, the board responsible for certifying the results of the vote on such race or measure shall order a recount of the votes cast with respect to such office or measure. A recount need not be ordered with respect to the returns for any office, however, if the candidate or candidates defeated or eliminated from contention for such office by one-half of a percent or less of the votes cast for such office request in writing that a recount not be made. Each canvassing board responsible for conducting a recount shall examine the counters on the machines or the tabulation of the ballots cast in each precinct in which the office or issue appeared on the ballot

and determine whether the returns correctly reflect the votes cast. If there is a discrepancy between the returns and the counters of the machines or the tabulation of the ballots cast, the counters of such machines or the tabulation of the ballots cast shall be presumed correct and such votes shall be canvassed accordingly.

(5) The canvassing board may employ such clerical help to assist with the work of the board as it deems necessary, with at least one member of the board present at all times, until the canvass of the returns is completed. The clerical help shall be paid from the same fund as inspectors and other necessary election officials.

(6) At the same time that the results of an election are certified to the Department of State, the county canvassing board shall file a report with the Division of Elections on the conduct of the election. The report shall contain information relating to any problems incurred as a result of equipment malfunctions either at the precinct level or at a counting location, any difficulties or unusual circumstances encountered by an election board or the canvassing board, and any other additional information which the canvassing board feels should be made a part of the official election record. Such reports shall be maintained on file in the Division of Elections and shall be available for public inspection. The division shall utilize the reports submitted by the canvassing boards to determine what problems may be likely to occur in other elections and disseminate such information, along with possible solutions, to the supervisors of elections.

102.166 Protest of election returns; procedure.--

(1) Any candidate for nomination or election, or any elector qualified to vote in the election related to such candidacy, shall have the right to protest the returns of the election as being erroneous by filing with the appropriate canvassing board a sworn, written protest.

(2) Such protest shall be filed with the canvassing board prior to the time the canvassing board certifies the results for the office being protested or within 5 days after midnight of the date the election is held, whichever occurs later.

(3) Before canvassing the returns of the election, the canvassing board shall:

(a) When paper ballots are used, examine the tabulation of the paper ballots cast.

(b) When voting machines are used, examine the counters on the machines of nonprinter machines or the printer-pac on printer machines. If there is a discrepancy between the returns and the counters of the machines or the printer-pac, the counters of such machines or the printer-pac shall be presumed correct.

(c) When electronic or electromechanical equipment is used, the canvassing board shall examine precinct records and election returns. If there is a clerical error, such error shall be corrected by the county canvassing board.

If there is a discrepancy which could affect the outcome of an election, the canvassing board may recount the ballots on the automatic tabulating equipment.

(4)(a)   Any candidate whose name appeared on the ballot, any political committee that supports or opposes an issue which appeared on the ballot, or any political party whose candidates' names appeared on the ballot may file a written request with the county canvassing board for a manual recount. The written request shall contain a statement of the reason the manual recount is being requested.

(b)   Such request must be filed with the canvassing board prior to the time the canvassing board certifies the results for the office being protested or within 72 hours after midnight of the date the election was held, whichever occurs later.

(c)   The county canvassing board may authorize a manual recount. If a manual recount is authorized, the county canvassing board shall make a reasonable effort to notify each candidate whose race is being recounted of the time and place of such recount.

(d)   The manual recount must include at least three precincts and at least 1 percent of the total votes cast for such candidate or issue. In the event there are less than three precincts involved in the election, all precincts shall be counted. The person who requested the recount shall choose three precincts to be recounted, and, if other precincts are recounted, the county canvassing board shall select the additional precincts.

(5)   If the manual recount indicates an error in the vote tabulation which could affect the outcome of the election, the county canvassing board shall:

(a)   Correct the error and recount the remaining precincts with the vote tabulation system;

(b)   Request the Department of State to verify the tabulation software; or

(c)   Manually recount all ballots.

(6)   Any manual recount shall be open to the public.

(7)   Procedures for a manual recount are as follows:

(a)   The county canvassing board shall appoint as many counting teams of at least two electors as is necessary to manually recount the ballots. A counting team must have, when possible, members of at least two political parties. A candidate involved in the race shall not be a member of the counting team.

(b)   If a counting team is unable to determine a voter's intent in casting a ballot, the ballot shall be presented to the county canvassing board for it to determine the voter's intent.

(8) If the county canvassing board determines the need to verify the tabulation software, the county canvassing board shall request in writing that the Department of State verify the software.

(9) When the Department of State verifies such software, the department shall:

(a)   Compare the software used to tabulate the votes with the software filed with the Department of State pursuant to s. 101.5607; and

(b)   Check the election parameters.

(10) The Department of State shall respond to the county canvassing board within 3 working days.

102.168 Contest of election.--

(1)   Except as provided in s. 102.171, the certification of election or nomination of any person to office, or of the result on any question submitted by referendum, may be contested in the circuit court by any unsuccessful candidate for such office or nomination thereto or by any elector qualified to vote in the election related to such candidacy, or by any taxpayer, respectively.

(2)   Such contestant shall file a complaint, together with the fees prescribed in chapter 28, with the clerk of the circuit court within 10 days after midnight of the date the last county canvassing board empowered to canvass the returns certifies the results of the election being contested or within 5 days after midnight of the date the last county canvassing board empowered to canvass the returns certifies the results of that particular election following a protest pursuant to s. 102.166(1), whichever occurs later.

(3)   The complaint shall set forth the grounds on which the contestant intends to establish his or her right to such office or set aside the result of the election on a submitted referendum. The grounds for contesting an election under this section are:

(a)   Misconduct, fraud, or corruption on the part of any election official or any member of the canvassing board sufficient to change or place in doubt the result of the election.

(b)   Ineligibility of the successful candidate for the nomination or office in dispute.

(c)   Receipt of a number of illegal votes or rejection of a number of legal votes sufficient to change or place in doubt the result of the election.

(d)   Proof that any elector, election official, or canvassing board member was given or offered a bribe or reward in money, property, or any other thing of value for the purpose of procuring the successful candidate's nomination or election or determining the result on any question submitted by referendum.

(e)   Any other cause or allegation which, if sustained, would show that a person other than the successful candidate was the person duly nominated or elected to the office in question or that the outcome of the election on a question submitted by referendum was contrary to the result declared by the canvassing board or election board.

(4)   The canvassing board or election board shall be the proper party defendant, and the successful candidate shall be an indispensable party to any action brought to contest the election or nomination of a candidate.

(5)   A statement of the grounds of contest may not be rejected, nor the proceedings dismissed, by the court for any want of form if the grounds of contest provided in the statement are sufficient to clearly inform the defendant of the particular proceeding or cause for which the nomination or election is contested.

(6)   A copy of the complaint shall be served upon the defendant and any other person named therein in the same manner as in other civil cases under the laws of this state. Within 10 days after the complaint has been served, the defendant must file an answer admitting or denying the allegations on which the contestant relies or stating that the defendant has no knowledge or information concerning the allegations, which shall be deemed a denial of the allegations, and must state any other defenses, in law or fact, on which the defendant relies. If an answer is not filed within the time prescribed, the defendant may not be granted a hearing in court to assert any claim or objection that is required by this subsection to be stated in an answer.

(7)   Any candidate, qualified elector, or taxpayer presenting such a contest to a circuit judge is entitled to an immediate hearing. However, the court in its discretion may limit the time to be consumed in taking testimony, with a view therein to the circumstances of the matter and to the proximity of any succeeding primary or other election.

(8)   The circuit judge to whom the contest is presented may fashion such orders as he or she deems necessary to ensure that each allegation in the complaint is investigated, examined, or checked, to prevent or correct any alleged wrong, and to provide any relief appropriate under such circumstances.

102.1685 Venue.--

The venue for contesting a nomination or election or the results of a referendum shall be in the county in which the contestant qualified or in the county in which the question was submitted for referendum or, if the election or referendum covered more than one county, then in Leon County.

102.171 Contest of election to Legislature.--

The jurisdiction to hear any contest of the election of a member to either house of the Legislature is vested in the applicable house, as each house, pursuant to s. 2, Art. III of the State Constitution, is the sole judge of the qualifications, elections, and returns of its members. Therefore, the certification of election of any person to the office of member of either house of the Legislature may only be contested in the applicable house by an unsuccessful candidate for such office, in accordance with the rules of that house. This section does not apply to any contest of the nomination of any person for the office of member of either house of the Legislature at any primary or special primary election in which only those qualified electors who are registered members of the political party holding such primary election may vote, as provided for in s. 5(b), Art. VI of the State Constitution. This section does apply to any contest of a primary or special primary election for the office of member of either house of the Legislature in which all qualified electors may vote, as provided for in s. 5(b), Art. VI of the State Constitution, and the recipient of the most votes is deemed to be elected according to applicable law.